Understanding Ada

A Software Engineering Approach

Understanding Ada

A Software Engineering Approach

Gary Bray

Intermetrics, Inc.

David Pokrass

Motorola, Inc.

John Wiley & Sons

New York   Chichester   Brisbane   Toronto   Singapore

Ada is a registered trademark of the U.S. government (Ada Joint Program Office).

Figure 3.2 illustration by John Heymann

Library of Congress Cataloging in Publication Data:

Bray, Gary.
    Understanding Ada.

    Includes indexes.
    1. Ada (Computer program language)   I. Pokrass, David.
II. Title.
QA76.73.A35B73   1985   001.64′24   84-26998

ISBN 0-471-87833-2

Printed in the United States of America

10 9 8 7 6 5 4 3 2 1

to
Adele and Charles
Marlys and Noah

P R E F A C E

Ada is a powerful, general-purpose, high-level programming language designed to support software engineering. Because of past disappointments, experienced programmers often are rightfully skeptical of an unfamiliar language billed as "new" and "powerful." Ada is different than many earlier languages in that the language power has been guided by a strong concern for reliability, readability, and maintainability. Influenced by the strengths of Pascal, Ada is designed to support software engineering principles that have proven effective in building software systems.

The application domain for Ada is broad and includes real-time systems, operating systems, numerical applications, and general system software. Because the application requirements are broad, Ada is a big language. The size, however, provides support and security, not potential programming traps that emerge only when the program is executed. Where Ada is complex, the complexity results from rules to enhance security while preserving expressiveness. Ada is not an amalgam of all-inclusive features, but rather consists of a set of cohesive, interwoven constructs that in conjunction support software engineering.

Sponsored by the U.S. Department of Defense (DoD), Ada was developed to stem soaring software costs. Historically these costs resulted in part from the use of about 500 programming languages, all mutually incompatible, for DoD systems. The costs associated with this horde of languages could be avoided, of course, by adopting a single programming language. Use of a single language unifies training, reduces maintenance, lowers the number of compiler errors and, most important, increases reuse of applications and support tools.

Unfortunately, no existing language met all the requirements of the application domain. The DoD therefore sponsored the design of a new programming language, with cooperation from much of the academic and professional computing community. The proposed designs were reviewed extensively by participants worldwide. After a design was selected, the language underwent thorough testing and evaluation. The resulting language was named Ada, in tribute to the nineteenth century mathematician Ada Lovelace, a colleague of the forefather of computing, Charles Babbage.

Interest in Ada is widespread and growing. The DoD has adopted Ada as the single language for embedded computer software, and DoD contracts require its use. In February 1983, Ada received standardization by the American National Standards Institute (ANSI).

No language by itself can reduce software costs and improve software quality. The quality of a software system ultimately depends upon the people who build it, as well as the methods they use. By applying methodical software engineering techniques, programmers are more likely to achieve a quality result, and Ada provides an excellent vehicle for applying modern software engineering techniques.

This book describes Ada, emphasizing the features that support software engineering. Our approach is informal, and we attempt to provide rationale, based on software engineering principles, for key parts of the language design. The reader thus will find a framework for understanding constructs, rather than an exhaustive list of language rules. Many examples are given throughout the book to illustrate important features. The examples often build upon one another, illustrating reuse of earlier program units. Although all major aspects of Ada are presented, we concentrate on features (e.g., packages, exceptions, generics, and tasks) not found in most widely-available languages. Our goal, then, is to convey the essence of Ada by showing how these novel features can contribute to improved software engineering.

The book is intended for the reader who wants an understanding of Ada without swimming through an ocean of details (which does not mean, however, that the water is shallow and swimming unnecessary). The book thus is appropriate for students of programming languages and software engineering and for professional programmers and managers who are, or are considering, using Ada. The reader is assumed to be familiar with a high-level language (e.g., C, Pascal, FORTRAN, PL/I, or COBOL) and to understand the steps of software development (design, coding, testing, and so forth). To readers with this background, the book should provide motivation for the design of Ada and a working knowledge for Ada programming.

We take a somewhat "bottom-up" approach. Chapter 0 sets the stage and previews issues developed in later chapters. Chapter 1 presents the basic Ada statements, such as the if, while, and case statements. Chapter 2 describes types, objects, and their associated operations. Chapter 3 describes subprograms and introduces packages, a key Ada construct for modularity. Chapter 4 describes exceptions, a flexible mechanism for handling errors that arise during execution. Chapter 5 describes generics, a powerful facility for building reusable program units. Chapter 6 describes tasks and rendezvous, the constructs for concurrent execution of cooperating program units. Chapter 7 describes the features for input-output. Chapter 8 describes the features for "bit level" representation specification. Chapter 9 ("The Big Picture") describes compilation and how the pieces of an Ada program fit together. Finally, Chapter 10 ("The Bigger Picture") discusses the Ada programming support environment, an integrated set of tools to promote Ada programming. Throughout these chapters, we attempt to demonstrate the cohesive support Ada provides for the programming of clear, correct, long-lived systems.

A number of people and organizations made valuable contributions during preparation of the manuscript. Chuck Shipley carefully reviewed our thinking and our prose, thereby clarifying both. In addition, helpful comments were made by Vicki Almstrum, Kele McGlohon, Lee McGraw, Anne Marie Murray, Lew Rosenthal, Software Leverage, Inc., and John Tempka. The Ada Systems Division of Intermetrics, Inc. and the Software Resources Development Department of Motorola, Inc. encouraged the pursuit of software engineering principles and practice. In addition, Intermetrics, Inc. allowed us the use of its facilities in preparing the manuscript. Carol Beasley of John Wiley & Sons was especially helpful throughout the writing and production of the book. Lorraine Mellon and Judith Watkins, also of John Wiley & Sons, were instrumental in obtaining the photographs reproduced in the book. Kay Newfie provided special encouragement, as well as diverting and welcome vacation suggestions. Many thanks to Marlys Pokrass for tracking even the "most elusive" printmakers.

Gary Bray
David Pokrass

C O N T E N T S

4.   **Error Handling**   107

5.   **Generics: No Wheels Reinvented Here**   127

Understanding Ada

A Software Engineering Approach

Roy Lichtenstein. Dawning. *1964. Oil and magna on canvas. Art Resource © Sotheby Parke–Bernet*

CHAPTER 0

Building on Ada

0.1 Climatic Changes

Software engineering is concerned with the orderly, methodical development of reliable, usable software. The Ada programming language has been designed for modern software engineering and includes direct support for its principles. Before describing the software engineering influence on Ada, several points illustrate why Ada is important.

Like the construction of a building, software development cannot be successful unless proven design principles and techniques are applied. Moreover, appropriate tools that implement and encourage sound design principles must be available to carry out the job. For building construction, sophisticated stress analysis and structural design principles are less useful if the only tools are saws, nails, and hammers. Similarly, software engineering is more difficult with languages that have not been designed to exploit its principles. To take full advantage of software engineering principles, a programmer must use a language that supports, encourages, and enforces these principles.

The plummeting cost of hardware has increased the need for software, which for some time has been more costly and slower to develop than hardware. The revolution in microprocessors also has made feasible larger and more ambitious systems, which require larger software systems to control them. New kinds of software are required for new hardware configurations (such as distributed computers communicating over a network) which were not common previously and therefore are not as well-understood. New software buildings must be constructed that are better suited to the changing computing climate. In some cases, we do not yet fully understand the new buildings, but flexible, general-purpose tools are needed to build them. Because of this need for software, the new tools must promote conservation of programming effort rather than conservation of bits.

Historically, software projects, particularly ones building large programs with large staffs, have been plagued with cost overruns, schedule slippage, poor documentation, and inadequate, unreliable, and difficult products. If software were buildings, the computing skyline would contain many unsightly, teetering, partially-complete facades. Indeed, software pundits and others often characterize the current state of software development in terms such as *problem* and *crisis*.

0.2 Tenets of Software Engineering

Many programming languages are ill-suited to human abilities for dealing with complexity. It is not surprising that software built using such languages often has been inadequate. People think and understand by means of abstractions, and abstraction is the major technique for understanding and inventing complex structures. An abstraction provides a simple view of a structure and summarizes its interesting and important properties. Each of the elements of an abstraction itself can be an abstraction for details at a lower (or higher) level. At a given level of abstraction, however, the view must be simple or the abstraction is inappropriate.

A primary emphasis of software engineering is the formulation of appropriate abstractions for the desired system (which we will call the *application*).

The benefits of structured control statements, such as if, while, and case statements, are almost universally acknowledged. A program that uses structured control statements is more clear and understandable than one that uses unrestricted control. More complicated control sequences can be constructed by composing the simple statements. Structured control statements are simple, readable abstractions for the actions in programs. Subprograms particularly are an important abstraction mechanism for a sequence of actions.

Most widely-available languages unfortunately do not provide comparable facilities for data abstraction. Data abstraction is the ability to define a type by specifying the operations that are meaningful for it, without exposing the representation of the type. In most languages, a predefined type for integers is a simple example of a data abstraction. Programmers may consider integer objects as having the properties and operations of mathematical integers, in most cases without concern for the bit strings that actually represent integers in hardware. A shortcoming of many languages is that they do not allow the programmer to define *new* data abstractions, in addition to those predefined in the language, suited to the application.

Languages such as Pascal allow programmers to define new data types, but the representation (e.g., whether it is an array or record) of the type is not hidden from other parts of the program. Because the representation is exposed, the abstract properties cannot be assured. Given an object of a programmer-defined type, other parts of the program can access the representation directly and hence can violate its abstract properties. The underlying representation can be directly accessed, and perhaps inadvertently misused, from anywhere the object is visible.

Data type abstraction requires that the programmer be able to define a new data type and its associated operations and, equally important, *to hide the type representation* from other parts of the program. If the representation is not hidden, consistency in the use of the type cannot be ensured, and further, changes in the type due to later correction or enhancement affect units that depend on the underlying representation. Without representation hiding, these other units then must be located and changed also, increasing the chance of error and the cost of the change.

This representation hiding for programmer-defined types is analogous to the way a high-level language compiler hides the representation of the primitive types, such as arrays and records. Should the compiler change its representation of arrays, a programmer must recompile but need not check all array uses to ensure that they are still correct.

Programming is much easier if a specialized language for building similar applications is available. The language supplies appropriate abstractions for the application domain, and a programmer simply selects and composes these high-level constructs to build an application. The primitive constructs in the language are application-level constructs. Although specialized languages are successful in a specific problem domain, they typically are less useful for other applications, and therefore applications (or parts of applications) are seldom reusable. To obtain the advantages of both specialized and general-purpose languages, it is possible to build the specialized language upon a more general base language, which is extensible.

For consistency, a programmer-defined type should be uniform with the types predefined by the language; that is, the language must be extensible so that facilities defined by the programmer in effect extend the language with application-specific types and operations. Rather than having a specialized language for every application, the basic language is extended with types and operations appropriate for the application. This approach enables the programmer to concentrate on the application domain, instead of remembering the details of how the language has been adapted to the application domain.

Every programmer knows that conventional programming is prone to errors, ranging from minor clerical slips to major logical pratfalls. Insofar as possible, a programmer should not pay dearly in development time for trivial oversights and lapses in attention, which are almost inevitable. After a program is written, there generally are three points at which an error can be detected: (1) during compilation, by the compiler, (2) during execution, by the program itself, and (3) after execution, by a person observing the behavior of the program. The most extreme case of this last possibility is that end-users of the program discover the error.

For example, the compiler can detect syntax errors and violations of semantic rules in the language. Other errors, such as an attempt to refer to an array component with an out-of-bounds index, in general can be detected only during program execution. Finally, logical errors, such as an incorrect algorithm to compute a fast Fourier transform, can be discovered only by someone observing the program behavior.

Of course, any kind of error is costly, but generally the earlier an error is detected the less costly it is to correct. For example, if a program eventually is to be mass-produced in read-only memory (ROM), an error discovered *after* the ROM is burned will be much more costly than one discovered at compile-time. Thus early error detection through extensive compiler checking of program consistency is crucial.

Much of software cost arises after the application has been built, when the application is maintained and enhanced. Often major changes are necessary because of errors, changes in requirements, and the need for more functionality. Such changes can have a widespread effect on the program if they have not been anticipated in the design.

Modularity is one technique that can be used to limit the rippling of program changes to other parts of the program. A well-designed module is a small, single-purpose program unit, which has a narrow interface to the rest of the program. A small, single-purpose module is easier to understand and to change than a large, multipurpose, tightly-interwoven one. One criteria for decomposing programs into modules is information hiding. A module hides a design decision from the rest of the program, so that only the module is affected if this design decision changes. The module thus hides information about the design decision from other modules. As noted above, hiding representation information is especially crucial to simplify maintenance and enhancement.

Modularity should allow fine control over the scope and visibility of objects and other declarations. The scope of an object is the region of the program where the object can be used. If an object is visible to many program units (such as global variables are in Pascal), there are many places potentially affected by changes. The uses of a global object can be determined only by scanning the entire program. Use of global variables makes interfaces wider and has been likened to the use of unstructured control statements in its effects on structure and clarity. By contrast, the places where a local object is used can be found (and therefore changed) much more easily. Locality of reference is an important property of readable and maintainable programs.

When an application is decomposed into modules, the interconnection between the modules is important so that the system can be configured easily. The specification of the interconnection of the modules in a system has been called *programming-in-the-large*. In the past, this interconnection has been performed manually or by secondary tools—not by the compiler. For ease of maintenance, however, programming-in-the-large should be an integral part of the language itself.

To someone who, as a result of feverish productivity, has completed an individual programming project in a short time, programmer productivity statistics seem astonishingly low. One study indicates that on average programmers perhaps produce as few as 5 lines of debugged code per day (Brooks, 1979). To someone who has participated in a large programming project, however, the statistics are more understandable. The communication and coordination required among project members consume a considerable portion of project time. Large programs require simple, clear interfaces, so that the need for direct communication is reduced.

Design methodologies can improve productivity by promoting good designs, which lead to programs that can be coded and debugged more readily. A more direct way of increasing productivity is to avoid building the entire system from scratch. Lawyers often prepare wills and contracts by piecing together standard paragraphs from a legal library. Ada is designed to help create programs by piecing together standard program units from an Ada library. Reusable software components are program units that can be applied to more than one program.

For reusability, a program unit must be portable; that is, one must be able to compile and run the unit on a different machine without major (preferably without any) modifications. Moreover, a program unit must not be overspecific. It must not contain unnecessary details that limit its generality.

0.3 Ada and Software Engineering

Ada was designed to support the principles of modern software engineering. Its application domain is embedded computers, that is, computers that are "embedded" within a larger physical system that the computer helps to control. Examples of systems that contain embedded computers are a spacecraft, a fleet of elevators, or an automated bank teller system. Embedded computer software tends to be very large, the number of source lines sometimes extending into the millions. The requirements of embedded computer programming are broad and, accordingly, Ada is a rich, expressive language useful for both general-purpose and specialized programming.

A guiding principle in Ada is that programming is a human activity. With most production programs, especially large ones, people read the program more often than they change it. Ada emphasizes program clarity and readability, rather than minimum keystrokes. Reserved words (with a few exceptions) are full English words; predefined declarations also generally have meaningful identifiers. This emphasis on readability makes programs more self-documenting and more maintainable. Hence Ada is best suited for writing production-quality systems, rather than throw-away, "write-only" programs.

Ada includes abstractions for both control and data. The control abstractions include procedures and functions, and also assignment statements, if statements, case statements, while statements, for statements, exit statements, return statements, and block statements.

To simplify programming robust systems that are reliable and recover from errors, Ada provides *exceptions*. Exceptions are a control construct that allows the normal flow of control to be transferred when an error or unusual condition is detected. Error handling is simplified, because error processing is localized to sections of the program called *exception handlers*. The actions for the normal cases do not have to be cluttered with error checking and processing.

Ada includes the common primitive data types and allows them to be composed to form composite types. The primitive data types include integers, enumerations (including characters and booleans), floating point numbers, fixed point numbers, and access types (pointers). Array and record types are the composite types, which contain other types as components.

Influenced by the success of Pascal, Ada is strongly typed, which means that the programmer specifies the type of every object, that the type cannot be changed, and that an object can be used only in operations defined for its type. In non-strongly typed languages, if two objects do not match in their types, the compiler implicitly converts one of the objects to make them match. Programs in such languages are more error-prone, difficult to debug, and have fewer errors detected at compile-time.

The Ada compiler does not perform implicit conversions in an attempt to make something meaningful out of what probably is a mistake. The compiler checks that objects are used consistently with their type. When using a strongly typed language, experienced programmers often find that the compiler detects most errors. Once it compiles without errors, the program is much more likely to be correct than one written in a weakly typed language.

To further refine the meaning of an object, the programmer can place *constraints* on the values an object may contain. The Ada compiler will check that these constraints are not violated, thereby ensuring the integrity of the object. Where necessary, the compiler will generate executable code to check the constraints during execution.

In addition to conventional data types, Ada provides an important data type abstraction facility called *private types*. A programmer uses a private type to define a new type whose representation is hidden from other program units. Other program units can use objects of a private type only through given operations and cannot access the underlying representation.

Most entities in an Ada program have *attributes,* which are properties that the programmer can reference. Attributes are an important feature that promote maintenance and reusability. They allow the properties of entities to be referenced, without redundantly repeating the details available from the definition of the entity.

There are four kinds of program units in Ada: subprograms, packages, tasks, and generics. Each unit generally is given in two parts—a specification and a body. The specification defines the logical interface to the unit. The logical interface is the set of services and facilities that the unit makes available (visible) to the rest of the program. The body defines the implementation details, which are hidden from the rest of the program. The separation of specifications and bodies in Ada can simplify the communication problems among members of a large project. A specification summarizes the interface, and the associated body is less important to users and can be developed independently.

Ada packages are a major construct to support abstraction, modularity, and reusability. A package is a logically related collection of declarations, which can include objects, types, and other program units. The declarations in the package specification are available to other program units, but the declarations in the body are hidden. A package can be used for a collection of related objects and types, for a collection of operations on a shared internal data structure (data object abstraction), and for the definition of new data types using private types (data type abstraction).

Embedded systems often involve many hardware processors that communicate to coordinate their actions. Even on a single processor, systems typically are partitioned into logically concurrent units. Ada tasks are program units that execute concurrently. Tasks are objects that execute in parallel with other tasks. Tasks communicate by means of *rendezvous,* which provides both synchronization and parameter passing between tasks. Task interaction through rendezvous is high level and relieves the programmer of low-level synchronization details. Without language-defined concurrency, each implementation defines its own executive interface, which has different calls, different semantics, and a range of services that differs from other implementations. Because tasking is defined within the language, Ada source code does not contain such implementation-dependent executive calls, and hence Ada concurrent programs are portable.

Ada defines an important and powerful capability to support reusability, called *generics.* Generics are parameterized program units that can be tailored to an application. Generics avoid the problem of overspecificity by allowing a unit to be parameterized by types and subprograms (as well as by objects). Thus general algorithms and data structures that are meaningful for classes of types and sub-programs can be developed as generics.

Because Ada encourages modular programming, it contains features for pro-gramming-in-the-large. Ada program units can be separately compiled, with no sacrifice in compiler checking. Programs compiled as separate compilation units are checked as thoroughly as a single compilation unit, eliminating module inter-face errors. Both top-down and bottom-up submission to the compiler are sup-ported. Top-down submission allows the high-level structure of the program to be compiled first, using *stubs* to substitute for implementations of the low-level pro-gram units. Bottom-up submission allows the low-level units to be compiled first, providing a proven foundation for building higher-level units.

Moreover, the dependences among program units are explicit in the Ada source code. Unlike many existing systems, the structure of an Ada system is *not* dis-persed among the source code, a run-time executive, and auxiliary system genera-tion tools. Ada system structure is defined *completely* by the source code. The Ada compiler ensures that units are compiled in a correct order and that an executable system is configured only from units that are up-to-date.

0.4 An Example of an Ada Program

Before plunging further into a description of Ada, we present a complete Ada program which shows that, although Ada is well-suited for large programs, Ada programs need not be large.

```
with TEXT_IO; use TEXT_IO;
procedure COPY_FILE is
     CH : CHARACTER;
begin
     while not END_OF_FILE loop
          GET(CH);
          PUT(CH);
     end loop;
end COPY_FILE;
```

This procedure declares a variable CH of type CHARACTER and loops reading a character from the default input file and writing it to the default output file, until the end of the input file. TEXT_IO is a predefined library package that contains the function END_OF_FILE and procedures GET, and PUT. Semicolons terminate dec-larations and statements. The program is readable, even though the details have not yet been presented. In later chapters, we describe more fully the constructs illustrated in this example.

0.5 Exercises

1. Assume you are a member of a project to build a large application for factory monitoring. Select your favorite programming language (if you know only one, it qualifies as your favorite by default) and describe its good and bad features for building a large application. What features would help you to adapt the language to the application? What features would help you interface your units with those of other project members? How much consistency checking would be done automatically across interfaces? What features would help you reuse units, built by other project members, that were not originally intended to be used with your units? Do your answers vary depending on the compiler for the language? Depending on the operating system?

2. Give three reasons why the hiding of representation details of data types is important. How does your favorite language support representation hiding?

Frank Stella. Hiraqla. 1968. *Graham Gund Collection, Museum of Fine Arts, Boston.*

CHAPTER 1

Basic
Statements

Ada programs are composed of two kinds of elements: declarations and statements. Declarations define the entities that will be used in a program; statements perform actions using the declared entities. Because statements in Ada are simpler than declarations, basic statements are presented in this chapter, followed by declarations in the next chapter. As a result of this presentation order, data types are mentioned in this chapter before they are fully described. We trust that the reader has sufficient background, so that these simple types will not prove daunting.

Although sometimes considered to be a conventional topic, statements can greatly affect the look and feel of a language. The choices taken in Ada for statements, as with other constructs, are guided by a strong concern for reliability, readability, and maintainability. As an introduction, we discuss some elementary concepts.

The actions of an Ada program are specified both by declarations and by statements; that is, an Ada program has an effect through elaboration of its declarations and execution of its statements. Declarations are given within program text called a declarative part, and they define the entities that a program will use. In contrast, statements are actions involving declared entities and occur within a statement part. Statements cannot appear in a declarative part, nor can declarations appear in a statement part.

In the most simple terms, the text of an Ada program is executed by a processor. For a concurrent program (discussed in Chapter 6), more than one processor conceptually can be executing. To execute a program, the processor steps sequentially through the program text from top to bottom, executing each declaration or statement before proceeding to the next one. When finished with one action, the processor by default performs the next action in the top-to-bottom sequence. This order is natural to many people, because top-to-bottom is the natural order of reading in the English language. Thus an Ada program is most easily understood by reading it in top-to-bottom order.

Certain kinds of statements, however, can cause the processor to branch to another part of the program text, rather than stepping sequentially to the next statement. With structured control statements, the destination of the branch (if taken) is clear from the kind of statement. Ada provides a full set of structured control statements, including if statements, loop statements, and case statements.

The processor itself may be implemented as a software interpreter which executes the Ada source text, as a hardware processor which executes the machine instructions that are a translated version of the Ada source text, or as some synthesis of hardware and software execution. Regardless of the implementation, the semantics (the meaning) of the program is the same.

Before a hardware processor can execute a translated version of an Ada program, the program first must be translated by another program called a *compiler*. Execution of a compiled program typically is more efficient than software interpretation of the corresponding source program. Because efficiency is important to embedded computer applications, our descriptions refer to an Ada compiler rather than an interpreter.

The following sections briefly introduce the basic Ada statements. Later chapters illustrate them more fully and discuss the more novel statements where appropriate.

1.1 Assignment Statement

A variable can be given a new value using the assignment statement, which has the following form:

```
A_VARIABLE := SOME_VALUE;    -- An assignment statement
```

The assignment delimiter, ":=", is read as "is assigned" or "gets the value." In this example, the current value of A_VARIABLE is replaced by the value of the expression SOME_VALUE. Rules concerning the types and possible values involved in an assignment statement are deferred until Chapter 2, where types and objects are discussed.

The example illustrates several points in addition to an assignment statement. An identifier, such as A_VARIABLE or SOME_VALUE, is a sequence of characters of arbitrary length (provided it fits on a line) which begins with a letter and can contain letters, digits, and underscores. An underscore must be preceded and followed by a letter or digit, and an identifier cannot contain two consecutive underscores, nor can it end with an underscore. All characters in an identifier are significant. Upper case and lower case letters are allowed and, as in ordinary English, represent the same letter. For example, A_VARIABLE and A_Variable are the same identifier. Finally, the above assignment statement also illustrates a comment. A comment begins with two adjacent dashes and extends to the end of the line.

1.2 Procedure Call Statement

A fundamental abstraction construct in most languages is the subprogram. A subprogram is a named sequence of actions that can be called from elsewhere in the program by writing the subprogram name. The subprogram is an abstraction for its sequence of actions. When a subprogram is called, the actions of the subprogram are executed, and when the subprogram completes, control returns to the next action following the subprogram call. Subprograms can have parameters, which are supplied when the subprogram is called. In Ada, a subprogram that is a statement is called a procedure (Ada also provides functions, which are subprograms that are expressions) and is invoked simply by writing its name. Two example procedure calls are:

```
A_PROCEDURE_CALL;
A_CALL_WITH_PARAMETERS(FIRST_PARAMETER,
                       SECOND_PARAMETER);
```

The first is a call of a parameterless procedure, and the second a call of a procedure with two parameters supplied in the call. Chapter 3 discusses subprograms and subprogram calls in detail. For now, in examples for the remaining basic statements, we use procedure calls with illustrative (and unrealistic) names wherever we need an arbitrary statement.

1.3 If Statement

An if statement provides conditional execution of a sequence of statements, based on the value of a BOOLEAN expression. Three examples of possible forms of if statements are shown below:

```
if   A_BOOLEAN_EXPRESSION then
        A_STATEMENT;
        ANOTHER_STATEMENT;
end  if;

if   A_BOOLEAN_EXPRESSION then
        A_SEQUENCE_OF_STATEMENTS;
else
        AN_ALTERNATIVE_SEQUENCE_OF_STATEMENTS;
end  if;

if   A_BOOLEAN_EXPRESSION then
        A_SEQUENCE_OF_STATEMENTS;
elsif ANOTHER_BOOLEAN_EXPRESSION  then
        ANOTHER_SEQUENCE_OF_STATEMENTS;
elsif YET_ANOTHER_BOOLEAN_EXPRESSION  then
        YET_ANOTHER_SEQUENCE_OF_STATEMENTS;
else
        STILL_ANOTHER_SEQUENCE_OF_STATEMENTS;
end  if;
```

Before describing the if statements, a word is in order about formatting style and lexical conventions, which are important influences on readability. In our examples, we adopt the style of the Reference Manual for the Ada Programming Language (Ada, 1983). In particular, we use lower case to write reserved words such as **if, then,** and **else,** and upper case for the names of types, objects, and other entities.

For the first form of if statement, the sequence of statements is executed only if A_BOOLEAN_EXPRESSION evaluates to TRUE. The second form is similar, except that the statements following the **else** (in this case AN_ALTERNATIVE_SEQUENCE_OF_STATEMENTS) are executed only if A_BOOLEAN_EXPRESSION evaluates to FALSE. In the third form, the **elsif** reserved word allows additional BOOLEAN conditions at the same level as the if statement; the first expression that evaluates to TRUE in top-to-bottom order determines the single statement sequence executed. The **elsif** construct makes the selection among mutually exclusive alternatives easier to read than the equivalent nested construction using only **if** and **else** clauses. For example, the if statement:

```
if  B1  then
       S1;
elsif  B2  then
       S2;
else
       S3;
end  if;
```

is easier to read than its equivalent nested form:

```
if  B1  then
       S1;
else
       if  B2  then
             S2;
       else
             S3;
       end  if;
end  if;
```

   The if statement is an example of a compound statement, that is, a statement that can contain other statements nested within it. As the if statement illustrates, compound statements in general are bracketed by an initial reserved word and a closing **end** followed by the repeated initial reserved word.

   Several features of Ada statements improve ease of writing and maintenance. As a rule, wherever a single statement is allowed, multiple statements also are allowed. Thus the introduction of bracketing constructs, such as the BEGIN-END pair of Pascal, is unnecessary when a single statement later must be changed to multiple statements, easing maintenance. Also, statements (and declarations) always are terminated by semicolons. Unlike Pascal, semicolons are terminators rather than separators. Ada thereby avoids a common problem with Pascal programs, which often require several compilations just to eliminate semicolon errors.

1.4 Case Statement

The case statement also provides conditional execution, depending on the value of an expression, which we call the *case selector*. It is illustrated below:

```
case AN_INTEGER_EXPRESSION is
   when 1         => STATEMENTS_FOR_VALUE_1;
   when 2 .. 6    => STATEMENTS_FOR_VALUES_2_THRU_6;
   when 8 | 11    => STATEMENTS_FOR_VALUES_8_OR_11;
   when others    => STATEMENTS_FOR_ALL_OTHER_VALUES;
end case;
```

In this example, the case selector is AN_INTEGER_EXPRESSION. This case state-
ment chooses one of the when clauses for execution, depending on the value of
AN_INTEGER_EXPRESSION. If the value is 1, STATEMENTS_FOR_VALUE_1 is
executed. If the value is within the range 2 to 6 inclusive, STATEMENTS_FOR_
VALUES_2_THRU_6 is executed. If the value is either 8 or 11, STATEMENTS_
FOR_VALUES_8_OR_11 is executed. If the value is none of those given by previ-
ous when clauses, the final **others** clause is chosen, in this case STATEMENTS_
FOR_ALL_OTHER_VALUES.

As the example illustrates, ranges of values are indicated by the symbol "..", and
alternatives are indicated by the symbol "|". The symbol "=>" indicates an associa-
tion; in this case, a set of values given by a when clause is associated with corresponding actions. Alternatives not explicitly specified are indicated by the reserved
word **others,** which (if used) must appear last. Ada follows the principle that similar
concepts should be expressed with a similar notation and dissimilar concepts should
be expressed with different notations. In later chapters, we will see that the above
notations are used to convey the same concepts in different Ada constructs.

The example above shows a case selector with (implied) type INTEGER. Case
selectors, and the corresponding values of the when clauses, are not restricted to
INTEGERs and can include any *discrete* type. Discrete types include enumeration
and integer types and are discussed further in Chapter 2.

Several rules about the case statement improve reliability and readability. First,
the when clauses of a case statement must provide for all the possible values of the
case selector. In the example, the others clause was necessary to account for the
possible values of AN_INTEGER_EXPRESSION not mentioned in the preceding
when clauses. This rule ensures that each of the possible values of the case selector
has an associated when clause, one of which will be chosen when the case statement is executed. This rule is checked during compilation, and thus during execution, it is impossible to "fall through" to the end of the case statement without
having chosen any of the when clauses. Of course, it is possible that indeed no
action is required for a given when clause, in which case the programmer must use
the null statement to indicate explicitly that nothing is to be done. The null statement is illustrated below:

```
case AN_INTEGER_EXPRESSION is
   when 1         => STATEMENTS_FOR_VALUE_1;
   when 2 .. 6    => STATEMENTS_FOR_VALUES_2_THRU_6;
   when 8 | 11    => STATEMENTS_FOR_VALUES_8_OR_11;
   when others    => null;
end case;
```

The explicit **null** informs a reader of the program that the associated choice has not been simply overlooked, but that indeed no action is necessary.

1.5 Loop and Exit Statements

Loop statements in Ada have a very regular form, illustrated in their simplest form below:

```
loop
      STATEMENTS_OF_LOOP_BODY;
end loop;
```

The initial **loop** indicates the top of the loop, and the final **end loop** indicates the bottom of the loop. For the execution of a loop statement, the statements of the loop body are executed repeatedly, and when the last statement of the body is executed, control resumes at the top of the loop.

The above loop cycles indefinitely, which sometimes is useful in operating systems and control programs. More often, however, the loop needs to complete. The exit statement allows a loop statement to complete. The following three loops illustrate several possible forms:

```
loop
      SOME_STATEMENTS;
      exit;
end loop;

loop
      SOME_STATEMENTS;
      exit when A_BOOLEAN_CONDITION;
end loop;

A_NAMED_LOOP:
   loop
      SOME_STATEMENTS;
      exit A_NAMED_LOOP when A_BOOLEAN_CONDITION;
   end loop A_NAMED_LOOP;
```

An exit statement can be placed anywhere in the loop body, and more than one exit can be included in the loop body. The first example illustrates an unconditional exit, which completes the loop. The second example illustrates a conditional exit that depends on the value of A_BOOLEAN_EXPRESSION. If A_BOOLEAN_EXPRESSION is TRUE, the loop completes; if FALSE, the exit has no effect. The intent of an exit statement with a when clause is more transparent than the equivalent if statement containing an exit statement:

```
if A_BOOLEAN_CONDITION then
    exit;
end if;
```

Using the conditional exit statement, a reader immediately grasps that a loop exit may occur, whereas with the if statement, the reader must look further to see the **exit** and also must notice that the if statement does nothing more than the loop exit.

The third example illustrates a *named loop* and an exit statement using the loop name. The loop name is the identifier A_NAMED_LOOP. When no loop name is given in an exit statement, the innermost loop is exited. An exit with a loop name completes the named loop, even if it is not the innermost loop. An exit statement can be used only to complete an enclosing loop.

Ada provides two additional forms of loop statements, the *while* statement and the *for* statement, for cases that commonly occur. With these loops, the basic loop statement is preceded by an *iteration scheme,* which specifies the conditions for executing the loop. These forms are illustrated below:

```
while A_BOOLEAN_EXPRESSION loop
    SOME_STATEMENTS;
end loop;

A_FORWARD_LOOP:
    for INDEX in 0 .. 10 loop
        SOME_STATEMENTS;
    end loop A_FORWARD_LOOP;

A_BACKWARDS_LOOP:
    for INDEX in reverse 0 .. 10 loop
        SOME_STATEMENTS;
    end loop A_BACKWARDS_LOOP;
```

A person reading the program text in top-to-bottom order knows at the top of the loop the conditions that govern execution of the loop. At the start of the each iteration, the while loop first evaluates the loop condition, A_BOOLEAN_EX-PRESSION, and executes the loop body if the condition is TRUE. The loop body is executed repeatedly until the condition evaluates to FALSE.

A for loop iterates over a discrete range. The **for** iteration scheme specifies a *loop parameter* and a discrete range. The body of the loop is executed once for each value in the discrete range. For each such iteration, the loop parameter is assigned the corresponding value of the discrete range. (If the upper limit is less than the lower limit, the loop does not execute at all.) A reverse iteration is similar, except that the iteration proceeds downward from the upper value of the discrete range to the lower value. Note that for a reverse iteration, the range is written in the same order as the forward iteration: The **reverse** indicates that iteration proceeds from the upper to the lower value of the discrete range.

To ensure the simple, intuitive meaning of a **for** iteration, Ada imposes several rules on the loop parameter. The loop parameter is declared *implicitly* by its occurrence in the iteration scheme. Unlike ordinary variables, which must be declared before they are used, the loop parameter is defined implicitly by the iteration scheme. The loop parameter does not exist outside the loop and thus cannot be referred to by statements outside the loop. In this way, Ada avoids the problem in Pascal that the value of the loop parameter is undefined, but nonetheless available, when the loop completes. Moreover, in Ada the loop parameter cannot be modified by the programmer. For example, an assignment statement that attempts to assign a value to the loop parameter is illegal. Hence Ada enforces the simplicity of a for iteration. If more complex loop iteration is required, the more general forms of loop statements should be used instead of the for iteration.

1.6 Block Statement

A *block statement* allows declarations and statements that are logically related to be grouped together. The declarations in a block statement are local to the block statement, and they cease to exist when the block completes. That is, declarations within a block statement are available only within the block. To illustrate, the following block statement declares two local variables, FOUND and COUNT, which are used in a while statement.

```
A_BLOCK_STATEMENT:            -- A block name
   declare
        FOUND : BOOLEAN := FALSE;     -- Local declarations
        COUNT : INTEGER  := 0;
   begin                       -- Begin the sequence of statements
        while not FOUND loop
            COUNT := COUNT + 1;
            FOUND := LOOK_FOR_IT;
        end loop;
   end A_BLOCK_STATEMENT; -- End the sequence of statements
```

FOUND has type BOOLEAN and is initialized to FALSE. COUNT has type INTEGER and is initialized to 0. The next chapter describes object declarations more fully; our purpose in this section is to illustrate declarations with local scope.

The *scope* of a declaration in a block statement is the region of program text that begins at the point the identifier is introduced and extends to the end of the block. For example, in the block statement above, the scope of FOUND extends to the end of the block statement, and FOUND thus can be used in the while loop. Outside the block statement, FOUND ceases to exist and cannot be referenced. The declaration is said to be local to the block statement.

A block allows the programmer to place a declaration close to where it is used, which ensures that it cannot be used inappropriately by other parts of the program. A local declaration also documents to program readers the extent of the declaration. As the example shows, a block statement, like a loop statement, can have a name, which is optional. Unlike a loop statement, a block cannot be completed by an exit statement.

In addition to allowing local variables to be introduced, block statements are useful for other reasons. In particular, they can have exception handlers associated with them. Exception handlers on block statements are discussed in Chapter 4.

Block statements and loop statements are the only statements that can be named. If a name is used, it must be repeated at the end of the statement. Statement names should not be confused with statement labels, which are illustrated in the following section.

1.7 Other Statements

Ada also provides a goto statement which transfers control unconditionally to a statement label, an identifier in eye-catching brackets:

```
<< START >>      -- A statement label is enclosed by "<<" and ">>"
    PAY_50_DOLLARS_FOR_POOR_PROGRAMMING_PRACTICE;
    DO_NOT_COLLECT_200_DOLLARS;
    goto START;
```

Several rules restrict the possible destinations of goto statements. For example, a goto cannot transfer control out of a subprogram nor into a branch of an if statement. Because Ada provides a full set of structured control statements, the goto statement generally should be avoided; we mention it only for completeness.

Ada has other statements related to more novel language features, which are discussed in later chapters. In particular, procedure calls and return statements are discussed in Chapter 3, raise statements in Chapter 4, and entry calls, accept statements, select statements, and delay statements in Chapter 6.

1.8 Exercises

1. In Pascal, the repeat statement is a looping construct that completes the loop when a condition at the bottom of the loop is true. Thus the loop is iterated at least once. Ada has no repeat statement. Write Ada statements equivalent to the Pascal repeat statement below:

```
REPEAT
    THE_LOOP_BODY
UNTIL A_CONDITION;
```

2. Ada comments extend to the end of the line. Many languages, including Pascal and C, have bracketed comments, which means that comments are begun and ended by special comment brackets. For example, Pascal comments are surrounded by "{" and "}". What are the advantages and disadvantages of the Ada style of comments?

3. Write a for loop that iterates from 1 to 99. Write a for loop that iterates from 99 to 1.

4. The increment (or decrement) of the for loop parameter is always 1. Describe the advantages and disadvantages of this rule and illustrate how increments other than 1 could be programmed in Ada.

5. Why does the following case statement cause a compilation error? Repair the error.

```
case AN_INTEGER_EXPRESSION is
    when 1 => ITS_ONE;
    when 2 => ITS_TWO;
end case;
```

6. Without moving the exit statement, rewrite the following loop so that the exit statement completes the outermost loop.

```
loop
    S1;
    loop
        S2;
        exit when B;
    end loop;
end loop;
```

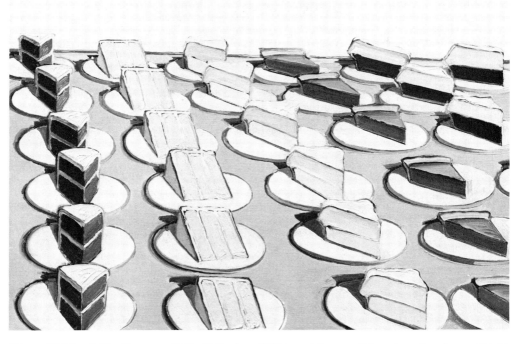

Wayne Thiebaud. Pie Counter. *1963. Collection of Whitney Museum of American Art, Larry Aldrich Foundation Fund Accounting #64.11*

CHAPTER 2

Types, Objects, and Subtypes

As Chapter 0 noted, a major goal of Ada is to allow the compiler to detect errors as early as possible by checking program consistency. Declarations are a key concept to support automatic error detection by the compiler. A declaration introduces an identifier and defines its meaning. An identifier denotes an entity in the program, which can be a type, an object, or one of the other constructs we will discuss. An identifier must be declared before it can be used, and uses of the identifier (and thereby of the denoted entity) must be consistent with its meaning. Consistency in the use of entities is checked automatically by the compiler.

Another important basis for compiler checking is the type concept. A *type* in Ada is a set of values, together with associated operations on those values. For example, INTEGER is a type that has the values ... -2, -1, 0, 1, 2 ... and operations such as addition, subtraction, multiplication, division, and the modulus operation.

Most early programming languages (such as FORTRAN and ALGOL 60) provided integers, real numbers, arrays, and booleans, but few other data types. More recent languages (and Ada is no exception) provide a richer assortment of predefined data types and, more important, facilities to allow the programmer to create *new* data types with associated operations.

Although almost all languages include a concept of types, the degree to which it affects the language differs. Some languages, such as Pascal and Ada, are called *strongly typed*. Strongly typed means that an object in the language has a single type, and language rules ensure that the object is used only in operations appropriate for its type. An Ada variable must be given a particular type before it can be used. The variable may be used only in operations appropriate for the type and may contain only values of the type. For example, an INTEGER variable cannot be assigned a BOOLEAN value. Similar rules apply to the operations of a type. For example, the INTEGER "+" binary operator must have two operands, both of type INTEGER.

Because the compiler enforces the type rules, programmers are protected from a large class of mistakes in the use of objects. In a strongly typed language, the compiler has available and uses more information about the program than is possible for nonstrongly typed languages. Armed with this information, the compiler can maximize the number of errors detected early, at compile-time.

This chapter describes Ada types and objects, emphasizing the influence of the goals of reliability, readability, expressiveness, and portability. Later chapters discuss declarations of other kinds of entities, such as subprograms, packages, and tasks.

2.1 Types and Objects

Figure 2.1 illustrates the six classes of Ada types: scalar types, array types, record types, access types, private types, and task types. The first four are described in this chapter, whereas private and task types will be discussed in Chapters 3 and 6, respectively.

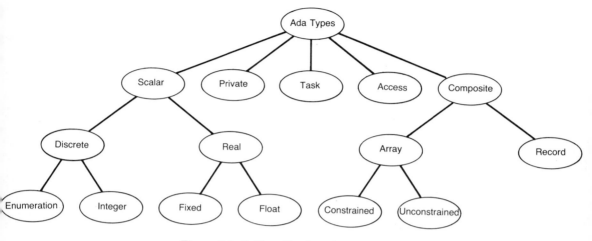

Figure 2.1 A Classification of Ada Types

The first class in Figure 2.1 is the *scalar* type, whose values are either numbers or enumerated values. The values of a scalar type are ordered, and therefore the relational operators, such as "=", "⟨", and "⟩", may be applied to any pair of values of the same scalar type. As the figure indicates, there are two subclasses of scalar types: *discrete* types and *real* types. For discrete types, which include integer and enumeration types, the concepts "next value" and "previous value" are meaningful. For example, given the INTEGER value 1, the next value is 2 and the previous is 0. Real types, on the other hand, represent the real numbers, which conceptually are a continuum.

Like most programming languages, Ada comes equipped with predefined types such as BOOLEAN, INTEGER, CHARACTER, and FLOAT. The type BOOLEAN has two associated values: FALSE and TRUE. The value returned by the ordinary relational operators

"=",   "/=",   "⟨",   "⟨=",   "⟩",   "⟩="

when applied to appropriate operands is of type BOOLEAN. These operators are, respectively, equality, inequality, less than, less than or equal, greater than, and greater than or equal. A BOOLEAN value is not numeric, and therefore arithmetic operations on objects of BOOLEAN type are illegal.

Ada predefines the type INTEGER. Some implementations also may include other predefined integer types such as SHORT_INTEGER and LONG_INTEGER, with shorter or longer ranges, respectively, than INTEGER. As stated above, the allowable operations on integers include addition, subtraction, multiplication, and division, written, respectively, as "+", "-", "*", and "/".

The predefined type CHARACTER contains the 128 characters of the standard ASCII character set. The printable ASCII characters are written as 'A', 'a', 'B', and so forth. The nonprintable characters are represented with special identifiers such as BS (backspace), LF (line feed), and CR (carriage return) declared in a predefined package named ASCII. As is the case with BOOLEANs, CHARACTERs are not numbers, and so arithmetic operations may not be performed upon them.

The predefined type FLOAT is used to represent real numbers, with associated operations of floating point arithmetic. This type and other real types will be covered in Section 2.3.

In Ada, an *object* is something that can contain a value. All objects are either *constants* or *variables*. The value of a variable can be changed during execution, whereas the value of a constant cannot change once the constant has been initialized.

Before an object can be used, it must be associated with a type. This association of a type with an object, called an *object declaration*, is fundamental to the goals of a strongly typed language, for it enables the compiler to check the consistency of subsequent operations upon the object.

Consider the following declarations:

```
COUNT : INTEGER;
RATE   : FLOAT;
```

The first declaration declares a variable COUNT and specifies that its type is INTEGER. The second specifies that the variable RATE has type FLOAT. The programmer must use these variables only in operations appropriate for their types. For example, the equality operation, "=", can be applied only to objects of the same type. Hence, an attempt to test the equality of COUNT and RATE as in the expression

```
COUNT = RATE
```

will cause a compilation error. (There is, however, a way to convert COUNT explicitly to a value of type FLOAT so that it then could be compared with RATE.) In a more weakly typed language, a comparison similar to the one above might be allowed. For example, in the language C, such an operation would be legal. The compiler would generate a run-time call to convert the integer portion of the expression to floating point. This conversion is transparent to the programmer.

Ada allows several objects to be declared with a single declaration:

```
RATE, DISTANCE, WEIGHT : FLOAT;
```

These declarations have the same effect as writing

```
RATE     : FLOAT;
DISTANCE : FLOAT;
WEIGHT   : FLOAT;
```

Constant declarations appear somewhat like variable declarations. A constant must be initialized in its declaration, and once initialized, its value cannot be changed. A constant is initialized by an expression given after the ":=" in the constant declaration, as illustrated below:

```
MAXIMUM_WITHDRAWAL : constant FLOAT    := 1000.00;
NUMBER_OF_TELLERS  : constant INTEGER := TELLER_COUNT;
```

MAXIMUM_WITHDRAWAL is declared as a constant of type FLOAT with value 1000.00. The declaration for NUMBER_OF_TELLERS illustrates that the value of a constant need not be determined at compile-time. For example, assuming TELLER_COUNT is the identifier of a function, NUMBER_OF_TELLERS is initialized to the value returned by the function call. (Functions will be discussed in Section 3.2.)

The process (during execution) by which a declaration achieves its effect is called *elaboration;* whereas a statement is said to be executed, a declaration is said to be elaborated. The elaboration of the variable COUNT above includes allocating storage to contain the value of the variable. The elaboration of the constant NUMBER_OF_TELLERS includes allocating storage, evaluating the expression TELLER_COUNT, and initializing the object.

Variables, like constants, also may be given an initial value within the declaration. A declaration such as

```
RATE    : FLOAT := 10.25;
```

creates a variable of type FLOAT and initializes it to 10.25. By initializing the variable in the declaration, it is impossible for the program to attempt to use the variable before it has been given a value. Forgetting to initialize variables is a common programming error. The ability to initialize a variable where it is declared keeps the declaration and its initial value together, making it easier to avoid uninitialized variables.

Ada provides a special kind of declaration for integer or real constants whose values are known at compile-time. Such constants are called *named numbers* and are illustrated below.

```
EULER_CONSTANT : constant := 0.57721;
LIGHT_YEAR     : constant := 5_878_000_000_000;
```

Named numbers may be used wherever a numeric literal can appear. As the example illustrates, underscores may be placed in numeric literals to improve their readability. Named numbers are not quite the same as ordinary constants: Note that there is no type explicitly given in these declarations. The Ada compiler associates a special type, either *universal integer* or *universal real*, depending on the value, with a named number. The universal types have arbitrarily fine precision, and arithmetic using them is exact. They are internal to the compiler, and therefore are not available to the programmer. An internal type is called an *anonymous type*, because the programmer cannot refer to it with a name. In cases where a universal number must be represented in the executable code, the compiler chooses an appropriate representation.

An important distinction between ordinary constants (e.g., NUMBER_OF_ TELLERS) and named numbers (e.g., EULER_CONSTANT) is that the value of a constant need not be determined until elaboration of the constant declaration, which occurs during program execution. On the other hand, the value of a named number is determined at compilation time.

One reason for using named numbers is to enhance portability. LIGHT_YEAR could have been declared as an ordinary INTEGER constant:

```
LIGHT_YEAR      : constant INTEGER := 5_878_000_000_000;
```

But this declaration is admissible only if the underlying implementation for INTE-GER contains values as large as the number of miles in a light year. Using the conventional implementation, this declaration of LIGHT_YEAR assumes at least a 44-bit representation for type INTEGER. On some machines this declaration will be valid, but on other machines the declaration perhaps would have to be rewritten as:

```
LIGHT_YEAR      : constant LONG_INTEGER := 5_878_000_000_000;
```

Hence the declaration is implementation-dependent. By using a named number declaration instead, the programmer avoids overspecification, which would result from using a particular integer type, thereby making the program more portable.

By default, numeric literals are base 10 numbers; however, they may be written with any base between 2 and 16, as illustrated below:

```
BASE_TWO      : constant := 2#1111_1111#;
BASE_SIXTEEN : constant := 16#FF#;
BASE_EIGHT    : constant := 8#377#;
```

The three named numbers above all have the decimal value 255.

2.2 Enumeration Types

In addition to the predefined types, the programmer also has available powerful type declaration facilities to create new data types more appropriate for the application. A programmer-defined type defines the properties of a class of objects in the application domain. The objects then can be understood more easily in terms of the application, rather than in terms of their representation in the language. A type definition collects these properties into a single place, both for documentation and easier modification. Because of these benefits of abstraction and documentation, well-written Ada programs extensively use the data type definition features.

Whereas an object declaration associates an object name with a type, a type declaration associates a type identifier with a type definition. A type declaration is introduced by the reserved word **type**. Type and object declarations can be interspersed, so that related types and objects can be grouped together.

One way for the programmer to declare a new type is by listing its values. For example, the following declaration

```
type DAY is (MONDAY, TUESDAY, WEDNESDAY, THURSDAY,
             FRIDAY, SATURDAY, SUNDAY);
```

defines a new type called DAY, which has seven values. A type defined by enumerating its values is called an *enumeration* type, and its values are called *enumeration literals*. The identifiers MONDAY, TUESDAY, and so forth are the literal values of the type DAY, just as 101, TRUE, and 'A' are literal values of the types INTEGER, BOOLEAN, and CHARACTER, respectively. The example below illustrates uses of the type DAY:

```
PAYDAY : constant DAY := FRIDAY;
TODAY  : DAY;
...

TODAY := MONDAY;
if TODAY = PAYDAY then
    GET_WEEKLY_REPORTS;
end if;
```

For simplicity of the examples in this chapter, where necessary we separate declarations from statements by an ellipsis ("...") which is not part of Ada. This program fragment declares a constant named PAYDAY and a variable named TODAY, both of type DAY. Following the two declarations is an assignment statement, which assigns the literal value MONDAY to the variable TODAY. The if statement uses the equality operator "=" to test if TODAY and PAYDAY have the same value. If the value returned by this operator is TRUE, the procedure GET_WEEKLY_REPORTS is called.

Note that we could have initialized the variable TODAY in its declaration:

```
PAYDAY : constant DAY := FRIDAY;
TODAY  :          DAY := MONDAY; -- initial value of TODAY
```

The clarity achieved by using enumeration types is striking: the above text is understandable even to someone not familiar with Ada. Without enumeration types, the programmer is forced to encode the days of the week into some other type (such as integers). Such an encoding would be far less clear and maintainable, because the program indeed is concerned with days of the week, not integers.

User-defined data types not only enhance program readability, they also facili-tate program development. The programmer can think in terms of the application domain, concentrating on the problem solution rather than on the underlying rep-resentation of entities such as FRIDAY. Of course, at a lower level the values of type DAY are represented as numbers. Representation is the concern of the com-piler, however, and the programmer can consider these values more abstractly as days of the week.

Next, consider the following enumeration type declarations:

```
type CUSTOMER_KIND is (INDIVIDUAL,  CORPORATE,  JOINT,
                          PARTNERSHIP);
type TREND          is (UP,  DOWN,  STABLE,      VOLATILE);
type PEST           is (MOSQUITO,  TERMITE,      CREDITOR);
type INTEREST_KIND  is (PRIME,     BONDS,        DISCOUNT);
type PLACE          is (BOSTON,    NEW_YORK,  PHILADELPHIA);
type PLANET         is (MERCURY,  VENUS,        EARTH,
                          MARS,     JUPITER,      SATURN,
                          URANUS,   NEPTUNE,    PLUTO);
```

Like type DAY above, these types define abstract values which can be used in oper-ations appropriate for enumeration types. The definition of the enumeration type indicates the order of the values. Therefore given the declaration and initialization:

```
MARKET : TREND := DOWN;
```

the relational expression

```
(MARKET < STABLE)
```

is legal as well as TRUE. The expression

```
MONDAY >= DOWN
```

is illegal, however, because MONDAY and DOWN belong to different types.

Although we usually think of enumeration types as user-defined, the predefined types BOOLEAN and CHARACTER are enumeration types as well. The predefined declaration of BOOLEAN is, in fact,

```
type BOOLEAN is (FALSE,  TRUE);
```

2.3 Real Types

The real numbers (in the mathematical sense) are the set of numbers used to per-form numeric calculations. These numbers include

$$2.0, \quad 3/32, \quad 1/3, \sqrt{2}, \quad \pi$$

Like the integers, only a finite subset of real numbers can actually be represented in a computer. For example, most computers are capable of representing the *exact* value of only the first two numbers in the above list. Hence in real-number computations we work with only approximations of most real values. Ada provides two classes of types, *floating point* types and *fixed point* types, that approximate real numbers.

Floating point numbers are expressed with a fractional part (called the mantissa) and an exponential part. With floating point numbers, the exponential is written as a power of some fixed base, usually 2 or 10, and the mantissa is limited to a fixed number of decimal places. For example, consider floating point numbers with four decimal places in the mantissa. One such number is 0.1235e2, which represents the number we normally write as 12.35. Another floating point number is 0.1235e7, which equals 1_235_000.0.

For a given number of decimal places in the mantissa, floating point numbers are more closely "packed" around zero than the numbers further away from zero. Consider, for example, that the next floating point number (having a four decimal mantissa) after 0.1235e2 is 0.1236e2, which lies a distance of 0.01 from its nearest neighbor. However, the larger number 0.1235e7 is a distance of 1000 from the next floating point number. Thus the accuracy of floating point numbers is relative: the accuracy is "fine" for small numbers, but the accuracy is "coarse" for large numbers. The advantage of floating point numbers is that both very large and very small numbers can be represented.

In the past, programmers had only indirect means for specifying the accuracy of real types used in a program. For example, in Pascal there is only one type for real arithmetic, which varies in accuracy among implementations. Other languages, such as FORTRAN and ALGOL 68, offer the programmer more than one real type, but no assurance of the precisions of these types.

Let us now look at the Ada definition of floating point types. All Ada compilers provide the predefined type FLOAT, introduced above, whose accuracy *is* implementation-dependent. A compiler may also provide other predefined (and implementation-dependent) types such as SHORT_FLOAT and LONG_FLOAT, which have "substantially" less or more accuracy.

Implementation-dependent, predefined types are inadequate for the creation of portable software. For portability, the programmer must be able to indicate explicitly the accuracy required in the application. Consider the floating point type declaration:

type DISTANCE **is digits** 6;

The type DISTANCE is required to have at least six decimal digits of accuracy in the mantissa. This declaration actually will be represented as one of the predefined floating point types. The particular predefined type is selected by the implementation, but the declaration guarantees that the type has the requested precision. If the compiler cannot support the requested precision, the declaration is rejected.

A declaration also may provide a *range constraint* as in

type MONEY_SUPPLY **is digits** 4 **range** 1.0e9..1.0e12;

which specifies that values of type MONEY_SUPPLY have at least four digits of accuracy, within the range 1.0e9..1.0e12. As we will see in the next section, range constraints also can be placed on discrete types.

In addition to the ordinary arithmetic operators ("+", "-", "*", and "/"), exponentiation ("**") is also allowed with floating point numbers. The right operand, the exponent, must be an integer.

```
2.0 ** (-1)      -- 0.5
2.0 ** 0         -- 1.0
2.0 ** 2         -- 4.0
```

When the exponent is positive, exponentiation is defined to be repeated multiplication of the left operand. When the exponent is negative, it is defined as the reciprocal of the value obtained by repeated multiplication. When the exponent is 0, the result is 1. Note that the exponent in the first of the above expressions is surrounded by parentheses, which are necessary because the operator "**" has higher precedence than the unary minus "-".

Fixed point types are the other class of real types. One of the rationales for including fixed point types in Ada is that the intended target machine may not support floating point operations in hardware. Unlike floating point types, the values of a fixed point type are evenly distributed. With a fixed point type the programmer specifies the distance, or *delta*, between successive numbers. The declarations

```
type INTEREST_RATE is delta 0.0001 range 4.0..30.0;
type DOLLAR        is delta 0.01   range 0.0..1.0e8;
```

define two fixed point types with values at least as "fine" as 0.0001 and 0.01, respectively. The declaration for INTEREST_RATE logically defines the values

4.0000, 4.0001, 4.0002, ... , 29.9999, 30.0000

A range constraint must always be provided in the declaration of a fixed point type.

Within a program, two identical definitions might be used to declare two different types. For example,

```
type UNEMPLOYMENT_RATE is delta 0.0001 range 0.0..100.0;
type HUMIDITY          is delta 0.0001 range 0.0..100.0;
```

Attaching a single name (such as HUMIDITY) to a type definition is an example of *factorization*. The advantages are twofold: When an object is declared, its intended use can be deduced from the type to which it belongs. Second, if the definition needs to be modified (say, from **delta** 0.0001 to **delta** 0.001), only one place in the program (at the site of the type declaration) must be changed. On the other hand, consider the difficulty of maintaining a program if only predefined floating point types (e.g., FLOAT and LONG_FLOAT) are allowed. Changing the type declarations for a collection of logically related objects would require searching the entire program text for the appropriate object declarations.

Addition, subtraction, multiplication, and division are valid operations for fixed point numbers. Addition and subtraction of two fixed point numbers of the same type result in a value of that type. Multiplication and division of two fixed point numbers, however, always result in a value of the predefined anonymous type *universal fixed*, which has an arbitrarily small delta. For multiplication or division, the result must be converted explicitly to the correct type before it can be assigned to a variable of a user-defined fixed point type. For example, assuming A_FIXED and B_FIXED are fixed point variables with type FINE_FIXED, the following assignments illustrate conversion of the result of fixed point operations:

```
A_FIXED :=  FINE_FIXED(A_FIXED * B_FIXED);
A_FIXED :=  FINE_FIXED(A_FIXED / B_FIXED);
```

The expression FINE_FIXED(...) is a *type conversion*. It explicitly converts the result of the operation to the type FINE_FIXED.

Certain arithmetic operators with fixed and integer operands also are predefined. For example, the following assignments are legal:

```
A_FIXED :=  A_FIXED * 3;   -- A_FIXED + A_FIXED + A_FIXED
A_FIXED :=  3 * A_FIXED;   -- A_FIXED + A_FIXED + A_FIXED
A_FIXED :=  A_FIXED / 3;
```

The first two operations yield the same value as adding A_FIXED three times. The third, however, yields a fixed point number that is an approximation of the quotient.

2.4 Subtypes

Given a predefined or user-defined type, the programmer can create *subtypes* of this type. A subtype associates a name with a subset of the values of a type; the subset is defined by placing a *constraint* upon the type, as in the examples below:

```
subtype BANKING_DAY      is DAY      range MONDAY..FRIDAY;
subtype WEEKEND          is DAY      range SATURDAY..SUNDAY;
subtype SHORT_TERM       is INTEGER  range 1..365;
subtype ACCOUNT_BALANCES is DOLLAR   range 100.00..100_000.00;
subtype ACCOUNT_ID       is POSITIVE range 1..1e9;
```

These subtypes have range constraints that indicate their value range. In addition to range constraints, other kinds of constraints are defined for arrays and records. A subtype declaration *does not* introduce a new type; rather, it puts a constraint on the values of an existing type, called the *base* type of the subtype. For SHORT_ TERM, the base type is INTEGER and the subset contains the values 1 through 365.

Given a subtype declaration, objects can be declared with this subtype:

```
EARLY_DAY : BANKING_DAY;
LATE_DAY  : WEEKEND;
S         : SHORT_TERM;
BALANCE   : ACCOUNT_BALANCES;
ID        : ACCOUNT_ID;
```

Because the subtype of S is SHORT_TERM, S cannot contain a value outside the range 1..365. The compiler ensures that, during execution, the value of S is within this range. An attempt to give S a value outside its subtype will cause a run-time error called CONSTRAINT_ERROR. (CONSTRAINT_ERROR is an example of the general Ada facility called exceptions, discussed in Chapter 4.)

The type of an object is the base type of its subtype. Hence, the type of variable S is INTEGER, and S can be used wherever an INTEGER can be used. For example, if the variable J has type INTEGER (with no constraint), J and S can be assigned to one another:

```
J := S;        -- cannot cause CONSTRAINT_ERROR
S := J;        -- must be checked at run-time
```

When executed, the assignment to S will check that the current value of J satisfies the subtype of S. The compiler arranges for this check, if necessary, by inserting additional machine code to check the value before performing the assignment.

A type permits compile-time checking that an object is used only in operations that are appropriate for it. A subtype permits run-time checking that an object contains only values that satisfy its constraint. The distinction is illustrated by the following assignment to S:

```
S := 0;        -- legal, but will cause CONSTRAINT_ERROR
```

This statement is legal, because assignment is defined for INTEGERs and 0 is an INTEGER. Because 0 does not satisfy the subtype of S, however, the statement will cause CONSTRAINT_ERROR when executed. The word *legal* in Ada means that the construct is acceptable to the compiler. It does not necessarily mean that the construct will not cause a run-time error.

A subtype declaration provides more information to the compiler so that the compiler can check uses of the subtype. Subtypes also make the program more self-documenting by indicating the intended use of an object. A person reading or modifying the program has more information about how the object is used. Types and subtypes both support the Ada philosophy that errors should be detected as early (and as automatically) as possible.

Ada provides operations called *membership tests* so that the programmer can test if a value belongs to a particular subtype or range. These operations return a value of type BOOLEAN. To illustrate, assume the variable TODAY has type DAY. The program might base its action on whether TODAY belongs to the subtype WEEK-END:

```
if TODAY in WEEKEND then              -- membership test
    SLEEP_LATE;
end if;
```

The value tested (in this case TODAY) must have the same type as the subtype or range that appears after the reserved word **in**. In this example, both TODAY and the subtype WEEKEND have type DAY.

The membership test **not in** may also be used to produce the complementary result to the membership test **in**. For example:

```
if TODAY not in WEEKEND then
    GO_TO_WORK;
end if;
```

When scalar types are involved, a range may be given on the right side of the membership test instead of a subtype name. It is legal, therefore, to write:

```
TODAY in TUESDAY..THURSDAY
```

In general, a discrete subtype identifier and the discrete range it denotes are interchangeable. For example, BANKING_DAY can be used as a shorthand for the range MONDAY .. FRIDAY, as illustrated by the statements below:

```
for I in BANKING_DAY loop             -- equivalent to MONDAY .. FRIDAY
    BE_OF_NOBLE_MIND;
end loop;
```

```
case TODAY is
    when BANKING_DAY  => SUFFER_SLINGS_AND_ARROWS;
    when WEEKEND      => PERCHANCE_TO_DREAM;
end case;
```

2.5 Attributes

Ada provides a collection of operations that can be used to determine certain properties of types, objects, and subtypes during program execution. These special operations are called *attributes*. There are several attributes in Ada; we will describe a few of the more common ones now, and others will be introduced later.

Two useful attributes are 'FIRST and 'LAST. Note that attributes are distinguished by an apostrophe preceding their name. These two attributes may be used with any scalar type or subtype. When used, they return the first and last values, respectively, of the type or subtype.

```
DAY'FIRST                -- same as MONDAY (see 2.2)
DAY'LAST                 -- same as SUNDAY
BANKING_DAY'FIRST        -- same as MONDAY (see 2.4)
BANKING_DAY'LAST         -- same as FRIDAY
SHORT_TERM'FIRST         -- same as 1       (see 2.4)
SHORT_TERM'LAST          -- same as 365
MONEY_SUPPLY'FIRST       -- same as 1.0e9  (see 2.3)
MONEY_SUPPLY'LAST        -- same as 1.0e12
```

An attribute is an expression and, like all expressions, yields a value. For example, the following declarations are predefined subtypes declared using an attribute of INTEGER:

```
subtype POSITIVE is INTEGER range 1 .. INTEGER'LAST;
subtype NATURAL  is INTEGER range 0 .. INTEGER'LAST;
```

The value INTEGER'LAST defines the upper bound of these subtypes.

For objects of a discrete type, the attributes 'SUCC and 'PRED return respectively the succeeding and preceding values of a given value of the type. For example:

```
DAY'SUCC(FRIDAY)            -- SATURDAY
BANKING_DAY'SUCC(FRIDAY)    -- also SATURDAY though not a
                           -- BANKING_DAY
DAY'PRED(TUESDAY)          -- MONDAY
DAY'PRED(MONDAY)           -- causes CONSTRAINT_ERROR
```

Observe that the attributes 'SUCC and 'PRED are functions, whereas 'FIRST and 'LAST are not.

Attributes allow a programmer to simplify maintenance by avoiding redundancy and overspecificity. For example, suppose we write:

```
subtype SHORT_TERM is INTEGER range 1..365;
```

and suppose that later (perhaps in another compilation unit) another programmer writes

```
INDEX : SHORT_TERM := 1;
...
while INDEX <= 365 loop
    -- some statements
end loop;
```

The intent of this fragment clearly is to perform some computation as long as INDEX remains in the range of SHORT_TERM. The initialization of INDEX and the while loop condition implicitly depend upon the range of SHORT_TERM. If SHORT_TERM later must be changed (perhaps to take account of leap years), we must search the program for all expressions that implicitly refer to properties of the old definition of SHORT_TERM, so that we can change them to be consistent with the new definition. Rather than changing only the subtype declaration, we also must locate and change all implicit uses of properties of the subtype declaration. Locating these dependences is tedious, and even when we locate them, we are prone to errors.

Because they repeat information defined by the subtype declaration, redundant literals such as 1 and 365 above make maintenance harder. The code is vulnerable if the subtype declaration later is changed. To avoid this problem, we can use attributes to make the dependencies upon the subtype definition explicit, rather than implicit:

```
INDEX : SHORT_TERM := SHORT_TERM'FIRST;
...
while INDEX <= SHORT_TERM'LAST loop
    -- some statements
end loop;
```

Later, if we modify the definition of SHORT_TERM, the compiler automatically will use the new values of the attributes SHORT_TERM'FIRST and SHORT_TERM'LAST. Using attributes, we avoid a tedious clerical task associated with changes.

2.6 Operators and Precedence

Operator precedence refers to the order in which operators are applied to their operands (in the absence of parentheses). The operator symbols, in order of increasing precedence, are given below:

logical operators	**and**	**or**	**xor**		
relational operators	=	/=	<	<=	>	>=
binary adding operators	+	-	&		
unary adding operators	+	-			
multiplying operators	*	/	**mod**	**rem**	
highest precedence operators	**	**abs**	**not**		

Table 2.1 Operator Precedences

The four logical operators are **and, or, xor**, and **not**. (Technically, **not** is considered a highest precedence operator.) An **and** returns TRUE if and only if each of its two operands is TRUE, and otherwise FALSE. The operators **or** and **xor** are "inclusive or" and "exclusive or," respectively. An **or** returns TRUE if at least one of its operands is TRUE. An **xor** returns TRUE if exactly one of its operands is TRUE. A **not** returns the logical negation of its operand.

When parentheses are not used to indicate evaluation order explicitly, the precedences determine the order. For example, because **not** has greater precedence than **or**, the expression

> **not** WEALTHY **or** WISE

means

> **(not** WEALTHY) **or** WISE   ,

and not

> **not** (WEALTHY **or** WISE)

If the last meaning is intended, parentheses are required.

Several other operators are noteworthy. Integer division, "/", always "truncates" toward zero, and so the following expressions are TRUE:

```
 11 /  5 =   2
-11 /  5 =  -2
 11 / -5 =  -2
-11 / -5 =   2
```

The operator **abs** may be applied to a numeric expression to return its absolute value:

```
abs 5   =   5
abs(-5) =  5
abs(5 - 10)  =  5
```

An operator related to integer division is the **rem** operator, which takes two operands, both of an integer type. The value of (M **rem** N) is the remainder left after dividing M by N with the same sign as that of M. For example, each of the following BOOLEAN expressions is TRUE:

```
10 rem 5  =   0
11 rem 5  =   1
12 rem 5  =   2
13 rem 5  =   3
14 rem 5  =   4
```

The **mod** operator is similar, except that the result has the sign of N, and its behavior is different than **rem** when the signs of A and B are different.

The "&" operator is the catenation operator. As we will see shortly, it is used with arrays.

Certain operations are not shown in the table. The membership tests **in** and **not in** have the same precedence as the relational operators. Two other operations not shown in the table are the short circuit control forms **and then** and **or else**. These forms are similar to **and** and **or** and have the same precedence. The difference is that the operands are evaluated serially, in the order they appear in the expression; that is, **and then** evaluates the second operand only if the first operand is true. Similarly, **or else** evaluates the second operand only if the first operand is FALSE. We will see shortly an example of the usefulness of the short circuit forms.

2.7 Arrays

Arrays are one of the composite types. An object of a composite type contains subobjects called *components*. In the case of arrays, the components must all be of the same type or subtype. Consider the following array type definitions:

```
type EUCLIDEAN_VECTOR     is array(1..3)              of FLOAT;
type YEARLY_DOLLAR_LIST   is array(1..365)           of DOLLAR;
type VARIABLE_DOLLAR_LIST is array(1..N)             of DOLLAR;
type DAILY_TREND          is array(BANKING_DAY)      of TREND;
type DAILY_DEPOSIT        is array(MONDAY..FRIDAY)
                             of ACCOUNT_BALANCES;
type DAILY_RATES          is array(INTEREST_KIND, BANKING_DAY)
                             of INTEREST_RATE;
```

These array declarations specify an *index constraint* and a component type or subtype. In the case of YEARLY_DOLLAR_LIST, the index constraint is 1..365 and the component type is DOLLAR. Objects of type YEARLY_DOLLAR_LIST, then, are arrays of 365 components, each of type DOLLAR. An array index type may be either integer or enumeration.

The size of an array type need not be known at compile-time. The index constraint is evaluated when the type declaration is elaborated. That is, the index constraint can be determined during execution at the point of the type declaration. For example, assuming N is a previously-declared INTEGER variable, the upper bound of the type VARIABLE_DOLLAR_LIST above is determined by the value of N when the declaration of VARIABLE_DOLLAR_LIST is elaborated. (If the value of N is less than 1 at this point, arrays of type VARIABLE_DOLLAR_LIST have no components; an array with no components is called a null array.)

DAILY_TREND and DAILY_DEPOSIT illustrate that an index constraint can be given by either a subtype name or a range. The last declaration has two index constraints and therefore defines a two-dimensional array. Ada places no restriction on the dimensionality of arrays. Figure 2.2 presents the logical view of two arrays.

Let us next consider some array object declarations:

```
ACCOUNT_HISTORY   : YEARLY_DOLLAR_LIST;
DAILY_BALANCES    : YEARLY_DOLLAR_LIST;
THIS_WEEKS_RATES  : DAILY_TREND;
```

The components of these arrays can be assigned values individually:

```
ACCOUNT_HISTORY(J)           := 500.50;
THIS_WEEKS_RATES(MONDAY) := UP;
```

The expression used as an index must satisfy the index constraint of the array; otherwise, the run-time error condition known as CONSTRAINT_ERROR occurs. Therefore the first assignment above is valid only if J is in the range 1..365. If J is outside this range, CONSTRAINT_ERROR occurs. Similarly, MONDAY is an admissible index for THIS_WEEKS_RATES, whereas using SATURDAY as an index would cause CONSTRAINT_ERROR.

Arrays also may be assigned by a single assignment statement:

```
ACCOUNT_HISTORY := DAILY_BALANCES;
```

This assignment statement assigns the 365 component values of DAILY_BALANCES to ACCOUNT_HISTORY.

In addition to being able to assign arrays with a single assignment statement, two arrays may also be tested for equality or inequality with a single operator. For example, after the preceding assignment, the expression

```
ACCOUNT_HISTORY = DAILY_BALANCES
```

yields the BOOLEAN value TRUE. These last comments are a corollary to the more general rule that assignment and equality testing are available for all types in Ada

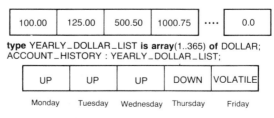

Figure 2.2 Logical View of Arrays

with the exception of a special class called limited types (to be discussed in Chapter 3).

Ordinarily, an object declaration must be preceded by the corresponding type declaration. With arrays, however, it is legal to combine these two steps into a single declaration, which defines the type and declares a single object:

```
GOOD_WEATHER : array(DAY)   of BOOLEAN;
LEDGER       : array(1..365) of DOLLAR;
```

Declarations such as these are useful when only one object of the array type is needed. With this kind of object declaration the compiler associates an anonymous type with the array object. A consequence is that if more than one array is declared, for example,

```
A, B : array (1..5) of INTEGER;
```

each has a different anonymous type, because the above declaration is equivalent to the two declarations

```
A : array (1..5) of INTEGER;
B : array (1..5) of INTEGER;
```

Readers familiar with Pascal will note that the meaning of an anonymous array in Ada is different than its meaning in Pascal. In Pascal, A and B have the same type; in Ada, A and B have different types.

As shown above, Ada allows entire arrays to be used in expressions and assignment statements. Ada also allows a contiguous subsequence of a one-dimensional array to be used similarly; this subsequence is called a *slice*. To illustrate:

```
DEPOSITS_1985, DEPOSITS_1986  : YEARLY_DOLLAR_LIST;
...
DEPOSITS_1986(1..31) := DEPOSITS_1985(335..365);
      -- DEC '85 to JAN '86
```

The last 31 components of the array on the right side of the assignment statement form the slice that is assigned to the slice on the left. In general, an assignment statement involving arrays is legal if both sides of the assignment have the same array type and the same number of components.

In some languages, a programmer has no way to construct explicitly the value of an entire array. Instead, array values can be created only by assigning values to each component, for example, within a loop statement or by a sequence of assignments. Construction of the array value therefore is more diffuse than a single assignment statement. Ada overcomes this limitation by providing a constructor for array values, called an *aggregate*. An aggregate is an array expression that includes a value for each component. The following declaration declares a EUCLIDEAN_ VECTOR and initializes it with an aggregate.

```
UNIT : EUCLIDEAN_VECTOR := (1.0, 0.0, 0.0);
```

The component values of the aggregate are listed in order. Therefore the above assignment is equivalent to a sequence of assignments for each component of the array:

```
UNIT(1) := 1.0;
UNIT(2) := 0.0;
UNIT(3) := 0.0;
```

The aggregate shown above might also have been written as

```
(1.0, others => 0.0)
```

The **others** part, if used, gives a value for components in the remainder of the array and must always appear at the end of the aggregate. The delimiter " => " can be read as "gets the value." An aggregate must give a complete value for the array: Every component must be given a value by the array aggregate, whether by explicit value or by an **others** clause.

Consider the following aggregates of type DAILY_TREND.

```
(UP, UP, UP, DOWN, VOLATILE)

(MONDAY .. WEDNESDAY => UP,
 THURSDAY            => DOWN,
 FRIDAY             => VOLATILE)

(THURSDAY           => DOWN,
 FRIDAY             => VOLATILE,
 MONDAY .. WEDNESDAY => UP)

(MONDAY | TUESDAY | WEDNESDAY => UP,
 THURSDAY            => DOWN,
 FRIDAY             => VOLATILE)
```

Each of these aggregates has the same value, which illustrates several alternative ways in which aggregates may be expressed. The first aggregate uses *positional association*, whereas the last three use *named association*. An association specifies a value for an array component (or components). With positional association, the component values are listed in order. With named association, a component value is associated with an index value, and the order of named associations is irrelevant. Positional and named associations may not be mixed in an array aggregate. Named associations make the association between a component and its value explicit and thereby improve readability.

Note that a named association may specify the value of a single component, a range of components (e.g., MONDAY .. WEDNESDAY), or a choice of components (e.g., MONDAY | TUESDAY | WEDNESDAY). In addition, as noted earlier, a subtype identifier can be used in place of its discrete range, which means the following aggregate also is allowed:

```
(BANKING_DAY  => UP)
```

The flexibility of named notation is useful when assigning values to large arrays.

An important use of aggregates is to initialize arrays. Arrays, like other kinds of objects, can be constants, and aggregates may be used to initialize them.

```
LAST_WEEK   : DAILY_TREND := (UP,UP,UP,DOWN,VOLATILE);
GOOD_WEEK : constant DAILY_TREND := (MONDAY..FRIDAY  => UP);
```

Constant arrays are useful for defining tables of values that will not change. Most languages can initialize large tables only by executing an assignment for each component in the array. Such initializations are awkward and do not allow the array to be declared constant.

2.8 Unconstrained Array Types

Arrays of type YEARLY_DOLLAR_LIST have 365 components, and arrays of type DAILY_TREND have 5 components. It might seem, then, that an array type always is "constrained" to have the same size. To avoid this restriction, Ada allows an array type to be *unconstrained*. An unconstrained array type can be used to create objects that have different sizes, but nevertheless have the same type. (Once declared, however, an array object cannot vary in size during execution.) Consider the following declaration:

```
type DOLLAR_LIST is array (INTEGER range <>) of DOLLAR;
```

The symbol "<>", pronounced "box," means the array type is unconstrained. This declaration specifies that the type DOLLAR_LIST contains components of type DOLLAR, and that the index type is INTEGER, but the index constraint (the array bounds) is not defined by the type. The index constraint must be supplied when an object of this type is declared. For example,

```
DEPOSITS_1987        : DOLLAR_LIST(1..365);
DEPOSITS_MARCH_1987 : DOLLAR_LIST(1..31);
```

These declarations say that DEPOSITS_1987 is an array of 365 components and DEPOSITS_MARCH_1987 is an array of 31 components. Both arrays have the *same* type; their index constraints, however, differ.

The reason for postponing the specification of the array bounds (rather than declaring them directly in the type declaration) may not be immediately obvious. In some strongly typed languages, it is impossible to write library subprograms that perform an operation on arrays of different sizes without sacrificing type security. Suppose, for example, a Pascal programmer needs to write a procedure to find the largest component in an arbitrary-size array of integer components. Such a procedure unfortunately is impossible, because in Pascal, arrays of the same type always have the same number of components. In Ada terms, the index subtypes of Pascal arrays are the same. Instead of one general array-handling procedure, a Pascal programmer must write a different procedure for each array size.

An Ada programmer, on the other hand, can write a general subprogram that operates on objects of a given unconstrained array type, say DOLLAR_LIST. The array bounds inside the subprogram are taken from the actual parameter passed to the subprogram; the bounds are not fixed when the subprogram is declared. For example, if the program was designed to find the largest component in the array, it then could be applied to DEPOSITS_1987 as well as DEPOSITS_MARCH_1987. Unconstrained array types promote reusability because a single subprogram can be used with array objects of the same unconstrained type.

To illustrate, consider the body of a subprogram to find the largest component in an array of the unconstrained type DOLLAR_LIST. Subprograms and parameters are discussed further in the next chapter, but for now, we assume that X is the name of a parameter of type DOLLAR_LIST. Because X is unconstrained, it acquires its bounds from the actual parameter passed to the subprogram. It is impossible to know the bounds before a call to the subprogram.

```
LARGEST_SO_FAR : DOLLAR := DOLLAR'FIRST;
...
for I in X'FIRST..X'LAST  loop
   if   X(I) ) LARGEST_SO_FAR  then
      LARGEST_SO_FAR := X(I);
   end  if;
end  loop;
```

This fragment finds the largest number in the array X by inspecting each component in the array and keeping the current largest number in a variable LARGEST_SO_FAR. The attribute DOLLAR'FIRST is the first value of the real type DOLLAR (i.e., 0.0) and is used to initialize LARGEST_SO_FAR.

Note the attributes 'FIRST and 'LAST used with the array object X. When used with an array name, these attributes evaluate to the first and last index values, respectively, in the index range. For example, if X is the array DEPOSITS_1987, then X'FIRST is 1 and X'LAST is 365. Since the attributes are evaluated during program execution, and yield the bounds of the actual array, the above algorithm is sufficiently general to process any array object of type DOLLAR_LIST. We will return to this example in the next chapter.

Arrays have an attribute 'RANGE, which is a shorthand for the range X'FIRST .. X'LAST. Hence the iteration scheme above could be written as:

for I **in** X'RANGE **loop**

Another useful attribute of array objects and constrained array subtypes is 'LENGTH, which yields the number of values in the index range of the array.

Finally, we must make a small confession. Strictly speaking, *all* array types in Ada are unconstrained. A constrained array declaration such as

type EUCLIDEAN_VECTOR **is array** (1..3) **of** FLOAT;

actually declares EUCLIDEAN_VECTOR to be a subtype of an anonymous unconstrained array type. Nonetheless, we usually refer to "type EUCLIDEAN_VECTOR" even though technically it is not precise.

2.9 Strings

One of the predefined types is an unconstrained array type called STRING. Its definition is:

type STRING **is array** (POSITIVE **range** ⟨⟩) **of** CHARACTER;

where POSITIVE is the predefined subtype containing the positive values of INTEGER. With unconstrained array types we observed that an object is given an index constraint in the object declaration. In many cases, a better approach is to create a subtype with the needed constraints. For example,

subtype PASSWORD_TYPE **is** STRING(1..8);
subtype CODE   **is** STRING(1..32);
subtype LINE   **is** STRING(1..80);

These subtypes are formed by placing an index constraint on an existing array type, much in the same way subtypes were formed by placing range constraints on scalar types. Declaring a constrained subtype is preferable if many objects will be declared with the constraint or if the subtype is to be used as the subtype of a subprogram formal parameter. Arrays now may be declared of subtype PASSWORD_TYPE in the usual manner:

CUSTOMER_PASSWORD : PASSWORD_TYPE;   -- an array of 8 characters

Because it is an array, a STRING object may be assigned a value using an aggregate:

```
CUSTOMER_PASSWORD : PASSWORD_TYPE := ('R','O','S','E','B','U','D',' ');
```

A more convenient way of constructing an aggregate for a character array (e.g., for a STRING) is to use double quotes:

```
CUSTOMER_PASSWORD : PASSWORD_TYPE := "ROSEBUD ";
QUERY_PASSWORD    : constant STRING  :=
                            "PLEASE ENTER YOUR PASSWORD";
```

Note the distinction between the kinds of quotes in the expressions 'R' and "R". The 'R' is a literal value of type CHARACTER. The "R" is an aggregate for an array of one character.

QUERY_PASSWORD illustrates a distinction between declaring variables and constants of an unconstrained type. For a variable, the index constraint must be given by the subtype or by an explicit constraint. For CUSTOMER_PASSWORD, the subtype PASSWORD_TYPE gives the index constraint. In contrast, for a constant, the index constraint can be given by the value of the initializing expression, as illustrated by QUERY_PASSWORD.

The component subtype of an array can be any type including another array type. For example,

```
type DEPOSITS is array(1980..2000) of YEARLY_DOLLAR_LIST;
```

is legal. The components, however, must all have the same subtype. When the components are themselves arrays, they must be constrained in the same way. Therefore a declaration such as

```
type RAGGED_PAGE is array(1..55) of STRING;      -- illegal
```

is illegal, because STRING is an unconstrained type. To correct this last declaration, we must constrain the component type:

```
type PAGE is array(1..55) of STRING(1..80);
     -- or
type PAGE is array(1..55) of LINE;
```

Note that it also is legal to declare an unconstrained array type whose components are arrays all having the same subtype. For example,

```
type FLEXIBLE_PAGE is array (POSITIVE range <>) of STRING(1..80);
```

Two useful attributes related to STRINGs are 'VALUE and 'IMAGE. The first of these attributes is a function that maps a value of type STRING into a corresponding value of a discrete type. For example,

```
I : INTEGER := INTEGER'VALUE("101");
J : INTEGER := 101;    -- I and J both have the value 101
```

In this example, the attribute INTEGER'VALUE maps the string "101" to the value 101. The attribute 'VALUE may also be used with enumeration types:

```
TODAY : DAY := DAY'VALUE("MONDAY");              -- MONDAY
```

The attribute 'IMAGE performs the inverse operation: it maps values of an enumeration or integer type into an expression of type STRING which represents its displayable format:

```
I              : INTEGER    := 101;
THREE_DIGITS : STRING(1..3) := INTEGER'IMAGE(I); -- "101"
```

A powerful array operator is "&"—the catenation operator. It can be applied to two operands of the same one-dimensional array type and its result is the array formed by the concatenation of the left array and the right array.

```
SALUTATION : constant STRING := "DEAR ";
NAME       :          STRING(1..4) := "JOHN";
GREETING   : constant STRING := SALUTATION & NAME;
                               -- "DEAR JOHN"
```

The catenation operator also can be used to concatenate an array with a value of the array component type.

The relational operators ($<$, $<=$, $=$, $/=$, $>$, $>=$) are defined for STRINGs and, as usual, return a BOOLEAN value. They perform a character-by-character comparison of the component values, starting at the first index position of each array. The result is determined by the component comparisons in order: if the arrays are unequal, the first unequal comparison determines the result. The following expressions illustrate:

```
"PI"           <   "SKY"          -- TRUE
"lower case" >     "UPPER CASE" -- TRUE; Ada uses ASCII
"Terrace"    >=  "Terrain"      -- FALSE
"WIDE"         <= "WIDEST"       -- TRUE
```

Although they are most useful for STRINGs, the relational operators are defined for any one-dimensional array of discrete type.

2.10 Records

A *record* is a composite type that contains a related set of named components. Records are called *structures* in some languages. Unlike arrays, the components of a record can have different types. The following type declaration defines a record type with three components:

```
type TRANSACTION is record
     ACCOUNT    : ACCOUNT_ID;                    -- Section 2.4
     PASSWORD   : PASSWORD_TYPE;                 -- Section 2.9
     AMOUNT     : DOLLAR           := 0.0; -- Section 2.3
end record;
```

Each record component is given by a component name followed by the name of the component type or subtype. In this example, the component AMOUNT also has a default initial value of 0.0. The default initial value specifies that when an object of type TRANSACTION is created, AMOUNT is given the value 0.0, unless the record object is initialized explicitly by the programmer.

Given a record object, a component of the record object can be selected using dot notation:

```
LAST_TRANSACTION : TRANSACTION;

...
LAST_TRANSACTION.ACCOUNT   := 55_238_1234;
LAST_TRANSACTION.AMOUNT    := 125.00;
LAST_TRANSACTION.PASSWORD := "ROSEBUD ";
```

Figure 2.3 provides a conceptual view of an object of type TRANSACTION. The programmer has considerable freedom to create new type definitions from already existing ones; that is, types may be composed from other types. For example, it is possible for a record type to include record or array types as components or for arrays to contain records.

The type of a record component must be an existing type or subtype; it cannot introduce a new type. For example, the following record declaration is illegal:

```
type ILLEGAL_RECORD is record
     A : array (1..10) of INTEGER;     -- Illegal component type
end record;
```

because the type of A cannot introduce a new type, in this case an anonymous array. A component subtype, however, can introduce an additional constraint on the values of the component:

```
type R is record
     SMALL_DOLLAR : DOLLAR range DOLLAR'FIRST .. 1.0e3;
     ...
end record;
```

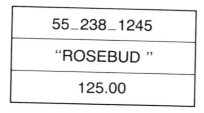

Figure 2.3 Type TRANSACTION

The component SMALL_DOLLAR in this example cannot be given a value larger than 1.0e3.

Like arrays, records also may be given values by using aggregates. The following two assignment statements illustrate both positional and named association; the same value is assigned in both cases.

```
THIS_TRANSACTION := (55_238_1245, "ROSEBUD ", 125.00);
THIS_TRANSACTION := (ACCOUNT    => 55_238_1245,
                     PASSWORD  => "ROSEBUD ",
                     AMOUNT    => 125.00);
```

With named association, each component is associated explicitly with a value. Both positional and named associations may be used in the same record aggregate, in which case positional associations must precede any named associations. As with array aggregates, the named association is somewhat more verbose but easier to read. A person reading the aggregate does not have to refer to the type declaration to know the values assigned to components. Record aggregates are "constructors" for building record values. Without aggregates, a record value could be constructed only by individual assignment statements for each component.

2.11 Discriminants

As defined above, the component PASSWORD of the record type TRANSACTION is a fixed-size array of characters. All objects of this type have passwords of 8 characters. To accommodate shorter passwords, the program would need to pad the array with spaces or perhaps insert a terminating character into the array.

To make records more flexible, Ada provides a mechanism called a *discriminant*, which parameterizes the record type and allows records of the same type to vary somewhat. A discriminant is a component of the record and appears in the record definition next to the name of the type. The discriminant must have a discrete type. Let us rewrite our declaration for TRANSACTION using a discriminant:

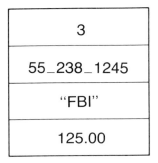

Figure 2.4 An Object of Type TRANSACTION, Including a Discriminant.

```
type TRANSACTION(PASSWORD_SIZE : POSITIVE) is record
     ACCOUNT     : ACCOUNT_ID;
     PASSWORD    : STRING(1..PASSWORD_SIZE);
     AMOUNT      : DOLLAR := 0.0;
end record;
```

This new version of TRANSACTION has a discriminant named PASSWORD_SIZE upon which the component PASSWORD *depends*. Individual records of type TRANSACTION may now be declared.

```
A1, A2   : TRANSACTION(3);                           -- have 3 character
                                                     -- PASSWORDs
B        : TRANSACTION(PASSWORD_SIZE => N);  -- has N character
                                                     -- PASSWORD


subtype SECRET_TRANSACTION is TRANSACTION(24);
C        : SECRET_TRANSACTION;                       -- has 24 character
                                                     -- PASSWORD
```

Each of the declarations using type TRANSACTION includes a *discriminant constraint*, which establishes the value of the discriminant. Figure 2.4 illustrates an object of this revised definition of TRANSACTION. The value of the discriminant determines the size of the component PASSWORD. Note that either positional or named associations may be used in discriminant constraints. We see that discriminant record types are similar to unconstrained array types: The type definition does not entirely define all the properties of the objects. The above objects each belong to the same type, but A1 and A2 have a different constraint than C. Assuming N is a variable, the constraint for B will not be known until the elaboration of the object declaration.

Constrained objects may be assigned only values that satisfy the same constraints. For example:

```
A1  :=  A2;                              -- ok
A1  :=  (3, 55_238_1245, "FBI", 125.00); -- ok
A1  :=  B;                               -- ok only if N is 3
A1  :=  C;                               -- causes CONSTRAINT_ERROR
```

Note that, because a discriminant is itself a component, a value for the discriminant must be supplied in an aggregate for a discriminant record.

Next, consider some declarations to describe house pets. For example, we might declare

```
type PET is (DOG, CAT, PARROT);
type HOUSE_PET is record
     KIND     : PET;
     AGE      : NATURAL;
end record;
```

As given above, the declaration for HOUSE_PET is not very flexible. It would be useful to include other information specific to each kind of pet. To allow associating different components with a type, the type can be defined as a *variant record*. To declare a record type with variants, we use a discriminant:

```
type HOUSE_PET(KIND : PET) is record
     AGE        : NATURAL;
     case KIND is
         when DOG =>
              HOUSEBROKEN : BOOLEAN;
         when CAT =>
              FUSSY : BOOLEAN;
         when PARROT =>
              VOCABULARY : NATURAL;
     end case;
end record;
```

Variant records provide additional flexibility by allowing alternative components to be associated with given values of the discriminant. Every object of type HOUSE_PET has a discriminant named KIND and a component named AGE. Note that the discriminant name KIND appears again after **case**, followed by three variants each preceded by **when**. Each variant gives a discriminant value (or values) and a list of components to be associated with objects that have that discriminant value. In this example, each object has either a component named HOUSEBROKEN, FUSSY, or VOCABULARY, depending on the value of the discriminant, KIND.

```
subtype CANINE is HOUSE_PET(KIND => DOG);
ROVER  : CANINE;
PIERRE : HOUSE_PET(CAT) := (CAT, 5, TRUE);
POLLY  : HOUSE_PET(PARROT);
```

ROVER, PIERRE, and POLLY all have the same type, but different constraints. The variable ROVER may be assigned only values that have the discriminant DOG. Similarly, PIERRE and POLLY are constrained to be a CAT and PARROT, respectively. Note that subtypes of variant records, such as CANINE, also can be declared. A record with variants may only be used in a manner consistent with the discriminant value:

```
ROVER.HOUSEBROKEN := TRUE;        -- ok
ROVER.VOCABULARY   := 5;          -- causes CONSTRAINT_ERROR
```

In a variant record declaration, *all* values of the discriminant subtype must be covered by the when clauses.[1] Recall that this rule is similar to the rule for case statements. Hence in the declaration of HOUSE_PET above, it would be illegal to omit, for example, the value PARROT from the when clauses of the variant part of the record.

As another example, U.S. pennies engraved with the head of Abraham Lincoln have been minted since 1909. Cities where the minting has occurred are Denver, Philadelphia, and San Francisco. An appropriate record type might be

```
type MINT is (D,P,S);
subtype PENNY_YEAR is POSITIVE range 1909..2000;
type LINCOLN_PENNY is
    record
        SITE : MINT;
        YEAR : PENNY_YEAR;
    end record;
```

To coin collectors, the information provided by this record type may not be sufficient. For certain years, additional information is necessary to describe pennies. For example, in 1909, some pennies were inscribed with "VDB," the initials of Victor D. Brenner, who designed the Lincoln cent. And in 1960, some pennies were minted with an unusually small date.

Let us rewrite this declaration using variants:

```
type LINCOLN_PENNY(YEAR : PENNY_YEAR) is
    record
        SITE : MINT;
        case YEAR is
            when 1909 =>
                VDB : BOOLEAN;
            when 1960 =>
                SMALL_DATE : BOOLEAN;
            when others =>
                null;
    end record;
```

---

[1] If the bounds of the subtype cannot be determined at compile-time, all values of the base type must be covered.

The choice **others** may only occur as the last variant and covers all values of the discriminant subtype not covered by previous choices. The others clause is convenient because most values of the discriminant subtype PENNY_YEAR will be treated in the same way. Note that the **null** component is given in this variant; it indicates that no component exists for this variant.

2.12 Unconstrained Records

In the above examples of records with discriminants, all objects are *constrained;* that is, the discriminant value is bound to the object and cannot be changed. Ada also allows records to be *unconstrained.* Consider another version of TRANSAC-TION:

```
type TRANSACTION(PASSWORD_SIZE : POSITIVE := 8) is record
    ACCOUNT     : ACCOUNT_ID;
    PASSWORD    : STRING(1..PASSWORD_SIZE);
    AMOUNT      : DOLLAR := 0.0;
end record;
```

This declaration appears much like the one before, except that the discriminant now has a *default expression.* The meaning of the default expression is that, if the object declaration does not specify a constraint, the discriminant value initially will be 8. Again, consider the following declarations:

```
X : TRANSACTION(10);        -- constrained
Y : TRANSACTION(K);         -- constrained
Z : TRANSACTION;            -- unconstrained
```

These declarations create three objects of type TRANSACTION. The first object is constrained and has a PASSWORD_SIZE of 10. The second object is constrained to the value of K when the object declaration is elaborated. Because it does not specify an explicit constraint in the object declaration, the third object is unconstrained. It initially has the default value 8, but it may be given other values during execution through full record assignments.

Assuming K is a variable, the declaration of Y is an example of a record whose discriminant is not known at compile-time. The declaration of Z, however, is an example of a record whose discriminant can vary during its existence.

Because the discriminant value of Z is not constrained, the following assignments are legal:

```
Z := X;        -- Z.PASSWORD now has size 10
Z := Y;        -- Z.PASSWORD now has size K
```

The following assignments, however, must be checked during execution to guarantee correct discriminant values:

```
X := Z;
Y := Z;
```

A variable declaration may be left unconstrained only if the record type definition has default values for its discriminants. This rule is in the spirit of software reliability, for it ensures that record discriminants always have a meaningful value.

Unconstrained objects also may be declared when the record has variants:

```
type HOUSE_PET(KIND : PET := DOG) is record
    AGE     : NATURAL;
    case KIND is
        when DOG    =>
            HOUSEBROKEN : BOOLEAN;
        when CAT    =>
            FUSSY : BOOLEAN;
        when PARROT =>
            VOCABULARY : NATURAL;
    end case;
end record;

MASCOT : HOUSE_PET(KIND => DOG);    -- constrained
OUR_PET : HOUSE_PET;                -- unconstrained, initially DOG


...


OUR_PET := (CAT, 2, TRUE);         -- now a cat
OUR_PET := MASCOT;                 -- now a dog
MASCOT.HOUSEBROKEN := FALSE;       -- legal
OUR_PET.VOCABULARY := 100;         -- ok if OUR_PET.KIND is
                                   -- PARROT
```

Note the potential danger of the last statement; if the component VOCABULARY does not exist, an attempt to access it, if permitted, could have unpredictable results.

To prevent such misuse of variant records, Ada provides several safeguards. First, a discriminant cannot be assigned a value in isolation; it may only receive a value through a complete record assignment. Therefore,

```
OUR_PET.KIND := PARROT;                    -- illegal
```

is illegal, but a complete record assignment to OUR_PET can change the discriminant (because it is unconstrained). With this rule, the compiler can ensure that the component values assigned to a variant record are consistent with the value of the discriminant. This rule prevents an object of type HOUSE_PET from becoming inconsistent, for example, by having a discriminant value of DOG, but (erroneously) a component value suitable for VOCABULARY. Second, as noted earlier, run-time discriminant checking ensures that only components consistent with the

discriminant are accessed. If a violation occurs during execution, CONSTRAINT_
ERROR will be raised.

2.13 Access Types

For many programs, the programmer does not know how much storage the program will require during execution, because of an inability to predict the program
input. For example, we may need a program to store a sequence of objects of type
TRANSACTION, but we may not know in advance how many objects there will be.

One solution is to declare an array of transactions, using an overestimate of the
number of transactions to define the maximum index of the array. If the estimate
is much larger than the required size, or if the desired list operations are inconvenient on arrays, this approach can be inefficient in space and time. An alternative
solution is to use *access* types.

Up to this point, the objects presented have had ordinary values such as
1000.00, 56, TRUE, MONDAY, (55_238_1245,"ROSEBUD ",125.00), and so forth.
In contrast, an access object, rather than containing "the real information," instead
provides access to this information. Access objects are called pointers or references
in some languages: they simply provide an indirect way of accessing other data.
The following declares an access type:

type TRANSACTION_NAME **is access** TRANSACTION;

This declaration defines a type, TRANSACTION_NAME, whose objects are references to objects of type TRANSACTION. The type TRANSACTION in this example
is the nondiscriminant version from Section 2.10. Figure 2.5 depicts the relationship between an access object and its designated object.

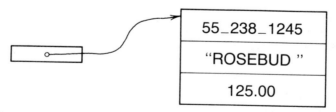

Figure 2.5 An Access Value with Designated Object

Given an access type, the program can allocate a new object "on the fly" as it
needs one. This dynamic allocation is accomplished by an expression called an
allocator. To illustrate, let us first declare a variable of type TRANSACTION_NAME:

THAT_TRANSACTION : TRANSACTION_NAME;

Next, we execute the following Ada statement:

```
THAT_TRANSACTION := new TRANSACTION;
```

The effect is that a new object having type TRANSACTION is created and an access value *designating* it is assigned to THAT_TRANSACTION. Because THAT_TRANS-ACTION now "points to" or designates the newly allocated record, we can access the record and its components.

The dot notation is used to access components. Thus

```
THAT_TRANSACTION.AMOUNT := 125.00;
```

assigns a value to the component named AMOUNT in the allocated record. Note that, in contrast to languages such as Pascal and C, no explicit dereference operator is required to refer to the designated object of an access variable. For example, in Pascal, if P is a pointer, the operator "^" is defined such that P^ is the object to which P points. In Ada, the dereference is implicit in the dot selection of an access variable.

The entire object (rather than a component) designated by an access value may be referred to by suffixing the access variable with **all** as in the following assignment:

```
THAT_TRANSACTION.all := LAST_TRANSACTION;
```

This last statement assigns the value of a declared record named LAST_TRANSAC-TION to a dynamically allocated record designated by THAT_TRANSACTION. Of course, a dynamically allocated object also may be assigned to another dynamically allocated object. If T1 and T2 both have type TRANSACTION_NAME, the statement

```
T1.all := T2.all;
```

assigns the value of the record designated by T2 to the record designated by T1. Component accesses also can use the **all** notation:

```
THAT_TRANSACTION.all.AMOUNT := 125.00;
```

This assignment is equivalent to the earlier assignment to the AMOUNT component.

Access variables themselves may be assigned. The statement

```
T1 := T2;
```

assigns to T1 the value of T2, thereby making T1 designate the object designated by T2. As elsewhere in Ada, an assignment such as above may take place only if both operands have the same type. In weakly typed languages (e.g., C) a single pointer may point to objects of many different types, a frequent source of errors.

Note that there are two kinds of objects: those that have a name and those that are designated by an access value. Objects that have a name are created by the elaboration of a declaration, whereas those that are accessed are created by allocation.

Access objects can refer only to objects created by an allocator and cannot refer to named objects:

```
THAT_TRANSACTION : TRANSACTION_NAME;
LAST_TRANSACTION : TRANSACTION;
...
THAT_TRANSACTION := new TRANSACTION;      -- legal
THAT_TRANSACTION := LAST_TRANSACTION;     -- illegal
```

Conversely, the only way a program may refer to an allocated object is with an access object.

Access variables may be assigned a special value written as **null**. This value indicates that the access variable designates no object. When access variables are first created, their value is **null** unless they are initialized otherwise. An attempt to access the designated object of a null access variable raises CONSTRAINT_ERROR, because there is no designated object to access.

Using access objects, we can build dynamic data structures, such as linked lists, by placing in the record a component whose type is an access type to the same kind of record. Many implementations of linked lists are possible; one example is to have the access component be a forward pointer to the next record in the list. Figure 2.6 illustrates this structure.

In effect, we want to define a self-referencing record type. In Ada, the relevant type declarations are given in three steps, as illustrated below:

```
type TRANSACTION_NODE;                        -- incomplete declaration.
type NODE_POINTER is access TRANSACTION_NODE;
type TRANSACTION_NODE is record              -- full declaration
     ACCOUNT           : ACCOUNT_ID;
     PASSWORD          : PASSWORD_TYPE;
     AMOUNT            : DOLLAR;
     NEXT_TRANSACTION  : NODE_POINTER;
end record;
```

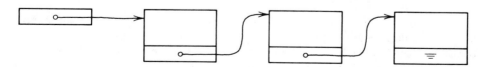

Figure 2.6 A Linked List of Records

The first declaration is called an *incomplete* declaration. It introduces the name of a type, but does not give its full definition. The full definition must be given in a later type declaration that uses the same type name. The second declaration defines an access type to objects of type TRANSACTION_NODE. Finally, the third declaration is the full declaration for the incomplete type. (In contrast, Pascal requires the pointer declaration first, rather than an incomplete declaration for the designated type.)

Given these declarations, the following fragment creates a linked list having N records.

```
START : NODE_POINTER :=  new TRANSACTION_NODE;
TAIL   : NODE_POINTER :=  START;
...
for I in 1..N-1 loop
    TAIL.NEXT_TRANSACTION :=  new TRANSACTION_NODE;
    TAIL :=  TAIL.NEXT_TRANSACTION;
end loop;
```

Note that **new** is used N times: once in the initialization of the variable START, and N-1 times within the loop. The variable TAIL is used to access the last record in the linked list. At the end of the for loop TAIL designates the N-th (and last) record in the list. START designates the first record. The forward pointer of the last record need not be assigned a null value because the default value of any access object is **null**.

To illustrate traversing the linked list, we search for the component AMOUNT that is greatest. We assume that the first record in the list is designated by START. Further we assume that the last record in the list can be recognized by its null value for NEXT_TRANSACTION.

```
CURRENT           : NODE_POINTER :=  START;      -- beginning of list
LARGEST_SO_FAR : DOLLAR :=  DOLLAR'FIRST;
...
while CURRENT /= null loop
    if CURRENT.AMOUNT > LARGEST_SO_FAR   then
        LARGEST_SO_FAR :=  CURRENT.AMOUNT;       -- update largest
                                                 -- value
    end if;
    CURRENT :=  CURRENT.NEXT_TRANSACTION; -- point to next node
end loop;
```

The while loop traverses the linked list of TRANSACTION_NODEs, maintaining in the variable LARGEST_SO_FAR the greatest value of AMOUNT so far encountered. The loop ends when the CURRENT access value is **null**. The while loop tests for this condition and causes the iteration to terminate when a null access value is encountered.

To illustrate a common situation that occurs with access types, suppose we would like to search a list for a record that satisfies some predicate. Specifically, assume we would like to find a record whose ACCOUNT is the same as that of a variable DESIRED_ACCOUNT. For speed of the search, if we find the record, we want to stop looking. Thus we do not want to traverse the entire list as we did in the above example. It is tempting to write:

```
while CURRENT /= null
   and CURRENT.ACCOUNT /= DESIRED_ACCOUNT
loop
      CURRENT := CURRENT.NEXT_TRANSACTION;
end loop;
```

This attempt may not be successful, however, because if CURRENT is **null**, CURRENT.ACCOUNT may raise CONSTRAINT_ERROR, because the **and** does not forbid evaluation of its second operand. For such situations, a short circuit operator is handy. The following fragment uses **and then** to ensure serial evaluation:

```
while CURRENT /= null
   and then CURRENT.ACCOUNT /= DESIRED_ACCOUNT
loop
      CURRENT := CURRENT.NEXT_TRANSACTION;
end loop;
```

Some languages require short circuit evaluation in all cases (i.e., the language has only **and then**). Depending on the implementation, however, compiler optimizations may be less effective for short circuit forms. Ada includes the "don't care" **and** for situations where evaluation order is irrelevant.

Ordinary objects can be initialized when they are declared. Similarly, the designated object of an access value can be initialized during allocation by use of a *qualified expression*, as shown below:

```
type TRANSACTION_NAME is access TRANSACTION;
THAT_TRANSACTION          : TRANSACTION_NAME;
...
THAT_TRANSACTION := new TRANSACTION'(                    -- see 2.11
                        PASSWORD_SIZE  => 14,
                        ACCOUNT        => 55_238_1234,
                        PASSWORD       => "ZOROASTRIANISM"
                        AMOUNT         => 125.00);
```

The qualified expression includes an aggregate that initializes the value of the designated TRANSACTION. The type TRANSACTION in this example is the discriminant version from Section 2.11. The discriminant alone can be initialized by including the discriminant constraint in the allocation:

```
THAT_TRANSACTION := new TRANSACTION(14);
```

In this example, PASSWORD_SIZE is constrained to the value 14, but other components are uninitialized. Note that the discriminant constraint is not a qualified expression.

To ensure that a discriminant always has a value, a discriminant record created by an allocator must be constrained, either by a qualified expression, by a discriminant constraint, or, in the case of unconstrained records, by default discriminant values.

Finally, a word is in order about deallocation. In Pascal, the built-in procedure DISPOSE can be used to deallocate a dynamically allocated object. The programmer passes to DISPOSE a pointer to the object to be deallocated. Allowing the programmer to deallocate objects explicitly is dangerous because of the possibility of *dangling pointers*. A dangling pointer occurs when two pointers both designate the same object, and the object then is deallocated using one of the pointers. The other pointer now designates deallocated storage. The program mistakenly may access the now-defunct object through this useless pointer, with unpredictable results.

Despite the dangers of explicit deallocation,Ada, like Pascal, makes it possible to deallocate objects. To enable deallocation, the programmer instantiates the predefined generic procedure UNCHECKED_DEALLOCATION. The concepts of generic procedures and their instantiation will be discussed in Chapter 5, and UNCHECKED_DEALLOCATION in particular will be discussed in Chapter 8.

2.14 Derived Types

Thus far we have examined several ways to define new types. Another way is to declare a new type to be identical to an existing type. The new type is called a *derived type*, and the existing type is said to be its *parent type*. Although they have identical values, operations, and properties, the two types are logically distinct. Consider the following derived type declaration:

```
type POPULATION is new INTEGER;
```

The declaration creates a new type POPULATION identical to its parent type INTEGER. INTEGER and POPULATION are distinct types, however, so if I has type INTEGER and P has type POPULATION, the following assignments are illegal:

```
I := P;
P := I;
```

If it is necessary to assign a value of type POPULATION to a variable of type INTEGER, or vice versa, then explicit conversion must be used:

```
I :=  INTEGER(P);
P :=  POPULATION(I);
```

If we define another type, say PET_POPULATION, derived from type POPULA-
TION, PET_POPULATION is said to be indirectly derived from INTEGER. Type
conversions are allowed between a type and all the types derived directly or indirectly from it and also between the derived types themselves. For example:

```
type PET_POPULATION is new POPULATION;
R : PET_POPULATION;
...
R :=  PET_POPULATION(P);
P :=  POPULATION(R);
R :=  PET_POPULATION(I);
```

As the last assignment illustrates, the conversion need not be fully qualified; that
is, the intervening type name POPULATION need not be given in converting an
INTEGER to PET_POPULATION.

The type POPULATION inherits from INTEGER the predefined operators, such
as "=", "+", and "*". Therefore the following is legal:

```
P1, P2 : POPULATION;
...
P1 :=  P1 + P2;
```

A derived type is a new type, although in general it is implemented the same as
the parent type. Derived types allow the programmer to keep different concepts
distinct, and thereby enable additional type checking.

Consider, next, the declaration

```
type POPULATION is range 1..100_000;
```

which appears like a subtype declaration but with no indication of the base type
between **is** and **range**. (Compare this declaration with that of SHORT_TERM in
Section 2.4.) This declaration is a shorthand for the following:

```
type anonymous is new predefined_integer_type;
subtype POPULATION is anonymous range 1..100_000;
```

Here, *anonymous* indicates a name, chosen by the compiler, that is unavailable to
the programmer. The parent type is a predefined integer type, chosen by the compiler, large enough to contain the range of values 1..100_000. For example, the
compiler could choose INTEGER if it has sufficient range, or if INTEGER has insufficient range, it could choose LONG_INTEGER (if provided). Thus POPULATION
is a subtype of a derived type of an unspecified predefined integer type. The phrase

integer types refers to the predefined integer types (if more than one) and all types derived from them.

This form of derived type is more portable than one that explicitly names the parent type. For example, consider the following subtype declaration:

 subtype POPULATION **is** INTEGER **range** 1..100_000;

This declaration is valid for a processor whose predefined INTEGER type includes the value 100_000. For another processor, however, INTEGER may have insufficient range, although the implementation might provide a predefined type LONG_INTEGER that could be used. Unfortunately, the subtype declaration would be rejected by the compiler for this second processor. The derived type declaration, however, is more portable: The compiler chooses the predefined type with sufficient range, if such a type is available in the implementation.

2.15 Summary

In Ada, types are a central theme. A type defines a set of values, operations, and rules. Ada provides predefined types such as INTEGER, FLOAT, CHARACTER, STRING, and BOOLEAN. More important, it provides facilities for the programmer to create new types tailored to a particular application. These facilities include enumeration types, real types, array types, record types, access types, and others. By defining new types the programmer can build abstraction into a program and can concentrate upon the application rather than upon the data representation.

Ada has many of the same features as Pascal and other high-level languages, but there are some important distinctions. The value of a constant or the constraint upon an object need not be known at compile-time, but instead can be determined when the declaration is elaborated during program execution. Unconstrained array types allow a type definition to be made without any constraint on the index, which enables general purpose array-handling routines to be written without specifying the array size in advance.

Subtypes are a way of specifying a constraint upon an already existing type. There are several ways to create subtypes. For example, a range constraint may be given to a scalar type (discrete type or numeric type). An index constraint may be placed on an unconstrained array type. A discriminant constraint may be given to a record type. These constraints are checked during execution to ensure that an object contains only meaningful values.

Records are composite objects whose components may have different types. Some records have a special component called a discriminant, which parameterizes the record type definition. One use of discriminants is to create records with an array component whose index constraint depends on the discriminant. Another use of discriminants is to create variant records whose components may vary during execution, depending on the discriminant.

Access objects are used to reference other objects which have been dynamically allocated through allocator expressions. Record types may be defined with components that are access types allowing self-referential structures such as linked lists to be defined. Access types allow complex data structures to be built dynamically.

A derived type is logically identical to its parent type, yet for purposes of type checking, it is distinct. Derived types can be used to increase abstraction and improve portability.

2.16 Exercises

1. Explain the concepts of types and subtypes.

2. Scalar types get their name from the fact that there is a natural order among the values of the type. What kinds of scalar types does Ada provide?

3. The concept of a type includes a set of values. How many values do each of the following types contain?

   (a) **type** DAY **is** (MONDAY, TUESDAY, etc..); see Section 2.2
   (b) **type** DAILY_TREND **is array**(BANKING_DAY) **of** TREND;   see
       Section 2.7
   (c) INTEGER   (*Hint*: attributes!)

4. Explain and illustrate how attributes assist in maintainability. Consider a loop statement that must iterate over all planets whose distance from the sun is greater than that of Mars:

   for WORLD **in** JUPITER .. PLUTO **loop**
   ...
   end loop;

   Rewrite this fragment using attributes.

5. What similarities and dissimilarities do unconstrained array types and discriminant record types have?

6. Write a fragment of Ada text that traverses the linked list shown in Figure 2.6 and deletes from the list the record whose AMOUNT component is greatest.

7. What is the effect of the following declaration and statements?

   P : NODE_POINTER;   -- see Section 2.13
   ...
   P := **new** TRANSACTION_NODE;
   P.NEXT_TRANSACTION := **new** TRANSACTION_NODE;
   P.NEXT_TRANSACTION.NEXT_TRANSACTION :=
                       new TRANSACTION_NODE;

8. Two uses of record discriminants were illustrated in this chapter. It was shown how discriminants can be used to parameterize a bound for an array component, and it was also shown how discriminants can be used to create variant records. Two further uses of discriminants are to give a default expression for a component and to provide a discriminant constraint for a component whose type has a discriminant. Explain and illustrate.

9. Record types are the only types whose objects can be given default values. Objects declared will assume any default component values unless they are overridden by initialization. In the following text, what is the initial value of X.J? What is the initial value of Y.J?

```
type T is record
    J : INTEGER := 1;
end record;

X : T;
Y : T := (J => 2);
```

10. Are the following declarations legal?

```
type R(J : POSITIVE) is record
    S : STRING(1..J);
end record;

A : array(1..10) of R;
```

11. Which of the assignment statements, if any, are legal? Explain.

```
type UA is array(INTEGER range <>) of INTEGER;
A : UA(1..5);
B : UA(1..5);
C : array(1..5) of INTEGER;
D : array(1..5) of INTEGER;
...
A := B;
A(1..3) := B(3..5);
C := A;
C := D;
```

12. Which of the assignment statements, if any, are legal? Explain.

```
type NEW_INT is new INTEGER;
type VERY_NEW_INT is new NEW_INT;
I   : INTEGER;
NI  : NEW_INT;
VNI : VERY_NEW_INT;
...
I   := NI;
```

```
NI  := 3;
I   := INTEGER(NI);
VNI := VERY_NEW_INT(I);
```

13. Design a discriminant record type modeled after the array type YEARLY_
    DOLLAR_LIST (see Section 2.7) but which is flexible enough to distinguish
    between leap years and nonleap years. Assume the only years of interest are
    those from 1984 through 2000.

14. Evaluate the following expressions:

    (a) MONDAY ⟨ TUESDAY   -- See Section 2.2
    (b) INTEGER'IMAGE(101) & " DALMATIANS"
    (c) DAY'SUCC(DAY'FIRST)   -- See Section 2.2

Ilya Bolotowsky Abstraction (No. 3). *1981. Museum of Art, Carnegie Institute, Pittsburgh. Gift of Kaufmann's and the Women's Committee of the Museum of Art*

CHAPTER 3

Subprograms and Packages

Chapters 1 and 2 have described statements and declarations, the elements of Ada programs. We now consider the larger structure of Ada programs. Ada programs are composed of building blocks called *program units*. Each program unit can be viewed as a provider of services to be used by other program units. These program units in turn provide services to other users.[1] Program units can be either subprograms, packages, tasks, or generic units. This chapter discusses subprograms and packages. Generic units and tasks are discussed in Chapters 5 and 6, respectively.

Almost every language provides some kind of subprogram facility. Whether they are called subprograms, subroutines, or procedures, the basic idea is the same: They are units that can be called from other points in the program. Once called, the subprogram executes and normally returns control to the point after the call in the caller. Usually, the language also provides a way to exchange information between the caller and the subprogram. Typically, the calling and the called subprograms pass information by *parameters*.

In Ada, there are two kinds of subprograms—procedures and functions. Functions are generally used to return a single value, such as a square root, the largest number in an array, or the last object in a list. The word *value* in Ada is quite general and refers to the value of entire arrays and records as well as scalars and other types. Procedures are usually used to perform more general actions, and therefore their parameter passing rules are more flexible than those for functions.

3.1 Procedures

The service provided by a procedure is described in a *procedure specification:*

```
procedure TRANSMIT(MESSAGE: in STRING; TO: in PLACE)
```

The specification gives the procedure name and its corresponding *formal parameters*. TRANSMIT has two formal parameters: the first is named MESSAGE and has type STRING, the second is named TO and has type PLACE. Formal parameters are objects that stand for the objects passed when the subprogram is called.

The actions performed by a procedure are given within the *procedure body*. (The procedure specification and its corresponding body can be compiled separately, as discussed in Chapter 9.) In general, a procedure body consists of the procedure specification, a declarative part, and a sequence of statements. Figure 3.1 illustrates the distinction between the specification and body. Consider a body for the procedure TRANSMIT:

---

[1] Unless stated otherwise, the word *user* will refer to a program unit that is utilizing another program unit.

```
procedure TRANSMIT(MESSAGE: in STRING; TO: in PLACE) is
    -- declarative part
begin
    -- some statements
end TRANSMIT;
```

procedure NAME (parameters);	Subprogram specification	**function** NAME (parameters) **return** TYPE_NAME;
procedure NAME (parameters) **is** -- local declarations **begin** -- statements **end** NAME;	Subprogram body	**function** NAME (parameters) **return** TYPENAME **is** -- local declarations **begin** -- statements -- must include return **end** NAME;

Figure 3.1 Subprogram Specification and Body

In addition to the parameter names and their types or subtypes, the specification also gives the *mode* of each parameter. The mode describes how the subprogram will use the parameter. Both parameters of TRANSMIT have mode **in**.

There are three parameter modes: **in, out**, and **in out**. Parameters of mode **in** are used to pass values (as opposed to variables) to a subprogram. Within the body of the subprogram, they are constants and therefore cannot be assigned values. If a parameter declaration does not include an indication of its mode, **in** is assumed.

Out parameters are used to return values to the caller. Such parameters might be used to return the result of a calculation or a status code. No initial value need be provided by the caller. The subprogram may assign a new value to the parameter but may not refer to it in an expression.[2] That is, the subprogram may not use the value of the parameter, although it can assign a value to it.

The third parameter mode, **in out**, is used to provide an initial value to the called subprogram and return a possibly updated value. A subprogram such as an array sort would use an **in out** parameter for the array to pass in the initial unsorted array and to pass back the same array sorted.

Of course, a subprogram need not have any formal parameters. Such a procedure might look like:

```
procedure INITIALIZE_DEVICES is
    -- some declarations
begin
    -- some statements
end;
```

[2] As a special case, discriminants and array bounds of **out** parameters may be read.

As this example illustrates, it is not required that the subprogram name be repeated at the end of its body.

Consider the following procedure body:

```
procedure ORDER(I, J : in out INTEGER) is
     TEMP : INTEGER;
begin
     if J ⟨ I then
          TEMP := I;
          I     := J;
          J     := TEMP;
     end if;
end ORDER;
```

The purpose of ORDER is to exchange the values of I and J, if necessary, so that I is less than or equal to J. Because the procedure uses the original parameter values, and possibly updates them, the parameter modes are **in out**; the procedure would not be correct otherwise. Had the parameters been declared mode **out**, there would have been no way for the calling subprogram to provide their initial values. Had they been declared mode **in**, the subprogram could not deliver the updated values back to the caller. Moreover, the compiler would have reported an error when an assignment was attempted to an **in** parameter, because an **in** parameter is a constant within the procedure.

The textual area of the procedure between the specification and the reserved word **begin** is called the declarative part of the procedure. Declarations made in the declarative part are *local* to the enclosing subprogram. In the case of ORDER, its declarative part consists of a single declaration for a variable named TEMP. This variable is created each time the procedure is called and is destroyed when the procedure completes execution. Furthermore, it may be accessed only by statements within ORDER. In other words, the scope of the variable begins at the beginning of its declaration and extends to the end of the enclosing body.

A procedure completes its execution normally in one of two ways: either it finishes executing the last statement in its body, or it executes a *return* statement, as illustrated in the following revision of ORDER:

```
procedure ORDER(I, J : in out INTEGER) is
     TEMP : INTEGER;
begin
     if I ⟨= J then        -- Nothing to do
          return;
     end if;
     TEMP := I;
     I     := J;
     J     := TEMP ;
end ORDER;
```

A procedure is called from elsewhere in the program by writing its name and supplying a set of *actual parameters*, each of which corresponds to one of the formal parameters. Actual parameters are the objects that the subprogram uses when it executes. For example,

```
TRANSMIT("HELLO", NEW_YORK);
TRANSMIT(NEXT_TRANSACTION.PASSWORD, PLACE'FIRST);
INITIALIZE_DEVICES;
ORDER(M, N);
FIND_ROOTS(SQUARE, CUBE, X*Y);
```

Actual parameters corresponding to formal parameters of mode **in** may be arbitrary expressions such as "HELLO", PLACE'FIRST, or X*Y. These values are given to the associated formal parameters when the subprogram call is made. Actual parameters corresponding to **out** or **in out** parameters must be variables. With **in out** parameters, the formal parameter is initialized to the value of the actual parameter. The actual variable corresponding to an **out** or **in out** parameter is updated with the value of the formal parameter when the procedure completes.[3]

Ada offers two styles of associating the formal and actual parameters, which resemble the alternate styles for writing record aggregates. The above procedure calls illustrated *positional* association. With positional association, the actual parameters are supplied in the same order that the formal parameters were declared. With *named* association, the actual parameters are explicitly associated with the formal parameters. The parameters may be written in a different order than the formal order. For example,

```
TRANSMIT(MESSAGE => "HELLO", TO => NEW_YORK);
    -- or
TRANSMIT(TO => NEW_YORK,    MESSAGE => "HELLO");
```

As with record aggregates, named association can improve the clarity of the subprogram call.

Another parallel between record components and subprogram parameters is the availability of *default expressions*. To illustrate, we might rewrite TRANSMIT as follows:

```
procedure TRANSMIT(MESSAGE: in STRING;
                   TO: in PLACE := NEW_YORK) is
    -- some declarations
begin
    -- some statements
end TRANSMIT;
```

---

[3] Two common parameter-passing implementations are pass-by-copy and pass-by-reference. Ada specifies that pass-by-copy must be used for scalar and access parameters; requiring copying avoids the problem known as aliasing (see Wulf, 1980). To avoid the expense of copying large objects, however, Ada permits the compiler to use pass-by-reference for parameters that are arrays or records.

Only **in** parameters may have default expressions. In such cases, the subprogram may be called without supplying the corresponding actual parameter:

```
TRANSMIT(MESSAGE  = > TEXT);                          -- to NEW_YORK
TRANSMIT(MESSAGE  = > TEXT, TO  = > BOSTON); -- to BOSTON
```

Default parameter expressions are a convenience to the programmer when writing a subprogram call that involves many parameters. For example, the procedure TRANSMIT could include many other parameters such as PARITY, DUPLEX, STOP_BITS, and so forth, which are of no concern to many programmers. In such situations, the presence of default values relieves the caller from having to supply an explicit parameter.

Consider now a more complete version of TRANSMIT.

```
procedure TRANSMIT(MESSAGE: in STRING; TO: in PLACE) is
      CH : CHARACTER;
begin
      MAKE_CONNECTION(TO);
      for I in MESSAGE'RANGE loop
            CH := MESSAGE(I);
            SEND(CH);                    -- transmit the character and
            ECHO(CH);                    -- echo it locally
      end loop;
end TRANSMIT;
```

Note that the statements within the for loop are executed for each integer value in the index range of the array MESSAGE. The attribute 'RANGE is useful to calculate the range of index values, because we cannot predict within TRANSMIT the size of the actual string. Recall that MESSAGE'RANGE evaluates to MES-SAGE'FIRST..MESSAGE'LAST.

Within TRANSMIT, calls are made to procedures MAKE_CONNECTION, SEND, and ECHO (not shown). Note that the parameter TO is passed further to MAKE_CONNECTION. The corresponding formal parameter of MAKE_CONNECTION must be an **in** parameter, because it is illegal to pass TO as an actual **out** or **in out** parameter. Inside TRANSMIT, TO is a constant, not a variable, so the compiler would not allow it to be passed to a subprogram that could attempt to update it.

3.2 Functions

Let us now examine functions, the other kind of subprogram. Functions are used to return a single value to the caller. Thus in addition to the formal parameter list, a function specification defines the type or subtype returned by the function. This subtype follows the reserved word **return** in the specification.

```
function LARGEST_DOLLAR(LIST : in DOLLAR_LIST) return DOLLAR is
    -- some declarations
begin
    -- some statements
end LARGEST_DOLLAR;
```

Aside from this additional piece of information in the specification, function bodies appear much like procedure bodies. There are, however, some important differences between procedures and functions. The chief difference is that a function call is an expression, whereas a procedure call is a statement. Consider the completed body of LARGEST_DOLLAR.

```
function LARGEST_DOLLAR(LIST : in DOLLAR_LIST) return DOLLAR is
    LARGEST_SO_FAR : DOLLAR := DOLLAR'FIRST;
begin
    for I in LIST'RANGE loop
        if   LIST(I) > LARGEST_SO_FAR then
            LARGEST_SO_FAR := LIST(I);
        end if;
    end loop;
    return LARGEST_SO_FAR;          -- value returned
end LARGEST_DOLLAR;
```

The executable portion of LARGEST_DOLLAR contains a loop to calculate the largest component in an array (it was illustrated in Section 2.8). Following the loop is a return statement that includes an expression, the variable LARGEST_SO_FAR. The final value of the variable LARGEST_SO_FAR is the value the function returns to the caller. Some example calls are shown below:

```
DEPOSITS, WITHDRAWALS : DOLLAR_LIST(1..365);
...
if   LARGEST_DOLLAR(DEPOSITS) < 1000.00 then
        FIRE_ADVERTISING_AGENCY;
elsif LARGEST_DOLLAR(WITHDRAWALS) > 100_000.00 then
        ADMONISH_BIG_SPENDERS;
else
        SOME_OTHER_IMPORTANT_ACT;
end if;
```

Note that the calls to LARGEST_DOLLAR occur within expressions such as

```
LARGEST_DOLLAR(DEPOSITS) < 1000.00
```

The value of the left side of this relational expression is the value returned by LARGEST_DOLLAR.

Functions and procedures have several other important differences in addition to the contexts in which they can be called. The formal parameters of functions may have only mode **in**. Moreover, a function must contain at least one return statement. A violation of either of these rules will result in a compilation error. The return statement of a function must contain an expression that is the function return value. Further, during execution, the function must execute one of these return statements. That is, unlike procedures, a function may not return to its caller by "falling off the bottom." An attempt to do so causes a predefined exception known as PROGRAM_ERROR (see Chapter 4) to be raised.

3.3 Subprograms and Reliability

We have discussed several Ada subprogram rules that promote reliability. For example, an **in** parameter is a constant within the subprogram, and may not be assigned a value nor passed to another subprogram except as another **in** parameter. These rules enable the compiler to check that the parameter conforms with the intended use of the formal parameter given in the subprogram specification.

The rules pertaining to function returns are another example of the emphasis on security. Recall that a function is not allowed to return to its caller except by executing a return statement containing an appropriate expression. If a function were allowed to return without an expression, the value returned to the site of the function call would be "garbage."

Subprogram calls are operations in the same sense that addition, multiplication, and assignment are operations. In the spirit of strong typing they, too, must obey type and subtype rules. Thus the type of an actual parameter must match the type of the corresponding formal parameter. An attempt to call

```
TRANSMIT(3.1415, BOSTON);                    -- illegal
```

would cause a compilation error because the first parameter does not have type STRING. These rules are crucial to preventing data structures and variables from being corrupted with meaningless values. In a weakly typed language that allowed the above procedure call, a real number mistakenly is interpreted as if it were a sequence of characters, with unpredictable results. Ada rules were largely influenced by the success of other strongly typed languages such as Pascal. This philosophy has proven effective in reducing errors and shortening the debugging cycle.

Subtype checking of parameter values also is performed. When **in** or **in out** actual parameters are supplied in a subprogram call, the Ada rules guarantee that any subtype constraints on the formal parameters are satisfied by the actual parameters. Upon return from the subprogram, any **out** or **in out** formal parameter values must satisfy any subtype constraints on the actual parameters. Therefore, given the function:

```
function FACTORIAL(N : in NATURAL) return POSITIVE is
begin
    --
end FACTORIAL;
```

CONSTRAINT_ERROR occurs if the following is executed:

```
K : INTEGER := -99;
...
J := FACTORIAL(K);
```

because K does not satisfy the subtype NATURAL (range 0 .. INTEGER'LAST) of the formal parameter N.

Finally, Ada requires that all subprograms be reentrant and permits them to be recursive. Reentrancy is the characteristic that allows a subprogram to be executed reliably by more than one concurrent process. Chapter 6 discusses reentrancy in more detail. A recursive subprogram invokes itself directly or indirectly, through intermediary subprogram calls. As an example, the familiar recursive formula for N! may be expressed in Ada as:

```
function FACTORIAL(N : in NATURAL) return POSITIVE is
begin
     if N = 0 then                    -- 0! = 1
          return 1;
     else                             -- N! = N * (N - 1)!
          return N * FACTORIAL(N-1);
     end if;
end FACTORIAL;
```

FACTORIAL is recursive, because it calls itself in the else clause of the if statement.

3.4 Subprogram Declarations and Scope

The declarative part of a subprogram is the region between the subprogram specification and the reserved word **begin**. As stated earlier, declarations made in this part are local to the subprogram. The kinds of declarations that can be given in the subprogram declarative part include types, constants, variables, named numbers, and other kinds of declarations yet to be discussed. Declarations of other subprograms can appear in a declarative part. Consider a new version of TRANSMIT:

```
procedure TRANSMIT(MESSAGE: in STRING; TO: in PLACE) is
     CH : CHARACTER;

     procedure SEND(C : in CHARACTER);        -- procedure declaration

     procedure SEND(C : in CHARACTER) is      -- corresponding body
          -- rest of body
     end SEND;
begin
     -- statements of TRANSMIT
end TRANSMIT;
```

Within the declarative part of TRANSMIT three items now appear: an object declaration for CH, a procedure declaration for SEND, and the corresponding body for
SEND. Note that the procedure declaration looks just like the procedure specification which appears later in the body.

Textually, the procedure SEND is *nested* within the procedure TRANSMIT. In
general, when any program unit appears textually within another program unit,
the first program unit is said to be nested within the second. Some program units
are not nested, but rather appear at the outermost textual level; such units are
called *library units*. A library unit is made visible to another unit by the **with** clause
as illustrated below:

```
with TRANSMIT;
procedure COMMUNICATE;
```

The **with** statement makes TRANSMIT visible within COMMUNICATE. (Chapter 9
discusses library units and visibility.)

In Chapter 1 we introduced the notion of scope and mentioned that the scope
of a declaration that occurs immediately within a block statement begins with the
declaration and extends to the end of the block. Similarly, the scope for a declaration that occurs in the declarative part of a subprogram begins with the declaration and extends to the end of the subprogram. This rule allows the variable CH in
the above example to be used by statements within the body of SEND. On the
other hand, entities within the declarative part of SEND cannot be used by statements of TRANSMIT. These scope rules are the ones associated with Pascal and
other languages descended from ALGOL 60.

Nested scopes support the principle of locality. Local declarations have smaller
scope, and therefore if the declaration is changed, the source text potentially affected by the change is small. Like unstructured control flow, global declarations
(declarations whose scope encompasses the entire program) can lead to programs
that are difficult to understand and to modify. To avoid problems when a program
later is modified, variables and other entities should be declared textually close to
where they are used.

In the above procedure, it may seem redundant to write a subprogram declaration followed by a body that contains the same information. In fact, a subprogram
declaration may be omitted in lieu of its complete body, except in a few cases. One
such case is when two subprograms are mutually recursive; the scope rules outlined above imply that the declaration of each subprogram must precede the call to
it. This arrangement is possible only if one declaration is made first, followed by
the corresponding bodies of both subprograms. The general rule is simply that a
declaration (or a subprogram body used in lieu of a declaration) must precede a
reference to it.

When a subprogram specification occurs in more than one place (e.g., in a declaration and then later in the body) the specifications must *conform*. Although minor variations are allowed, conformance effectively means that the two specifications must be identical. For example, suppose the subprogram declaration

procedure ORDER(I, J: **in out** INTEGER);

appears in a declarative part, and the following body is given:

```
procedure ORDER(I: in out INTEGER; J: in out INTEGER) is
begin
    --
end ORDER;
```

Although each specification by itself is legal, the two specifications do not conform.

The scope of a declaration is an area within which the declared entity may be used, subject to certain rules. There may be a subregion within the declaration scope where the declaration is *hidden*. For example, a variable declared within an inner scope hides a variable within an outer scope if the names of the two variables are the same.

```
procedure TRANSMIT(...) is
    CH : CHARACTER;

    procedure SEND(...) is
        CH : CHARACTER;
    begin
        --
        CH := 'A';                   -- inner CH
        TRANSMIT.CH := 'C';          -- outer CH
        --
    end SEND;
begin
    CH := 'B';                       -- outer CH
end TRANSMIT;
```

As this example illustrates, within the scope of the inner declaration of CH, the outer declaration of CH is hidden. The use of the identifier CH within the body of SEND refers to the inner variable. The outer CH may be accessed from inside SEND with the notation TRANSMIT.CH. As we will see in Section 3.6, certain entities can have the same name without hiding one another.

3.5 Operators

Ada encourages the programmer to define new data types and operations suited to the application. For consistency and extensibility, these programmer-defined types and operations should be consistent with the predefined types and operations. Such consistency can be used by a programmer to draw analogies, to exploit similarities, and to build upon existing concepts. Through analogy and generalization from well-understood concepts, the final product can be simpler and easier to understand. One way that Ada supports this programming style is by allowing a programmer to define new operators, which can be used in the same way as the predefined operators.

As we have seen, a function declaration defines a computation that returns a value. A function call is an expression that returns the value computed by the function. Thus functions are similar to the predefined operators, such as "+" for INTEGERs. Indeed, the predefined declaration for INTEGER "+" can be expressed as:

```
function "+" (LEFT, RIGHT : INTEGER) return INTEGER;
```

The operator symbol enclosed in double quotes is the function "identifier," in this case "+". Ada makes the uniformity between operators and functions explicit by allowing the programmer to declare operators for new data types.

The functions we have seen earlier were called using *prefix* notation, with the function identifier before its operands enclosed in parentheses. An operator, however, typically is called using *infix* notation, with the operator symbol between its operands. Operators also can be called with prefix notation, with some loss of readability. For example, assuming I is an INTEGER, these two calls both add one to I:

```
I := "+"(I, 1);

I := I + 1;
```

The second version in infix notation is more familiar and clear.

Ada allows the programmer to declare operators for new data types created for an application. Like the predefined operators, these new operators can be called using infix notation. For example, we could declare a new type:

```
type COMPLEX is record
     REAL_PART      : FLOAT;
     IMAGINARY_PART : FLOAT;
end record;

C, D, E, F, SUM : COMPLEX;
```

define an addition operation:

```
function "+" (LEFT, RIGHT : COMPLEX) return COMPLEX is
begin
     return (LEFT.REAL_PART      +  RIGHT.REAL_PART,
             LEFT.IMAGINARY_PART +  RIGHT.IMAGINARY_PART);
     -- These additions use the "+" for FLOATs
end "+";
```

and then use the operation as if the type and operation were predefined in the language:

```
SUM := C + D + E + F;
```

The infix expression is easier to read than a prefix expression such as:

```
SUM := ADD_COMPLEX(F, ADD_COMPLEX(E, ADD_COMPLEX(C, D)));
```

In the body of " + ", the components of the result are added using the " + "operator for FLOATs; that is, the " + " operations in the return statement are not recursive calls. The precedence of programmer-defined operators is the same as that for predefined operators. The operator symbols that the programmer can use to define new functions are those given in the precedence table in Section 2.6.[4]

Using operator declarations, the programmer can employ conventional infix notation where appropriate. Because the programmer can declare new data types, it is impossible for the language to predefine operators for the new types. The operator symbols, however, are applicable to many types (such as vectors and matrices) that are not predefined. Ada enables the programmer to tailor the language to the application by declaring both new types *and* their associated operators. These new constructs then can be used in a way consistent with the predefined constructs. The language thereby is *extended* to be more natural for the application.

3.6 Overloading

The ability to declare operators brings up an interesting point: there are many meanings of the operator " + ". The " + " denotes a number of functions, one for INTEGER, another for FLOAT and, given the above declaration, still another for COMPLEX. As we saw in the previous section, the " + " for FLOATs was used in the body of the " + " for COMPLEX. The " + " function is said to be *overloaded*, because it has multiple meanings.

Most languages define overloaded operators for predefined types. The meaning of operator use is determined by the (predefined) types of its operands. Few languages, however, allow the programmer to overload subprograms for programmer-defined types. Unlike these languages, Ada allows certain entities to be overloaded. Overloading is allowed for operators, subprogram identifiers, task entry identifiers, and enumeration literals. Overloading is not allowed for objects and types.

The importance of overloading is evident from the fact that most languages overload predefined operations. Because programmer-defined types are central to Ada, the programmer also should be able to overload operations on these new types. Like the ability to define infix operators, overloading promotes extensibility

---

[4] The "/=" operator cannot be declared explicitly, and "=" can be declared only for limited types, discussed in Section 3.12.

and consistency. Overloading also is important for building large programs, in which many subprograms are declared, perhaps by many programmers. The likelihood of naming problems is reduced if subprograms can be overloaded. The meaning of a subprogram call is determined (resolved) by the types of the parameters and also by the result type in the case of functions.

The following two type declarations illustrate overloading for enumeration literals:

```
type BEEF            is (STANDARD, GOOD, CHOICE, PRIME);
type INTEREST_KIND is (PRIME, BONDS, DISCOUNT);
```

The identifier PRIME is a literal of both BEEF and INTEREST_KIND and hence is overloaded. If PRIME occurs in an expression, the compiler determines the intended enumeration literal based on context. For example, if variable MYSTERY_MEAT has type BEEF, the assignment below refers to the PRIME of BEEF.

```
MYSTERY_MEAT := PRIME;
```

The context, the assignment statement, determines the meaning of PRIME.

A subprogram identifier can be overloaded, provided that none of the subprograms with that identifier have the same *parameter and result type profile*. The parameter and result type profile is defined by the base type and order of each of the formal parameters (and the result type in the case of functions) in the subprogram specification. The profile does not consider the names, modes, or subtypes of the formal parameters, nor whether the formal parameters have default expressions. For a call to an overloaded subprogram, the meaning of the call is determined by the parameter types and the result type.

For example, the following two procedure declarations define overloadings of the identifier ORDER.

```
procedure ORDER(I, J  : in out INTEGER);
procedure ORDER(X, Y : in out FLOAT);
```

The first procedure orders INTEGERs; the second orders FLOATs. Because the parameter and result type profiles are different, the declarations are legal.

Both procedures are available to be called by other program units. For a call, the compiler resolves the intended procedure by analyzing the actual parameters. For example, in the call:

```
N1, N2 : POSITIVE;
...
ORDER(N1, N2);
```

the compiler resolves the call to the ORDER for INTEGERs, because the base type of POSITIVE is INTEGER. Although the compiler typically can resolve an overloaded subprogram call, ambiguous calls, which the compiler cannot resolve, are possible. In such cases, the call is illegal and the programmer must remove the ambiguity explicitly.

The programmer can resolve the call explicitly by using named parameter association (if the formal parameter names are different) or by using a qualified expression to indicate the type of a parameter. A qualified expression indicates explicitly the type of an expression. (Section 2.13 introduced qualified expressions in connection with initial values of allocated objects.) The example below illustrates disambiguation:

```
procedure PROCESS(THE_CUT   : BEEF);
procedure PROCESS(THE_RATE : INTEREST_KIND);
...
PROCESS(PRIME);                   -- illegal
PROCESS(BEEF'(PRIME));            -- legal
PROCESS(THE_RATE  =〉 PRIME);     -- legal
```

Note that although formal parameter names are not part of the parameter and result type profile, which means that they are not considered in determining if overloaded *declarations* are legal, the programmer nevertheless can use them to resolve *calls* to overloaded subprograms. In practice, ambiguous calls seldom occur.

To avoid more complex rules, overloading is not allowed for object and type identifiers. Therefore the following two declarations are illegal in the same declarative part:

```
I : INTEGER;
I : FLOAT;                  -- illegal
```

Allowing such overloading would offer little benefit in return for considerable complexity. An object conceptually represents a single, unique entity that should not share its identifier with other objects. In contrast, a single operation can be applicable to different types of objects. Hence it is more intuitive to allow overloading for operations but not for objects.

Like any language feature, overloading can be misused, but appropriate use of overloading can enhance clarity. Overloading can be used to highlight symmetry, similarity, and regularity. The programmer has greater freedom in choosing identifiers, with less worry about naming problems. Awkward names such as ADD_VECTOR, ADD_MATRIX, and ADD_COMPLEX can be avoided in favor of more natural names such as an overloaded "+".

3.7 An Example: Automatic Tellers with Queues

To provide a framework for our ideas let us consider an automatic banking center (see Figure 3.2) that allows bank customers to make withdrawals, deposits, inquiries, and account transfers. If the center is in a heavily traveled area such as an airport, it may even include several human-machine interfaces so that more than one person can be serviced simultaneously. To use the banking center, a customer approaches a "teller" (depicted in Figure 3.2) and makes a request for a transaction. Before the transaction can begin, the teller asks the customer to insert a magnetic banking card encoded with the customer's account number. The teller then asks the customer to type in a password associated with the account, and finally the teller prompts for the kind of transaction. Let us suppose that the software for this device is to be designed in Ada.

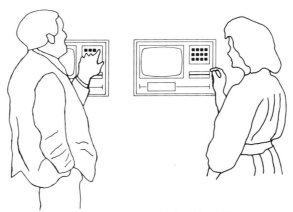

Figure 3.2 An Automatic Banking Center

Customer requests for transactions may flood the banking center faster than they can be processed. To manage the difference in the speed at which the requests can be processed and the rate at which the requests are made, we provide a data structure known as a *queue* in which the transaction requests can reside until the system has time to process them. This data structure usually implies two operations for accessing its members. The first operation inserts a new piece of data into the structure, whereas the second operation retrieves the datum that has been waiting in the queue for the greatest length of time. Let us examine the queue data structure in more detail.

One implementation of a queue is known as a *circular array*. As Figure 3.3 illustrates, the queue is envisioned as a circular structure containing a finite number of storage "cells." Data items that are waiting in the queue occupy a contiguous section of these cells. In addition to the object used to store the data, three variables are used to manage the data in the queue. When the queue is not empty, the variable HEAD references the front of the queue (the element that will be the next to leave), whereas TAIL references the cell where the next data item will be stored. Initially, when the queue is empty, both HEAD and TAIL reference the same cell. Finally, a variable named COUNT keeps the current number of elements in the queue.

An implementation of a queue as a circular array is given by the following declarations:

```
SIZE : constant POSITIVE := 8;
subtype INDEX is INTEGER range 1..SIZE;
type     SPACE is array(INDEX) of TRANSACTION;

type QUEUE_TYPE is record
      ITEMS  : SPACE;
      HEAD   : INDEX := 1;        -- next value to leave
      TAIL   : INDEX := 1;        -- next available slot
      COUNT : INTEGER range 0..SIZE := 0;
end record;

QUEUE : QUEUE_TYPE;
```

The variable QUEUE is declared to be a record of type QUEUE_TYPE. Hence
QUEUE.ITEMS is an array of TRANSACTION records indexed from 1..8. The components QUEUE.HEAD and QUEUE.TAIL are integers constrained to be in the
range 1..8. Finally, QUEUE.COUNT is constrained to be 0..8. Note the default
values for HEAD, TAIL, and COUNT.

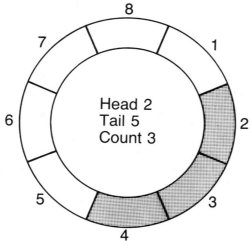

Figure 3.3 A Queue as a Circular Array

Let us consider two procedures called ENTER and REMOVE, which might be
called from various places within the automatic banking system to insert and retrieve transactions.

```
procedure ENTER (T : in TRANSACTION) is
begin
      if QUEUE.COUNT /= SIZE then           -- If the queue is not full
          QUEUE.ITEMS(QUEUE.TAIL) := T;     -- enter the new transaction
          QUEUE.TAIL    := (QUEUE.TAIL rem SIZE) + 1;
          QUEUE.COUNT := QUEUE.COUNT + 1;
      end if;
end ENTER;
```

The algorithm for ENTER checks first to see that QUEUE is not full. If there is room available, the parameter T is assigned to the next available slot in ITEMS, namely QUEUE.ITEMS(QUEUE.TAIL). Finally, the tail and count components are adjusted to reflect this new entry. Note that QUEUE.TAIL "wraps around" to 1 if its previous value was SIZE. Hence its correct new value is

```
(QUEUE.TAIL rem SIZE) +   1
```

The procedure REMOVE, whose logic mirrors ENTER, now follows.

```
procedure REMOVE (T : out TRANSACTION) is
begin
    if QUEUE.COUNT /= 0 then               -- If the queue is nonempty
        T :=  QUEUE.ITEMS(QUEUE.HEAD);    -- remove first transaction
        QUEUE.HEAD   := (QUEUE.HEAD rem SIZE) + 1;
        QUEUE.COUNT := QUEUE.COUNT - 1;
    end if;
end REMOVE;
```

Although this queue example has illustrated many of the concepts presented so far, there is an unsettling aspect to its design. Note that the object named QUEUE needs to be visible to both ENTER and REMOVE. According to the scope rules explained thus far, the declaration of QUEUE_TYPE must be made *global* to both procedures. A procedure in the scope of ENTER and REMOVE also will be in the scope of QUEUE. Such a procedure therefore could enter and remove items in the queue by directly accessing the variable QUEUE. Ideally, we would like the users of the queue to view it as an "abstract object" or "black box", which hides its underlying details and algorithms. Before describing the Ada features for information hiding, we illustrate further what we mean by abstraction.

3.8 Abstraction

One of the important themes of this chapter (and indeed this book) is abstraction. The definition of abstraction given in Hibbard (1981) is useful: An abstraction is a simplified description of a system that emphasizes certain properties while hiding or suppressing other properties.

Abstractions play an important part of everyday life. For example, consider cars, which are commonplace, although complex, systems. A car is comprised of an engine, a transmission, an electrical system, a cooling system, and much more. Despite this complexity, even people with little mechanical inclination can learn to drive. This situation is possible because we can treat the car as an abstraction. We need not know the mechanical and hydraulic details of the brake system; we merely must know that depressing the brake pedal causes the car to slow down. We simplify a car by viewing it as a collection of resources (such as ignition, steering wheel, brakes), operations performed on those resources (insert key, rotate counterclockwise, depress brake), and the effect of those operations (start engine, turn left, slow down).

Abstractions are central to all intellectual activity. For example, mathematicians often take a well-known structure and create an abstraction of it by listing a set of axioms believed to be important properties of the structure. The axioms of ring theory (commutativity, associativity, and so forth) are an important abstraction of the integers. A good abstraction emphasizes the important properties of the underlying structure. When developing the abstraction, however, the important properties often are not obvious. The main challenge in all fields of science and engineering is identifying simple and fruitful abstractions.

Subprograms traditionally have been the chief abstraction mechanism in programming. Subprograms can be used to group a sequence of actions into a single abstraction which can be executed by other parts of a program. Consider a programmer who groups a sequence of initialization statements into a procedure called INITIALIZE_DEVICES. The sequence of statements could have been coded inline. It is easier and more manageable, however, to defer the issue of initialization using a subprogram call to a (perhaps yet unwritten) procedure. By doing so, the programmer concentrates on the task at hand rather than worrying about the details of device initialization. The name of the subprogram becomes an abstraction for its actions. The procedure call, in effect, becomes a powerful statement in the programming language.

In Chapter 2 we pointed out that programmer-defined types are an abstraction tool as well. A programmer who uses the type DAY need not be concerned with the machine representation of values of type DAY. Programmer-defined types often must be more complicated than a simple enumeration. It is important to be able to define abstractions for these more complicated structures as well.

We attempted earlier to build an abstraction for a queue by providing operations ENTER and REMOVE. As we noted, there unfortunately appeared to be no way of enforcing the abstract view of the queue. The subprograms that call ENTER and REMOVE also could perform operations directly upon the object. These operations could be erroneous, perhaps by violating a subtle assumption about the object. For better abstraction, the programmer also needs the ability to restrict the allowed operations. Packages, as we will see, can be used to hide information and representation, enabling better abstraction.

3.9 Packages

A key Ada construct to support abstraction, information hiding, and modularity is the *package*. Packages are program units used to group logically related data and associated operations into a single abstraction. In general, a package has two parts: a *package specification* and *package body*, although the package body sometimes is unnecessary. The following package specification groups together the type declaration for TRANSACTION presented earlier and declarations for the subprograms illustrated in Section 3.7.

```
package QUEUE_PACKAGE is

    type TRANSACTION is record
            ACCOUNT    : ACCOUNT_ID;
            PASSWORD : PASSWORD_TYPE;
            AMOUNT     : DOLLAR;
    end record;

    procedure ENTER  (T :  in TRANSACTION);
    procedure REMOVE(T : out TRANSACTION);

end QUEUE_PACKAGE;
```

Packages are collections of resources that can be made available to other parts of the program. The declarations in the package specification are said to be *visible* to other program units. QUEUE_PACKAGE provides three resources: a type TRANSACTION, a procedure ENTER, and a procedure REMOVE. A program unit that uses QUEUE_PACKAGE can declare new objects of type TRANSACTION and can call the procedures ENTER and REMOVE.

As we said above, packages generally come in two parts: a specification (which was illustrated above) and a package body, as shown in Figure 3.4. The purpose of the package body is to give the implementation of those entities (e.g., procedures and functions) whose specification appears in the package specification. In the case of QUEUE_PACKAGE, its body must contain the corresponding bodies for ENTER and REMOVE. Bodies of program units cannot appear in a package specification; they must always be placed in the corresponding package body.

Package bodies also may contain other entities such as objects and subprograms whose declarations did not appear in the specification. The scope of such entities is limited to the package body. Therefore these items may be used only within the package body, and not by the user of the package. Ada is designed to simplify the

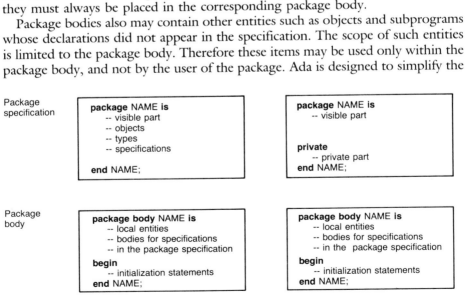

Figure 3.4 Package Specification and Body

creation of large programs that require many programmers. Hiding information in the package body helps to protect users from changes in the package implementation that otherwise could ripple throughout the application.

Consider, then, the body of QUEUE_PACKAGE:

```
package body QUEUE_PACKAGE is

    SIZE : constant POSITIVE := 10;
    subtype INDEX is INTEGER range 1..SIZE;
    type SPACE is array(INDEX) of TRANSACTION;

    type QUEUE_TYPE is record
        ITEMS  : SPACE;
        HEAD   : INDEX := 1;        -- next value to leave
        TAIL   : INDEX := 1;        -- next available slot
        COUNT : INTEGER range 0..SIZE := 0;
    end record;

    QUEUE   : QUEUE_TYPE;

    procedure ENTER (T : in TRANSACTION) is
    begin ... end;      -- same as before

    procedure REMOVE (T : out TRANSACTION) is
    begin ... end;      -- same as before

end QUEUE_PACKAGE;
```

The user of the package may use only the declarations visible in the package specification. The package body, which provides the implementation details of the specification, may also contain other declarations. These details are not visible to the user of the package. Returning to our car analogy, the package specification is like the dashboard of a car, whereas the body is like the sensors and devices under the hood. A user of QUEUE_PACKAGE can use the names TRANSACTION, ENTER, and REMOVE. But the user could not, for example, refer to QUEUE, because it is declared in the package body and not in the specification.

Objects within a package body retain their values between calls to subprograms within the package. In the case of QUEUE_PACKAGE, the variable QUEUE will retain its value between calls to REMOVE and ENTER.

A package body has a structure similar to a subprogram body in that both have a declarative part. In the case of subprograms, a sequence of statements (with at least one statement) must follow. For package bodies, however, the sequence of statements is optional. When statements are present, the reserved word **begin** is placed after the declarative part, followed by the statements. The statements may be used for initialization. Had QUEUE_PACKAGE needed such initialization, the body would have had the following form:

```
package body QUEUE_PACKAGE is
    -- declarative part
begin
    -- initialization statements
end QUEUE_PACKAGE;
```

We have said that, in some cases, a package may consist of a specification without requiring a body. A body is unnecessary when the resources made visible by the specification do not themselves require bodies. For example, if a package specification includes only type declarations and object declarations, a body is unnecessary. But if a subprogram specification appears in the package specification, its body[5] must be given in the corresponding package body. Other entities that require implementation in the package body include tasks (Chapter 6), generic program units (Chapter 5), and other packages having bodies. To illustrate, the package below contains no declarations that require a body:

```
package SOLAR_SYSTEM is

    type PLANET is (MERCURY, VENUS,    EARTH,
                    MARS,     JUPITER,  SATURN,
                    URANUS,   NEPTUNE,  PLUTO);

    subtype TERRESTRIAL_PLANET is PLANET range MERCURY..MARS;
    subtype JOVIAN_PLANET      is PLANET range JUPITER..NEPTUNE;

    type MILES        is digits 5 range 0.0..5.0e9;
    type PLANET_FACTS is array  (PLANET) of MILES;

    DISTANCE_TO_SUN : constant PLANET_FACTS :=
    (MERCURY => 36.0e6,   VENUS   => 67.2e6,  EARTH  => 93.0e6,
     MARS    => 141.7e6,  JUPITER => 484.0e6, SATURN => 887.0e6,
     URANUS  => 1787.0e6, NEPTUNE => 2797.0e6,PLUTO  => 3675.0e6);

    DIAMETER : constant PLANET_FACTS :=
    (MERCURY => 3100.0,   VENUS   => 7700.0,  EARTH  => 7918.0,
     MARS    => 4220.0,   JUPITER => 88700.0, SATURN => 71600.0,
     URANUS  => 32000.0,  NEPTUNE => 31000.0, PLUTO  => 3600.0);

    NUMBER_OF_MOONS : constant array (PLANET) of NATURAL :=
    (MERCURY => 0,        VENUS   => 0,       EARTH  => 1,
     MARS    => 2,        JUPITER => 12,      SATURN => 10,
     URANUS  => 5,        NEPTUNE => 2,       PLUTO  => 0);

end SOLAR_SYSTEM;
```

This package consists only of types and objects, and thus a body is unnecessary. Even if one is not required, a package body nevertheless can be supplied. For

[5] The body may be a body stub, discussed in Section 9.3.

example, a package whose specification declares a complex object could be given a body to initialize the object.

3.10 Packages and Visibility

Recall that a library unit is a program unit not nested within another unit. A package may be a library unit or it may be nested within other program units. For example:

```
procedure A(...) is
      package QUEUE_PACKAGE is          -- declare a package and
            ...                          -- two procedures
      end QUEUE_PACKAGE;

      procedure B(...);
      procedure C(...);

      package body QUEUE_PACKAGE is     -- provide their bodies
            ...
      end QUEUE_PACKAGE;

      procedure B(...) is
      begin ... end;

      procedure C(...) is
      begin ... end;

begin
      ...
end A;
```

The package specification of QUEUE_PACKAGE appears as another declarative item in the declarative part of procedure A. In this example, declarations in QUEUE_PACKAGE can be used at places within its scope, which includes procedures B, C, and the sequence of statements in procedure A.

A program unit (e.g., procedure B) within the scope of QUEUE_PACKAGE might use it in the following way:

```
procedure B(...) is
      NEXT_TRANSACTION : QUEUE_PACKAGE.TRANSACTION;
begin
      ...
      NEXT_TRANSACTION.AMOUNT := 125.00;
      QUEUE_PACKAGE.ENTER(NEXT_TRANSACTION);
      ...
end B;
```

This example illustrates two uses of dot selection: to specify declarations within a package and to select components of a record. Note that the uses of TRANSAC-TION and ENTER require prefixing their names with the package name, separated by a dot. Such names are called *expanded names*. The "." which appears on the left side of the assignment statement has a different meaning: it selects a component from the record NEXT_TRANSACTION.

Prefixing each name by the package name can be tedious if declarations in a package are used often. As a convenience, Ada provides the *use* clause.

```
use  QUEUE_PACKAGE;
procedure  B(...)  is
      NEXT_TRANSACTION  :  TRANSACTION;
begin
      ...
      NEXT_TRANSACTION.AMOUNT  :=  125.00;
      ENTER(NEXT_TRANSACTION);
      ...
end  B;
```

The use clause makes the names within the package specification *directly visible* so that the dot notation is no longer necessary.

We have observed that a declaration within a block or subprogram is visible only within the enclosing block or subprogram. For example, a variable declared within a procedure may be used only within that procedure. A declaration in a package specification, however, is visible wherever the package is visible. A procedure name declared within a package specification, for example, may be used outside the package wherever the name of the package is visible. On the other hand, declarations within a package body can be used only within the package body. Therefore outside the body of QUEUE_PACKAGE, an attempt to assign a value to QUEUE is illegal and will result in a compilation error.

3.11 Data Object Abstraction

Packages are an abstraction mechanism. The user of a package may use only the declarations that appear in the package specification. The user is prohibited by the compiler from using the underlying details in the package body.

In the QUEUE_PACKAGE example the variable QUEUE is inaccessible except from within the package body. Thus the only subprograms in the entire program that can access these objects directly are ENTER and REMOVE. The technique of hiding objects in a package body and making visible only well-understood operations or subprograms to access the objects is sometimes called *data object abstraction*. The idea is that the user of the package cannot make direct use of the underlying objects. Accessing them can be accomplished only indirectly through the sub-programs given in the package specification. Note that the queue becomes an abstract object in that the user knows how to use it but is not concerned about whether its implementation is a linked list, a circular array, or some other data structure. Analogously, the motorist knows how to use the brakes but need not be concerned about whether they are drum or disc.

Violating the assumptions of data structures is a common source of errors. Consider what would happen if a subprogram inserted a new record into QUEUE.ITEMS but neglected to increment QUEUE.TAIL: The next insertion would "clobber" this new record. The effect is that the record entered in the queue can never be retrieved.

One major benefit of hiding objects in a package body is that we can be more assured of program reliability. In the case of QUEUE_PACKAGE, if we can demonstrate the correctness of ENTER and REMOVE, we know that all attempts to access the queue also are correct.

We can have no such assurance for the unpackaged version of QUEUE, illustrated in Section 3.7. Consider a large program, for example, in which many subprograms access QUEUE directly. Even if we demonstrate that the existing subprograms use QUEUE correctly, our conviction is suspect the moment a new subprogram is added. The new subprogram may manipulate the exposed QUEUE directly and it may do so erroneously.

Another major benefit of data object abstraction is that it frees the user of the data objects from having to concentrate on their implementation details. The user needs to know only the manner in which to call the visible subprograms.

The specification of a package and the corresponding body may appear as separate compilation units. The Ada compiler is responsible for ensuring that the resources visible in the specification are indeed implemented in the package body. Chapter 9 discusses separate compilation in more detail.

Another important benefit of packages is that they can simplify maintenance and enhancement. For example, as a result of changing requirements or the need to improve efficiency, the implementor of QUEUE_PACKAGE may wish to change the queue data structure and the algorithms of ENTER and REMOVE. Because the program units that use QUEUE_PACKAGE do not depend on the implementations of ENTER and REMOVE, the change has no effect on these units. The only unit affected is the body of QUEUE_PACKAGE.

One drawback of the current version of QUEUE_PACKAGE is that there is no way for a subprogram which uses the package to "know" when the queue is full or empty. The reason, of course, is that the data structure (including the record components COUNT, HEAD, and TAIL) is hidden in the package body. It is important to be able to detect these conditions, because the package user should not call ENTER when the queue is full, nor call REMOVE when the queue is empty. To allow users to detect these conditions, we add two functions to the package specification: IS_EMPTY and IS_FULL, which return BOOLEAN values that indicate the state of the queue. The new version of the package is shown in outline below:

```
package QUEUE_PACKAGE is
    type TRANSACTION is ...

    procedure ENTER  (T :  in TRANSACTION);
    procedure REMOVE(T : out TRANSACTION);

    function  IS_EMPTY return BOOLEAN;
    function  IS_FULL  return BOOLEAN;

end QUEUE_PACKAGE;

package body QUEUE_PACKAGE is

    -- Declarations for SIZE, INDEX, SPACE, QUEUE_TYPE, and QUEUE.

    procedure ENTER  (T :  in TRANSACTION) is ...
    procedure REMOVE(T : out TRANSACTION) is ...

    function IS_EMPTY return BOOLEAN is
    begin
        return QUEUE.COUNT = 0;
    end;

    function IS_FULL return BOOLEAN is
    begin
        return QUEUE.COUNT = SIZE;
    end;

end QUEUE_PACKAGE;
```

This new version is the same as the old one except for the two new functions.

3.12 Data Type Abstraction: Private Types

In the automatic banking application, more than one queue of TRANSACTION records may be needed. The version of the package given in the previous section unfortunately provides only one queue. A more general approach is for the package specification to export a type for the QUEUE. Users of the package then could declare queue objects using this type. A first attempt at such a package is given below.

```
package EXPOSED_QUEUE_PACKAGE is
    type TRANSACTION is ...

    SIZE : constant POSITIVE := 10;
    subtype INDEX is INTEGER range 1..SIZE;
    type SPACE is array(INDEX) of TRANSACTION;
```

```
type QUEUE_TYPE is record
    ITEMS  : SPACE;
    HEAD   : INDEX := 1;          -- next value to leave
    TAIL   : INDEX := 1;          -- next available slot
    COUNT : INTEGER range 0..SIZE := 0;
end record;

procedure ENTER   (Q : in out QUEUE_TYPE;
                   T : in TRANSACTION);
procedure REMOVE (Q : in out QUEUE_TYPE;
                   T : out TRANSACTION);

function  IS_EMPTY (Q : QUEUE_TYPE) return BOOLEAN;
function  IS_FULL  (Q : QUEUE_TYPE) return BOOLEAN;

end EXPOSED_QUEUE_PACKAGE;
```

The body of EXPOSED_QUEUE_PACKAGE will contain the complete bodies for the four subprograms given in the package specification. Unlike previous packages, however, no object declarations appear in the body, because this package is designed to enable users to declare the queues. To accommodate this change, each subprogram has an extra parameter: The caller now must pass to the subprogram the queue to be accessed. Note also that in the case of ENTER and REMOVE this parameter has mode **in out**, because these subprograms must be able to read and update the actual queue.

Let us now use this new version of EXPOSED_QUEUE_PACKAGE and declare some queues.

```
use EXPOSED_QUEUE_PACKAGE;
...
REQUEST_QUEUE       : QUEUE_TYPE; -- declare some queues
REPLY_QUEUE         : QUEUE_TYPE;
LATEST_TRANSACTION : TRANSACTION; -- and a record
...
while not IS_EMPTY(REQUEST_QUEUE)
      and not IS_FULL(REPLY_QUEUE) loop
    REMOVE(REQUEST_QUEUE, LATEST_TRANSACTION);
    ENTER(REPLY_QUEUE, LATEST_TRANSACTION);
end loop;
```

Note that EXPOSED_QUEUE_PACKAGE provides more flexibility than previous packages but, regrettably, less abstraction. Package users no longer are required to view queues as abstract objects and now can access directly the details of queue objects. An assignment statement that changes the state of the queue, for example,

```
REQUEST_QUEUE.HEAD := REQUEST_QUEUE.TAIL;
```

is permissible outside the package, even though it probably makes the program incorrect. (Erroneous uses of objects are likely to be more subtle than this example.) Because the definition of QUEUE_TYPE is visible, the user is free to manipulate its internal structure.

Ada gives us a way out of this dilemma. To define an abstract type, we must be able to declare the type without exposing its actual structure. To enable this hiding of the implementation details of types, Ada provides *private types*.

```
package QUEUE_PACKAGE is
    type TRANSACTION is ...

    type QUEUE_TYPE is private;        -- private type declaration

    procedure ENTER    (Q : in out QUEUE_TYPE;
                        T : in TRANSACTION);
    procedure REMOVE  (Q : in out QUEUE_TYPE;
                        T : out TRANSACTION);

    function  IS_EMPTY (Q : QUEUE_TYPE) return BOOLEAN;
    function  IS_FULL  (Q : QUEUE_TYPE) return BOOLEAN;

private                               -- package private part
    SIZE : constant POSITIVE := 10;
    subtype INDEX is INTEGER range 1..SIZE;
    type    SPACE is array(INDEX) of TRANSACTION;

    type QUEUE_TYPE is record -- full declaration
        ITEMS  : SPACE;
        HEAD   : INDEX := 1;          -- next value to leave
        TAIL   : INDEX := 1;          -- next available slot
        COUNT : INTEGER range 0..SIZE := 0;
    end record;

end QUEUE_PACKAGE;
```

Recall that a package has two parts: a specification and a body. We now see that the specification itself can have two parts: a visible part and a *private part*. Our prior examples of package specifications have had only a visible part, but the specification of this latest refinement of QUEUE_PACKAGE has both a visible part and a private part.

The distinction is that the visible part contains declarations visible to the package user, whereas the private part contains declarations that implement the private types declared in the visible part. The name of a private type is visible to users, but its complete definition is not available.

In this example, QUEUE_TYPE is declared to be a private type in the visible part of the package. Its full declaration occurs in the private part. If a package declares a private type in the visible part, it must include a private part containing the full type declaration. The full type declaration need not be a record, as it is in our example; it could be another kind of type such as an INTEGER, an enumeration, or an array.

Initially, it may seem curious that the private part of the specification is necessary at all, on the presumption that the full declaration of QUEUE_TYPE could be given in the package body, which also hides details outside the package. Ada chose to require the full declaration in the private part for efficiency. If the full type could be deferred until the package body, which may be compiled separately after other units that use the specification, the compiler would not know the internal structure of QUEUE_TYPE. The compiler hence could not know the amount of storage to allocate for objects of type QUEUE_TYPE declared in other units. To avoid a host of associated problems, Ada requires the full declaration in the private part.

The purpose of private types is to restrict the operations available outside of the package body. A private type may be used in the normal way to declare objects, but its implementation (e.g., array, record, or integer) given by the full declaration in the private part may not be exploited outside the package.

An object whose type is private may be passed as a parameter to a subprogram declared in the package specification. In addition, the predefined operations "=" (equality), "/=" (inequality), and ":=" (assignment) can be used. Outside the package, the only operations on a private type are these three operations and the subprograms visible to users of the package.

Sometimes it is useful to disallow even the three predefined operations. For example, a user of QUEUE_PACKAGE probably should not be allowed to compare two objects of type QUEUE_TYPE with predefined "=". The problem is: Are two queues equal if they have the same values stored in the same logical order? Or are they equal if the underlying objects (the internal records) that represent them are equal? The user of the package probably understands equality as the first definition, whereas the predefined equality operator on the underlying record type yields the second definition. Because the definition is not intuitive, it is sensible to disallow users from comparing queues with predefined "=".

To enforce this policy, Ada allows types to be *limited private*. A more appropriate declaration for QUEUE_TYPE in the package visible part is:

```
type QUEUE_TYPE is limited private;    -- limited private
```

With this declaration, the user of the package still may declare objects of type QUEUE_TYPE, but may not apply the operations "=", "/=", or ":=" to the objects. The full specification and body for QUEUE_PACKAGE using the limited private type is shown below:

```
package QUEUE_PACKAGE is
    type TRANSACTION is record
         ACCOUNT   : ACCOUNT_ID;
         PASSWORD : PASSWORD_TYPE;
         AMOUNT    : DOLLAR;
    end record;
```

```ada
type QUEUE_TYPE is limited private;

procedure ENTER    (Q : in out QUEUE_TYPE;
                     T : in TRANSACTION);
procedure REMOVE (Q : in out QUEUE_TYPE;
                   T : out TRANSACTION);

function  IS_EMPTY (Q : QUEUE_TYPE) return BOOLEAN;
function  IS_FULL   (Q : QUEUE_TYPE) return BOOLEAN;

private
    SIZE : constant POSITIVE := 10;
    subtype INDEX is INTEGER range 1..SIZE;
    type    SPACE is array(INDEX) of TRANSACTION;

    type QUEUE_TYPE is record
        ITEMS  : SPACE;
        HEAD  : INDEX := 1;      -- next value to leave
        TAIL   : INDEX := 1;      -- next available slot
        COUNT : INTEGER range 0..SIZE := 0;
    end record;

end QUEUE_PACKAGE;

package body QUEUE_PACKAGE is

    procedure ENTER    (Q : in out QUEUE_TYPE;
                        T :  in TRANSACTION) is
    begin
        if Q.COUNT /= SIZE then
            Q.ITEMS(Q.TAIL) := T;
            Q.TAIL          := (Q.TAIL rem SIZE) + 1;
            Q.COUNT         := Q.COUNT + 1;
        end if;
    end ENTER;

    procedure REMOVE (Q : in out QUEUE_TYPE;
                       T : out TRANSACTION) is
    begin
        if Q.COUNT /= 0 then
            T        := Q.ITEMS(Q.HEAD);
            Q.HEAD  := (Q.HEAD rem SIZE) + 1;
            Q.COUNT := Q.COUNT - 1;
        end if;
    end REMOVE;

    function  IS_EMPTY (Q : QUEUE_TYPE) return BOOLEAN is
    begin
        return Q.COUNT = 0;
    end;
```

```
function   IS_FULL   (Q : QUEUE_TYPE) return BOOLEAN is
begin
      return Q.COUNT = SIZE;
end;

end QUEUE_PACKAGE;
```

Earlier we noted that certain operator symbols (such as "$<$", "$+$") are overloaded with more than one meaning, and that the programmer may declare additional overloaded declarations using these symbols. Ordinarily, the equality operator "$=$" may not be overloaded explicitly by the programmer. An exception to this rule, however, allows explicit declaration of an equality operator if the operand type is limited private. Thus this new package specification of QUEUE_PACKAGE could include the declaration:

```
function "="(A, B : QUEUE_TYPE) return BOOLEAN;
```

The corresponding body of this function would then be implemented in the body of QUEUE_PACKAGE and could be tailored to correspond to the "natural" definition rather than the predefined one for the Ada representation. The "$/=$" function is defined implicitly as the negation of the "$=$" function; it cannot be declared explicitly.

Our QUEUE_PACKAGE refinements have been somewhat restrictive in that all queues declared using QUEUE_TYPE must be the same size. As we saw in Section 2.11, discriminant records allow additional flexibility in object declarations. A discriminant can be used to establish the size of a array component within the record. To make this capability available for private types as well, a private type also can have a discriminant part:

```
type QUEUE_TYPE (Q_SIZE : POSITIVE) is private;
   -- or
type QUEUE_TYPE (Q_SIZE : POSITIVE) is limited private;
```

For a private type with a discriminant part, the full declaration must be a discriminant record. The details of a discriminant version of QUEUE_TYPE are the subject of an exercise at the end of the chapter.

In Chapter 2 we stated that Ada allows programmers to create new types with associated operations. QUEUE_TYPE is an example of an abstract data type. A programmer who uses QUEUE_PACKAGE can declare abstract objects of type QUEUE_TYPE and also can use the operations provided by the package, such as REMOVE and ENTER. Because the implementation details of QUEUE_TYPE are hidden outside the package, it follows that only these operations can manipulate such objects directly. As noted previously, the creation of a data type with associated operations is called data type abstraction. It is more general than data object abstraction: Rather than encapsulating a single object within a package body, a new abstract type is created. Objects of the new abstract type can be declared, without exposing the internal structure of the type. These objects can be used only in operations defined for the new type.

3.13 Limited Private Types and Software Engineering

We conclude this chapter with an illustration of using limited private types to enhance reliability. Consider the following package specification:

```
package CUSTOMER_INTERFACE is
    type WINDOW is limited private;

    procedure OPEN (THE_WINDOW : in out WINDOW);
    procedure CLOSE(THE_WINDOW : in out WINDOW);

    procedure GET_REQUEST(FROM : in WINDOW; REQUEST : out ...);
    procedure GIVE_REPLY  (TO   : in WINDOW; REPLY   : in  ...);

private
    ...
end CUSTOMER_INTERFACE;
```

Users of the package can declare objects of type WINDOW and can call the procedures given in the specification. A WINDOW is considered to be either "open" or "closed". Initially a WINDOW is closed, and the procedure OPEN must be called before other operations using it are permissible. Similarly, CLOSE is called to close the window. OPEN may be called only if THE_WINDOW is closed, and CLOSE may be called only if THE_WINDOW is open.

It is convenient to represent the type WINDOW internally as an integer, so that values could be used to index into a table of WINDOWs. Assuming this representation, OPEN assigns a unique positive integer to the actual parameter, and CLOSE resets it to zero.

Thus the full declaration for WINDOW in the package private part could be:

```
type WINDOW is new NATURAL;
```

The problem with this definition is that there is no guarantee that a WINDOW initially is closed (i.e., has value zero). For example, a programmer could declare a WINDOW and then mistakenly call GET_REQUEST before OPEN had been called. When called with an uninitialized WINDOW, GET_REQUEST has no reliable way of determining the call is erroneous. If the uninitialized value for THE_WINDOW happens to satisfy the constraint for NATURAL, GET_REQUEST cannot detect that the proper sequence of operations has been violated.

A better approach is to declare the full type as follows:

```
type WINDOW is record
   INTERNAL_VALUE : NATURAL := 0;
end record;
```

Using a record component with a default initial value guarantees that objects of type WINDOW will have a meaningful value for the component INTERNAL_VALUE.

The protocol for using the operations also should be considered in writing the specifications for the operations. For example, the following declaration

```
procedure OPEN(THE_WINDOW :    out WINDOW);
```

uses the formal parameter mode **out**, which at first glance may seem appropriate, because OPEN returns an initialized value for THE_WINDOW. A better approach, however, is to use the **in out** formal parameter mode. Using mode **in out**, the body of OPEN can test the value of the actual parameter to ensure that an OPEN is not attempted on a WINDOW that already is open.

These techniques help the package body ensure that operations are performed according to the protocol. Default initial values for components, together with the lack of explicit assignment for limited types, help guarantee that objects of type WINDOW always have a meaningful value. Objects of type WINDOW will be nonzero only by calling OPEN, and will be zero either through default initialization or by calling CLOSE.

Finally, Ada does not allow a formal parameter of a limited private type to have mode **out** unless the procedure is declared in the same package that defines the type. For example,

```
package CUSTOMER_INTERFACE is
   -- as above
end CUSTOMER_INTERFACE;
```

```
procedure ILLEGAL(W : out CUSTOMER_INTERFACE.WINDOW) is ... end;
```

is not allowed. A reason for this restriction is that the above procedure could fail to give the formal parameter W a meaningful value. If parameter passing in this case were implemented by copy-out, the actual parameter could become garbage upon return from ILLEGAL.

3.14 Summary

Subprograms are an abstraction for a sequence of actions. The specification of a subprogram contains the information necessary for other program units to call it. This includes the subprogram name, the formal parameter names, their types or subtypes, their modes, and in the case of functions, the return type. There are three parameter passing modes: **in**, **out**, and **in out**.

A subprogram body contains the specification, any local declarations, and a sequence of statements. The local entities declared within the subprogram body may be types or objects, as well as nested program units.

A package is a collection of resources that can be used by other program units. These resources may include constant and variable declarations, type declarations, procedures, functions, other packages, exceptions, tasks, and generic units. Usually the package comes in two main parts—the package specification and the package body. The package specification contains items visible to the users of the package. Generally, the package body is needed to implement those "executable" entities, such as functions and procedures, whose declarations appeared in the package specification. A package body is sometimes unnecessary, such as when the specification contains only type and object declarations.[6]

Packages can be designed to accomplish several goals. A package containing only type and object declarations may be used to group a collection of logically related items. Packages also can be used to create "abstract data objects," which make visible in the package specification a set of subprograms to operate upon the abstract object. By declaring the data structure in the package body, the package designer not only can hide the implementation details of the subprograms, but also the implementation details of the data object as well.

Ada private types can be used to build abstract data types, which make visible the name of a type in the package specification but not the complete definition. The type definition is hidden in a special area called the private part. The user of the package then is free to declare objects of this new type. However, the operations on these objects are limited to the subprograms that appear in the package specification. If the type is private, the operations ":=", "=", and "/=" may be used. If the type is limited private, no operations are available, other than those declared in the package specification.

3.15 Exercises

1. Write an Ada function whose specification part appears below. The function has two formal parameters of type STRING and CHARACTER and determines if the character occurs within the string.

   function PRESENT(LOCATE : CHARACTER; WITHIN : STRING)
   return BOOLEAN;

---

[6] An exception is that for an incomplete type declared in a package private part, the full declaration can be deferred until the package body. In this case, a body must be given and must contain the full declaration for the incomplete type. This feature is illustrated in Chapter 5.

2. Write an Ada procedure that "pads" the last N characters of a string with the given fill character.

```
procedure PAD(N : POSITIVE; FILL : CHARACTER ;
              WITHIN : in out STRING);
```

3. Rewrite the declarations associated with type QUEUE_TYPE (see Section 3.7) so that the size of the array ITEMS is determined by a discriminant.

4. Add to the package QUEUE_PACKAGE (see Section 3.12) another function called PRESENT which checks if a record with a given ACCOUNT is waiting in the queue. A declaration for PRESENT might be:

```
function PRESENT(Q : QUEUE_TYPE; WHO : ACCOUNT_ID)
   return BOOLEAN;
```

5. The Ada Reference Manual (Section 7.4.1) states that the full type declaration for a private type may not be an unconstrained array type. Illustrate what is prohibited and describe the reason for the restriction.

6. In Chapter 2 it was illustrated how records could be linked using access values. However, we might wish to change the implementation of our queue in the body of QUEUE_PACKAGE (see Section 3.12) so that the records are stored in a linked list. What effect, if any, would there be upon the users of the package?

7. What are the benefits of the Ada parameter passing modes for reliability and documentation?

8. Declarations are elaborated in the order in which they appear. Consider the following fragment:

```
J : INTEGER := 1;
...
begin
   declare
       K : INTEGER := J;
       J : INTEGER := 2;
   begin
       ...
   end;
...
end;
```

What is the initial value of K in the block statement? What would be the initial value of K if the two inner declarations were reversed?

9. Using the declaration:

```
type SQUARE_MATRIX is array(1..SIZE, 1..SIZE) of FLOAT;
```

write an Ada function "*" which returns the matrix product of two such values. The matrix product of two matrices A and B is the matrix C where the element in the ith row and jth column is the dot product of the ith row of A with the jth column of B.

10. The exponentiation operator requires its right operand to be an integer. Therefore an expression such as X**(0.5) may not be used to find a square root. Design a function that computes the square root of a nonnegative number of type FLOAT.

11. Write the body of a function named DAY_AFTER which is passed a parameter of type DAY (see Section 2.2) and returns the day that chronologically follows.

12. Design a package that utilizes the idea of data object abstraction. The package should make visible two subprograms named INSERT and RETRIEVE, which manipulate a "table" containing records of type TRANSACTION. The subprogram INSERT stores a new record in the table. The subprogram RETRIEVE is passed a value of type ACCOUNT_ID and passes back a record of type TRANSACTION that has the given account number, if such a record exists in the table.

13. Generalize the design in exercise 12 by making TABLE a limited private type, and modifying the subprograms so that they manipulate **in out** parameters having type TABLE.

14. Implement the function discussed in Section 3.12 whose specification is shown below:

function "="(A, B : QUEUE_TYPE) **return** BOOLEAN;

15. Rewrite the body of package QUEUE_PACKAGE (Section 3.12) so that the queue is implemented as a linked list. Assume for now that there is no need to deallocate memory after it has been used.

16. Generalize exercise 9 to compute the product of any two compatible matrices A and B whose type is:

type MATRIX **is array** (INTEGER **range** $\langle \rangle$, INTEGER **range** $\langle \rangle$)
    of FLOAT;

Recall that A * B is defined if the number of columns in A equals the number of rows in B.

Edward Munch The Scream. *Collection of Philip and Lynn Straus*

CHAPTER 4

Error Handling

A program is more robust, reliable, and usable if it anticipates errors during execution and attempts to recover from them. Programs that rely on the underlying operating system or hardware to detect and recover from errors are difficult to use and to maintain. Ada provides a facility called *exceptions* for error handling which can simplify programming of robust programs.

Errors arise from many sources, such as programming and design mistakes, input data errors, hardware errors, user errors, and support software errors. Anticipation of all possible errors is clearly infeasible, but typically certain classes of errors are identifiable and meaningful to a program, and it is important to attempt graceful recovery from such errors.

Error recovery is especially important for interactive programs, such as editors, word processors, data base query interpreters, and electronic mail. Users will make unavoidable clerical and logical errors, and programs should recover from user mistakes, preserving as much of the program state as possible. Error detection and recovery is equally important for real-time programs, which often must continue operating even in the presence of errors. For example, the passengers in an airplane depend upon the navigation system to withstand occasional errors in input sensors.

Before discussing Ada exceptions, we review several conventional error-handling schemes. We refer to the "calling" and "called" program units involved in an interaction. A major concern of error handling is to communicate errors between such interacting program units.

4.1 Earlier Approaches

The previous comments about the importance of error handling have long been obvious to programmers, and a variety of techniques has been developed to facilitate error recovery. In earlier languages, goto statements were a common technique for transferring control to a program section to handle errors. Using this technique, a program that detects an error executes a goto statement to a program section that handles the error.

In addition to the difficulties of understanding programs with unrestricted goto statements, the disadvantage of this technique is that returning control to the calling subprogram is more difficult. Typically, the program must return from error processing to a fixed place to continue processing. Often the full significance of an error is known only in the calling subprogram, and the most effective recovery can be made at this higher level, not at the level at which the error was detected. For this sort of error recovery, the goto approach is inappropriate. Without adding complexity and obscurity (e.g., by using assigned goto statements in FORTRAN), error handling with goto statements is relatively inflexible. Goto statements are especially ill-suited in a language such as Ada, which has excellent constructs for modularity.

A more flexible technique that works well with structured programs is passing status flags between procedures. In this approach, a subprogram that can detect an

error has a formal parameter that is assigned the result status from the subprogram. For a program as crucial as an editor, every procedure may have a status
parameter that returns a value of success or an appropriate error value if an error is
detected. To detect errors and recover from them, the calling subprogram must
check the status parameter returned by the called subprogram. If an error occurred, the calling subprogram has an indication of the error and can direct its
processing accordingly.

To illustrate, we return to our earlier formulation of a queue package from
Chapter 3. It showed four subprograms: IS_EMPTY, IS_FULL, ENTER, and RE-
MOVE. For this package specification (although not for others we will develop), it
is erroneous to perform an ENTER operation on a full queue or a REMOVE operation on an empty queue. To use the status parameter method of error handling, a
formal parameter is added to each of the subprograms whose call may be invalid
for some state of the queue. For example, the specification of the ENTER operation in QUEUE_PACKAGE could be changed to:

```
procedure ENTER (Q    : in out QUEUE_TYPE;
                 T    : in     TRANSACTION;
                 FULL :    out BOOLEAN);
```

A use of the procedure in this case would be:

```
ENTER(Q    => A_QUEUE,
      T    => AN_ITEM,
      FULL => QUEUE_WAS_FULL);

if QUEUE_WAS_FULL then
     RECOVER; -- do something to recover from the error
end if;
```

The example assumes appropriate prior declarations of the actual parameters A_
QUEUE, AN_ITEM, and QUEUE_WAS_FULL and also a subprogram RECOVER,
which performs the actual recovery actions. The action taken to service the error,
of course, depends upon the application; for example, it may be possible to remove elements from the queue so that ENTER may be called again.

Another possible style for using this package, one that does not require changing the subprogram declarations, is to precede calls to ENTER and REMOVE with
calls to the functions IS_FULL and IS_EMPTY. Thus calls on QUEUE_PACKAGE
have this style:

```
if not IS_FULL(A_QUEUE) then
     ENTER(A_QUEUE, AN_ITEM);
else
     RECOVER; -- do something to recover from the error
end if;
```

This scheme requires that a check be made before each call of ENTER. This approach is advantageous because the check is performed before the call to ENTER, so that the call does not occur at all if the queue is full. The prior check may be crucial if the package implementor describes in the documentation that an ENTER operation on a full queue is undefined. Although the package may do something reasonable in undefined cases, (such as leaving the queue itself unchanged) users of such a package should not depend upon undefined actions.

These techniques require that a check be made for each call of the subprogram. If the check is omitted, and the queue is full, the program nevertheless continues to execute until the undetected error causes an error elsewhere in the program. Correlating this later error with the original error often can be very difficult.

4.2 Exceptions

Ada provides an alternative, called *exceptions*, to the error-handling approaches outlined above. An exception is a control construct that promotes flexible response to run-time events, typically errors such as hardware overflow or attempting to remove an element from an empty queue. Exceptions provide an alternative way of naming an error condition and transferring control to handle that error condition.

Exceptions in Ada are intended to be used to handle errors and also infrequent events. They are a convenient method of indicating to calling subprograms that an error has occurred. Exceptions are a generalization and an abstraction of the idea of a trap. A trap is a synchronous event which halts an operation that is no longer meaningful. The term *synchronous* means that, if the program is executed with the same data, the event will always occur, always at the same place in the program. (Ada facilities for handling asynchronous events, i.e., events that occur at unpredictable times, are discussed in Chapter 6.)

4.3 Exception Declarations

The following example illustrates the queue package augmented with exception declarations.

```
package QUEUE_PACKAGE is

    type TRANSACTION is record ... end record;
    type QUEUE_TYPE is limited private;

    function  IS_EMPTY(Q : in QUEUE_TYPE) return BOOLEAN;
    function  IS_FULL  (Q : in QUEUE_TYPE) return BOOLEAN;

    procedure ENTER    (Q : in out QUEUE_TYPE;
                        T : in   TRANSACTION);
    QUEUE_IS_FULL : exception; -- can be raised by ENTER
```

```
        procedure REMOVE (Q : in out QUEUE_TYPE;
                          T : out TRANSACTION);
        QUEUE_IS_EMPTY : exception; -- can be raised by REMOVE
private

        SIZE : constant := 10;
        subtype INDEX is INTEGER range 1 .. SIZE;
        type SPACE is array(INDEX) of TRANSACTION;
        type QUEUE_TYPE is record
            ITEMS  : SPACE;
            HEAD   : INDEX := 1;
            TAIL   : INDEX := 1;
            COUNT  : INTEGER range 0..SIZE := 0;
        end record;

    end QUEUE_PACKAGE;
```

The additions to the previous package are the two exception declarations. An exception is declared by introducing the name of the exception, followed by the reserved word **exception**. Although the programmer can place exception declarations anywhere in the specification, we adopt the convention of placing an exception declaration after the subprogram that can detect the error condition named by the exception. This convention emphasizes the exceptions that potentially are raised by a call to a subprogram within the package. These declarations merely make the exception name visible to package users and the package body.

An exception declaration appears similar to an object declaration, but an exception is not an object. An exception is the name of a condition; this name can be used in *raise statements* and in *exception handlers*. Typically, the subprograms implemented within the package body use these names to raise an exception, and users of the package declare exception handlers using these names. We now describe the concepts of exception raising and exception handling.

4.4 Raising an Exception

QUEUE_IS_FULL names an exception that is detected by ENTER, and QUEUE_IS_EMPTY names an exception that is detected by REMOVE. Detecting an exception and alerting the calling subprogram is called *raising the exception*. The raise statement is illustrated below:

```
procedure ENTER(Q : in out QUEUE_TYPE; T : in TRANSACTION) is
begin
    if Q.COUNT >= SIZE then
        raise QUEUE_IS_FULL; -- notify caller of error
    end if;

    -- other ENTER statements
end ENTER;
```

In this example, if no empty slots remain in Q, the operations to insert the new element must not be performed because they would overwrite an existing element. Before placing the new T in Q, ENTER checks that Q has enough room for the new element. If Q is full, ENTER executes the **raise** statement, which includes the name of the exception, QUEUE_IS_FULL, that it has detected. In Chapter 3, we saw that a subprogram completes execution normally by either executing a **return** statement or (in the case of procedures) by executing the last statement of the body. In this case, ENTER completes by executing the **raise** statement.

Note that ENTER is a relatively low-level operation on the queue, and therefore in general it cannot know the higher-level significance of the error. Depending on the context of the error, it may be possible for the higher level calling subprogram to recover gracefully from this error—for example, by removing elements from the queue for processing.

4.5 Handling a Raised Exception

A subprogram that uses the above package can provide exception handlers for these exceptions, as illustrated below.

```
with QUEUE_PACKAGE; use QUEUE_PACKAGE;
procedure FILL_QUEUE is
    A_QUEUE : QUEUE_TYPE;
    AN_ITEM : TRANSACTION;
begin
    -- other statements filling the queue

    ENTER(A_QUEUE, AN_ITEM); -- may raise QUEUE_IS_FULL

exception
    when QUEUE_IS_FULL =>
        RECOVER; -- do something to recover from the error

end FILL_QUEUE;
```

The procedure declares its exception handlers following the reserved word **exception**. An exception handler can be associated with any block, that is, a subprogram body, package body, task body, or block statement. Our description of exception handling is given in terms of subprogram bodies. Special rules for exceptions involving tasks are discussed in Chapter 6.

The statement part of bodies (whether a subprogram body, package body, or task body) in general have the following form:

```
begin
    -- statements
exception
    -- exception handlers
end;
```

As we have seen in Chapter 3, the exception handlers section of the body can be omitted.

The exception clause of a block has a structure similar to that of a case statement. It consists of a sequence of exception handlers. Each handler specifies an exception name (inside a when clause) together with statements to be executed when that exception is raised. The statements within an exception handler are executed only if the corresponding exception is raised; that is, control does not "fall through" from the statements of the block into the statements of the exception handler. In this case, the statements after the **when** clause that names QUEUE_IS_FULL will be executed only if the ENTER operation raises QUEUE_IS_FULL. These statements complete the execution of the block; control does not return to the point where the exception was raised.[1]

Consider a subprogram called SEND_MESSAGE that calls ENTER. If ENTER raises QUEUE_IS_FULL and SEND_MESSAGE does not declare an exception handler for QUEUE_IS_FULL, execution of SEND_MESSAGE is said to be *abandoned*, which means that SEND_MESSAGE is immediately completed.

When a subprogram is abandoned because of an unhandled exception, the exception *propagates* to the previously executing subprogram. Propagation means that the exception is raised in the calling subprogram at the point of the subprogram call. Similarly, if the calling subprogram has no handler for the exception, the exception in turn propagates to its caller. (Even though a block statement has no caller, it may be considered an anonymous subprogram called from only one point in the program, i.e., the point at which the block textually appears.) This process continues until either a subprogram with an exception handler is found in the calling sequence, or the entire program is abandoned because no subprogram in the calling sequence handled the exception. (In the latter case, a friendly implementation will at least indicate the exception that caused termination).

For example, consider a subprogram A, which is the main program, that calls a subprogram B, which raises the exception ERROR. Figure 4.1 illustrates the different control transfers that can occur, depending on the exception handlers declared.

In Figure 4.1 (a), B declares a local handler for ERROR, which is executed. Execution of the exception handler completes B, at which point B returns normally to A. In (b), subprogram B has no handler, so the exception propagates to A. A has a handler for ERROR which then is executed as a result of the propagation of ERROR, and this handler completes the execution of A. In (c), neither A nor B have a handler for ERROR, so both are abandoned when the exception is raised, and because A is the main program, the entire program is abandoned.

A subprogram can handle an exception without explicitly naming the exception by use of the *others* handler. An others handler placed at the end of the exception

---

[1] Readers familiar with PL/I will recognize a similarity of purpose between Ada exceptions and PL/I ON conditions. The similarity is more one of purpose than of semantics, however, because a PL/I condition handler is established dynamically, and after its execution, control returns to the point of the error. An Ada exception handler is statically established, and its execution completes execution of its containing block.

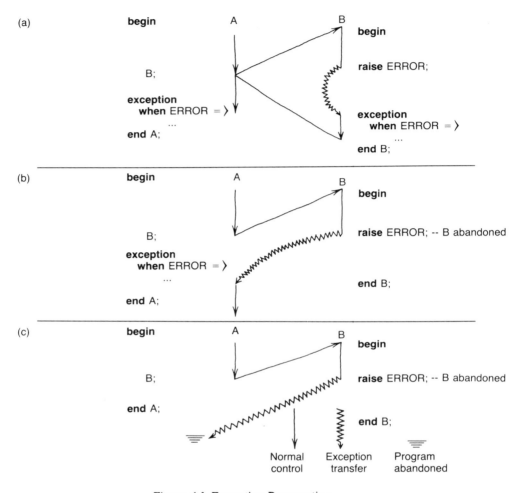

Figure 4.1 Exception Propagation.

clause handles exceptions that the subprogram does not name specifically. For example, the above exception clause could be changed to handle any exceptions raised by subprograms it calls as follows:

```
with QUEUE_PACKAGE; use QUEUE_PACKAGE;
procedure FILL_QUEUE is
    A_QUEUE : QUEUE_TYPE;
    AN_ITEM  : TRANSACTION;
begin
    -- other statements filling the queue

    ENTER(A_QUEUE, AN_ITEM); -- may raise QUEUE_IS_FULL
```

```
exception
    when QUEUE_IS_FULL =>
        RECOVER;              -- do something to recover from the error
    when others =>
        OTHER_RECOVER; -- recovery for other errors

end FILL_QUEUE;
```

In this case, the subprogram OTHER_RECOVER will be invoked if an exception other than QUEUE_IS_FULL is raised. Only one **others** handler is allowed and it must be the last handler of the exception clause.

Depending on the application, it may be desirable for a block to handle an exception locally and, after this local handling is complete, to propagate the exception to the caller. The local handling typically must restore a consistent state to data structures the block manipulates, before propagating the exception to its caller.

A common example is a subprogram that opens an external file which must be closed before the subprogram completes. If an exception is raised during execution of the subprogram, it must close the file and then propagate the exception to its caller, thereby notifying the caller of the error it encountered.

To perform this reraising of an exception, a statement within a handler can be itself a raise statement. If the handler specifies **others**, however, the name of the exception is not available to the handler, and therefore the reraise statement cannot name the exception. To allow reraising the same exception in this case, the raise statement can omit the exception name. Omitting the exception name is allowed only for raise statements within an exception handler. This form of raise statement reraises the same exception, causing it to propagate to the caller.

To illustrate with our queue example, the handler given above can be changed to reraise the same exception as follows:

```
with QUEUE_PACKAGE; use QUEUE_PACKAGE;
procedure FILL_QUEUE is
    A_QUEUE : QUEUE_TYPE;
    AN_ITEM  : TRANSACTION;
begin
    -- other statements filling the queue

    ENTER(A_QUEUE, AN_ITEM); -- may raise QUEUE_IS_FULL

exception
    when QUEUE_IS_FULL =>
        RECOVER;
        raise;                    -- reraise QUEUE_IS_FULL
    when others =>
        OTHER_RECOVER;     -- recovery for other errors
        raise;                    -- reraise whatever exception occurred
end FILL_QUEUE;
```

It is interesting to note an equivalence between a block with no exception handlers and a block with a single handler for **others** that simply reraises the exception; that is, with regard to exception propagation, the following blocks are equivalent:

```
BLOCK_ONE:
begin
      -- Some statements
end BLOCK_ONE;        -- no exception handlers


BLOCK_TWO:
begin
      -- Some statements
exception
      when others =>
            raise;        -- reraise the exception
end BLOCK_TWO;
```

A block with no exception handlers will propagate exceptions in the same way as a block with a single handler for **others** that performs a reraise of the same exception. The example above illustrates another aspect of blocks: they need not introduce local declarations, in which case the **declare** is omitted.

4.6 Retrying an Operation

Because exception handlers can be associated with block statements, as well as with program unit bodies, block statements often are used to interpose an exception handler within a sequence of statements. This use of blocks is important when the enclosing body needs to perform more processing, regardless of whether an exception is raised. Thus block statements are handy both to introduce declarations that have local scope and to introduce exception handlers within a sequence of statements.

To illustrate this use of block statements, consider the problem of recovering from interactive user input errors. The following loop illustrates retrying an operation until it succeeds. Assume that GET_RESPONSE is a subprogram that raises the exception USER_ERROR if A_RESPONSE is invalid. TEXT_IO.PUT_LINE is a predefined procedure (described more fully in Chapter 7) to output a STRING.

```
procedure INQUIRE(A_RESPONSE : out RESPONSE) is
begin
      INQUIRY_LOOP:
      loop
            begin
                  GET_RESPONSE(A_RESPONSE);
                  exit;
```

```
     exception
         when USER_ERROR =>
             TEXT_IO.PUT_LINE("Try again.");
     end;
   end loop INQUIRY_LOOP;
 end INQUIRE;
```

If GET_RESPONSE raises USER_ERROR, the exception handler executes, prompting the user to try again. The loop keeps calling GET_RESPONSE until USER_ERROR is not raised, in which case control reaches the exit statement.

INQUIRY_LOOP above is somewhat inflexible because INQUIRE will not complete unless it receives a valid response. Sometimes it is plausible to try an operation repeatedly up to some maximum number of times. When this number is reached, the operation is abandoned to allow the program to continue. One way to program such an algorithm is as follows:

```
procedure INQUIRE(A_RESPONSE : out RESPONSE) is
    MAXIMUM_TRYS : constant := 5;
begin
    INQUIRY_LOOP:
    for I in 1 .. MAXIMUM_TRYS loop
        begin
            GET_RESPONSE(A_RESPONSE);
            return;
        exception
            when USER_ERROR =>
                TEXT_IO.PUT_LINE("Try again.");
        end;
    end loop INQUIRY_LOOP;
    raise UNCOOPERATIVE_USER;
end INQUIRE;
```

For this example, assume visible declarations for GET_RESPONSE and for the exceptions USER_ERROR and UNCOOPERATIVE_USER. INQUIRE declares a constant MAXIMUM_TRYS, which defines the number of times that GET_RESPONSE will be tried. When GET_RESPONSE does not raise an exception, control flows to the return statement following the call to GET_RESPONSE, and INQUIRE completes. If GET_RESPONSE raises the exception USER_ERROR, the exception handler gains control, a message is printed, and control flows to the end of the loop for the next iteration. After MAXIMUM_TRYS attempts, INQUIRY_LOOP completes, control flows to the next statement after the loop, which raises the exception UNCOOPERATIVE_USER.

4.7 Predefined Exceptions

Ada predefines a number of exceptions that may be raised implicitly during program execution. By implicit raising, we mean the underlying implementation performs the raise statement, without the programmer explicitly writing a raise statement. The compiler generates instructions to check the consistency of the program during execution and to raise a predefined exception if a check fails. These exceptions are defined to indicate program errors that are detectable by an implementation only during execution. They are raised if an executing program violates certain Ada rules or if it exceeds implementation-defined limits. Users may declare exception handlers for predefined, as well as user-defined, exceptions. Although predefined exceptions generally are raised by the implementation, a programmer also can raise a predefined exception explicitly.

The predefined exceptions are:

```
NUMERIC_ERROR      : exception;
PROGRAM_ERROR      : exception;
STORAGE_ERROR      : exception;
TASKING_ERROR      : exception;
CONSTRAINT_ERROR : exception;
```

These exceptions are declared in the predefined package STANDARD (discussed further in Chapter 9).

NUMERIC_ERROR is raised for division by zero and for numeric overflow. The common error that raises PROGRAM_ERROR is leaving a function without executing a return statement, that is, by falling through to the end of the function body. STORAGE_ERROR is raised if an object is allocated using **new**, and no memory is available to hold the object. It also is raised if the memory for the data area of a task or subprogram is exceeded. TASKING_ERROR is raised if certain errors occur during communication between tasks. Discussion of Ada tasks and intertask communication is deferred until Chapter 6.

CONSTRAINT_ERROR is raised in several error circumstances; the most common are: (1) attempting to access the designated object of a null access value, (2) assigning to a variable a value outside the variable subtype, (3) referring to a nonexistent component of a variant record object, and (4) indexing an array with an index outside the index subtype. Each of these errors is illustrated below (using declarations from Chapter 2):

```
procedure CONTAINS_CONSTRAINT_ERRORS is

        A_TRANSACTION    : TRANSACTION_NAME; -- see 2.13
        WORK_DAY         : BANKING_DAY;      -- see 2.4
        UNIT             : EUCLIDEAN_VECTOR; -- see 2.7
        FRIEND           : HOUSE_PET;        -- see 2.11

        WITHDRAWAL       : DOLLAR := A_TRANSACTION.AMOUNT;
            -- case (1), A_TRANSACTION is null

        WORKDAY          : BANKING_DAY := SATURDAY;
            -- case (2), BANKING_DAY is range MONDAY .. FRIDAY
```

```
USE_DRIED_FOOD   : BOOLEAN := not FRIEND.FUSSY;
    -- case (3), FUSSY nonexistent for DOG discriminant

COUNTER              : INTEGER := 0;

begin

UNIT(4)                 := UNIT(4) + 1.0;
    -- case (4), index subtype is 1..3

exception
    when CONSTRAINT_ERROR =>
        null;
        -- Exceptions in statements are handled here,
        -- but exceptions in declarations are propagated.
end CONTAINS_CONSTRAINT_ERRORS;
```

Each of the four causes of CONSTRAINT_ERROR mentioned above is illustrated in this example.

The example also illustrates another property of exceptions. Notice in this example that exceptions can be raised in the declarations by the initialization expressions. Previously, we have seen exceptions raised only within the statements of a block. If the handler within CONTAINS_CONSTRAINT_ERRORS were executed for exceptions raised in declarations, the handler could access entities, such as COUNTER, that had not yet been elaborated. Recall that elaboration establishes a declaration and performs any initializations and that this process occurs in the order in which the declarations appear. If a declaration raises an exception, declarations later in the block are not yet elaborated. Accessing unelaborated declarations could cause erroneous results. For example, if the handler used COUNTER to guide its actions, it would be using an uninitialized value, even though COUNTER appears to be initialized from looking at the program text.

Ada avoids this problem by specifying that an exception raised within declarations immediately propagates to the calling subprogram (or in the case of a block statement to the enclosing block). Thus in the example, the handler for CONSTRAINT_ERROR would not be executed when the exception in the declaration of WITHDRAWAL occurs; instead the exception is propagated to the caller of CONTAINS_CONSTRAINT_ERRORS. When this first exception is raised, CONTAINS_CONSTRAINT_ERRORS would be abandoned.

4.8 Input-output Exceptions

Ada also predefines packages for input-output, which contain exceptions for common input-output errors, such as input data format errors (called DATA_ERROR) and attempts to read past end-of-file (END_ERROR). For example, several common input-output exceptions are illustrated by the following subprogram.

```
with TEXT_IO;              -- predefined package for text input-output
with TRANSACTIONS;         -- application-defined package
                           -- with type TRANSACTION
with TRANSACTION_IO;  -- application-defined transaction file input-output
with REPORT;               -- application-defined subprogram

procedure DAILY_REPORT is
    use TRANSACTIONS;
    use TRANSACTION_IO; -- makes declarations directly visible
    TRANSACTION_FILE   : FILE_TYPE;
    NEXT_TRANSACTION : TRANSACTION;
begin
    OPEN(FILE  = > TRANSACTION_FILE,
         MODE  = > IN_FILE,
         NAME  = > "TODAYS_TRANSACTIONS");
    while not END_OF_FILE(TRANSACTION_FILE) loop
        READ(TRANSACTION_FILE, NEXT_TRANSACTION);
        REPORT(NEXT_TRANSACTION);
    end loop;
exception
    when NAME_ERROR    = > -- can be raised by OPEN
        TEXT_IO.PUT_LINE("Could not open transaction file");
    when STATUS_ERROR = > -- can be raised by OPEN
        TEXT_IO.PUT_LINE("Transaction file already open");
    when DATA_ERROR    = > -- can be raised by READ
        TEXT_IO.PUT_LINE("Input format error");
        TEXT_IO.PUT_LINE("Check TODAYS_TRANSACTIONS file");
end DAILY_REPORT;
```

Although Ada input-output has not yet been discussed, this example nevertheless is sufficiently readable to illustrate several points about input-output exceptions. The procedure OPEN associates an external file, named by a STRING parameter ("TODAYS_TRANSACTIONS"), with an internal file object (TRANSACTION_FILE). NAME_ERROR is raised by OPEN if the string NAME does not identify an external file. STATUS_ERROR is raised by OPEN if the file object is already open. DATA_ERROR is raised by READ if a record in the opened file has an invalid input format, for example, if the file contains text instead of TRANSACTIONs. This example is explained more fully in Chapter 7.

Note that separating normal input-output processing from the error cases enhances the clarity of the central algorithm, in this case a simple loop. The normal processing is written as straight-line code, without the intrusion of checking explicitly for unusual events. Without exceptions, each input-output operation would have to check for valid results, which would obscure the simple intent of the loop.

The enhanced readability of exceptions is especially useful for programs that manipulate files and do frequent input-output, because input-output is especially prone to errors. Thus exceptions provide a uniform, readable mechanism for recovery from both predefined and user-defined conditions.

The example also shows that exceptions support incremental development and maintenance. The basic algorithm can be written initially without concern for possible errors that might arise. Once the basic algorithm is correct and tested, exception handling can be added *without changing the code that already works*. In languages without exceptions, the logic of the basic algorithm must be modified to add the necessary error checks. As every programmer knows, logic modifications are the bane of working code. This use of exceptions of course does not mean that a programmer can ignore possible errors but that concern about errors can be separated more easily from concern about the normal cases.

4.9 Suppressing Exceptions

The checking implicitly performed by an implementation is an invaluable aid to increasing reliability. Such checking prevents an error from remaining undetected until it causes another, seemingly unrelated, error. Not only is the checking valuable during development, it can also be useful during production use of the program.

In some applications, however, memory and processing resources are extremely limited. Because run-time checking requires additional executable code, a program tends to execute slower and requires more storage than one without checking. It is inadvisable to suppress run-time checking, even in production versions, but in those rare cases in which it is mandatory, the programmer can give the compiler permission to omit run-time checking. This permission is given by means of a statement called a *pragma*. A pragma is a directive to the compiler which gives information about how a given compilation unit is to be compiled. A pragma has the general form given below:

pragma *identifier*;

where *identifier* is the name of the pragma. Ada predefines a number of pragmas; an implementation can define pragmas in addition to the predefined ones.

The pragma that permits the compiler not to generate run-time checks is called SUPPRESS. Two examples of the SUPPRESS pragma are given below:

```
pragma SUPPRESS(INDEX_CHECK);
     -- no index checking on array indexing
pragma SUPPRESS(RANGE_CHECK, ON = ) WORKING_DAY);
     -- no range check on the variable WORKING_DAY
```

Other run-time checks also can be suppressed. Although SUPPRESS gives the compiler permission to omit checking, the compiler can ignore the pragma if omitting the check is impossible or too inefficient.

4.10 Advantages of Exceptions

Using exceptions for error processing has several advantages over gotos and status flags. Errors can be detected in a subprogram and handled in the context of the calling subprogram, which may have a more meaningful interpretation for the error than the detecting subprogram does. The same exception can be handled differently by the various calling subprograms, giving the same flexibility of status flags. Unlike status flags, however, the exception handling mechanism does not require the calling subprogram to check a flag after *each* call.

A further advantage of exceptions is that error processing is clearly isolated within the exception clause of the block. It is not interspersed with normal processing, obscuring the intent for the typical, nonerroneous case. For most programs, the main concern is processing for cases that are not erroneous, even though error checking code often can far exceed the code for the nonerroneous cases.

By using exceptions, these cases can be programmed without undue clutter from error recovery actions. They allow the clear separation of ordinary, normal processing from unusual, infrequent, or erroneous events. Using exceptions, the programmer can separate the concern with the primary problem from concern with error cases. The error cases are clearly distinguished from the normal processing by being in a separate section of the block, which is executed only if a designated exception is raised. Thus source code for the nonerroneous cases can be more readable.

In addition to improving readability and letting the programmer separate error processing, exceptions improve reliability. The executing program cannot "ignore" the error condition, as it can status flags, because if a handler is not provided, the exception causes the program to terminate. Thus an error cannot remain undetected and thereby either cause other, seemingly unrelated execution errors or cause incorrect results.

4.11 Summary

Exceptions are an important feature to support building robust systems for real-time, embedded applications. An exception is a name, which can be used in raise statements and within exception handlers. Using exceptions, it is possible to transfer control when an error is detected to another program section to handle the error. Transferring control is called raising an exception. An exception may be raised by the program executing a raise statement. For certain errors, one of the predefined exceptions can be raised implicitly by the generated executable code or by the run-time system.

The program section that receives control when an exception is raised is called an exception handler. The exception handler executed depends on where the exception is raised. Exceptions in declarations cause the exception to be propagated to the calling program unit. In the case of a block statement, the caller is considered to be the enclosing block. For an exception raised within statements, the exception handler (if any) within the current block is executed. If the current block contains no handler, the exception propagates to the calling program unit.

The SUPPRESS pragma can be used to turn off the run-time checking that otherwise would occur to detect predefined exceptions. Because the SUPPRESS pragma circumvents an important reliability feature of Ada, it should be used with caution.

4.12 Exercises

1. What are the advantages of using exceptions rather than status flags? Are there advantages to using status flags instead of exceptions?

2. Although an exception appears similar to an object declaration, the exception handling facility is a mechanism of control rather than data. What are the implications of this characteristic? For example, can an exception be a component of an array?

3. What is the difference in the effect of the two exception handlers below?

```
exception
    when others  => raise;
end;
```

```
exception
    when others  => raise FATAL_ERROR;
end;
```

4. What predefined exception (if any) does each of the following code fragments raise?

(a)
```
declare
        X : array (1..3) of INTEGER;
        I : INTEGER := 0;
begin
        X(I) := X(X'FIRST);
end;
```

(b)
```
declare
        type INTEGER_ACCESS is access INTEGER;
        INTEGER_NAME : INTEGER_ACCESS;
begin
        INTEGER_NAME.all := 0;
end;
```

(c) **declare**
    TODAY : WEEKEND := WEEKEND'SUCC(SATURDAY);
            -- from Section 2.4
  begin
      null;
  end;

(d) X := Y / 0.0;

5. If the following subprogram is executed, what does it output?

```
with TEXT_IO; use TEXT_IO;
procedure P is
    I : INTEGER range 0..9;
begin
    declare
        J : INTEGER range 1..9 := 1;
    begin
        J := 10;
    exception
        when CONSTRAINT_ERROR =>
            PUT_LINE("Exception handled in block.");
        when others =>
            PUT_LINE("Some other exception.");
    end;

    I := 10;
exception
    when CONSTRAINT_ERROR =>
        PUT_LINE("Exception handled in P.");
end P;
```

6. How many exception handlers are executed if MAIN is called?

```
procedure MAIN is
    PANIC : exception;

    procedure A is
    begin
        raise PANIC;
    end A;

    procedure B is
    begin
        A;
    exception
        when others => raise PANIC;
```

```
    end B;

    procedure C is
    begin
        B;
    exception
        when PANIC  => null;
        when others => raise;
    end;

begin
    C;
exception
    when PANIC => null;
end MAIN;
```

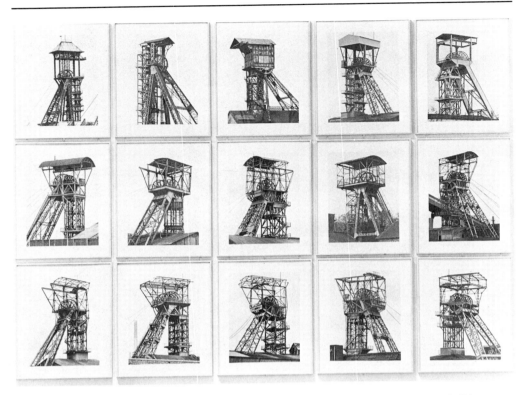

Bernd and Hilla Becher. Pitheads—Perspective Views. *Collection of the Art Institute of Chicago*

CHAPTER 5

Generics: No Wheels Reinvented Here

edial wheelwrights spent much of their lives duplicating previous work. Although the design of the wheel was well-understood, wheelwrights continued to construct wheels by hand. Later, due to industrial automation, their skills became obsolete. Like ancient wheelwrights, programmers spend much time redoing what already has been done. In this chapter, we examine a powerful Ada mechanism, called generics, to help make programming more automatic. Before Ada, facilities similar to generics were available only in research languages. Building upon the success of these languages, Ada generics offer the opportunity to apply new and powerful techniques to program development.

Recall that in Chapter 3 we presented a function called LARGEST_DOLLAR, which returned the largest value in an array of type DOLLAR_LIST. Because DOLLAR_LIST is an unconstrained array type, the function behaves correctly on any array of type DOLLAR_LIST, regardless of its bounds.

Suppose that upon further developing our application the need arises for a function to select the largest value in an array of INTEGERs. It is clear that the algorithm for finding the largest value is the same, regardless of whether the array component type is DOLLAR or INTEGER. It also is clear, however, that LARGEST_DOLLAR cannot be used, because its specification requires a parameter of type DOLLAR_LIST.

In many programming languages, it is necessary to write a new function, perhaps called LARGEST_INTEGER, to compute the largest value in an array of INTEGERs. Having to write this new function is unfortunate, because its algorithm is the same as that of LARGEST_DOLLAR. If it were possible to abstract, or factor out, the type of the array from the algorithm, we could reuse the same algorithm. The only requirement of the algorithm itself is that we must be able to decide if one array component is less (or greater) than another.

What we need is a "machine" that contains the algorithm for finding the largest element in an array type. The array type, however, should not be contained in the machine; it should be supplied by the programmer who uses the machine. The machine itself is not an ordinary function; rather it can create ordinary functions. Once the machine is built, the programmer can use it to create functions automatically to find the largest value in an array, regardless of the component type. For example, the programmer can create functions such as LARGEST_DOLLAR, LARGEST_INTEGER, and LARGEST_POPULATION.

In Ada, such machines are called *generic program units*. This chapter describes generic program units (generics for short) and then presents generic formulations of several common data structures. Generics are best described using examples, and accordingly this chapter discusses several moderate-size examples.

5.1 Generic Declarations

To provide a way of parameterizing program units by types and subprograms (as well as by objects), Ada enables packages and subprograms to be generic. Generics allow more abstract specifications than nongeneric program units. Like other program units, generics are declared in two parts: a specification and a body, as illustrated in Figure 5.1.

Once written, the generic can be used to create new program units tailored to a particular application. These new program units are called *instances* of the generic.

To illustrate, we change the procedure ORDER from Section 3.1 into a generic by factoring out the type of the objects and the "⟨" operation. Recall that the ORDER procedure orders its two parameters (which must have type INTEGER in the earlier version) so that the smaller value is placed in the left parameter and the larger in the right. We will change ORDER so that it can order values not only of INTEGERs, but of any assignable type. A generic declaration for this new procedure, called ORDER_MAKER, is given below:

```
generic
     type ITEM is private;
     with function "⟨"(LEFT, RIGHT : ITEM) return BOOLEAN is ⟨⟩;
procedure ORDER_MAKER(I, J : in out ITEM);
```

A generic program unit is introduced by the reserved word **generic**. The declarations between the **generic** and the procedure specification are the *generic formal parameters*, which can be objects, types, and subprograms. A generic is a *template* which can be parameterized; that is, a generic defines a class of program units, with certain features factored out. The features factored out are given by the generic formal parameters. In this example, the two generic formal parameters are the type ITEM and the function "⟨".

The generic formal parameters provide the information needed by the compiler to check the types and operations within the generic declaration and body. Although they appear similar to ordinary declarations, they are parameter declarations because they appear after the reserved word *generic*; that is, these declarations do not define particular objects, types, and subprograms, but instead define the kinds of *actual parameters* that the programmer must provide to declare an instance.

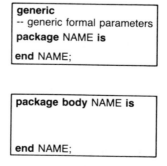

Figure 5.1 A Generic Program Unit

An instance is declared by *instantiating* the generic with actual parameters. *Instantiation* is a word coined by Ada to describe the process of making an instance of a generic. This process is illustrated in Figure 5.2.

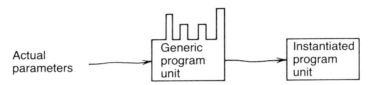

Figure 5.2 Generic Instantiation

The generic template is used to create the new program unit, which has the actual parameters substituted in place of the generic formal parameters in the template. An instantiation of ORDER_MAKER is given below:

```
procedure ORDER is new ORDER_MAKER(
     ITEM  => INTEGER,
     "<"    => "<");
```

An instantiation is the declaration of a new program unit. A programmer instantiates a generic by giving a name to the new program unit and actual parameters for any generic formal parameters. In this example, the new procedure is named ORDER and the actual parameters are INTEGER and the "<" function for INTEGERs. As with subprogram calls, named parameter associations are allowed for instantiations, and positional associations (if any) must appear before any named associations.

In general, the reserved word **new** in Ada indicates the creation of a new entity, based upon an existing entity. In Chapter 2 we saw two uses of **new**: the creation of a new object by means of an allocator and the creation of a new type by means of a derived type declaration. For generic instantiation, the **new** creates a new program unit, based upon the generic template.

The actual parameters supplied in the instantiation are used in the creation of the new program unit. These actual parameters are substituted in the instance for the generic formal parameters in the template; that is, the above instantiation conceptually creates a new procedure with the following specification:

```
procedure ORDER(I, J : in out INTEGER);
```

Generics are not ordinary program units in that they cannot be called. They can be instantiated, however, and the resulting instance is an ordinary program unit that can be called. Thus ORDER is an ordinary procedure for ordering INTEGER values identical to the one given in Section 3.1. This instance can be called, just as other program units can be called, as shown on the following page:

```
M, N : INTEGER;
...
ORDER(M, N);
```

Given ORDER_MAKER, we can create other instances as illustrated below:

```
procedure ORDER        is new ORDER_MAKER(
    ITEM => FLOAT,
    "⟨"  => "⟨");

procedure ORDER        is new ORDER_MAKER(
    ITEM => ACCOUNT_BALANCES,
    "⟨"  => "⟨");

procedure TALL_ORDER is new ORDER_MAKER(
    ITEM => HEIGHT,
    "⟨"  => "⟨");
```

The body for a generic program unit is no different in appearance than one for a nongeneric unit. The names of generic formal parameters are available for use (i.e., they are visible) within the body. The body of ORDER_MAKER is given below:

```
procedure ORDER_MAKER(I, J : in out ITEM) is
    TEMP : ITEM;
begin
    if J ⟨ I then        -- the formal operator "⟨"
        TEMP := I;
        I    := J;
        J    := TEMP;
    end if;
end ORDER_MAKER;
```

Note that the body does not mention it is generic, nor does it distinguish its generic formal parameters. Unlike ordinary subprograms (which in some cases can consist solely of a body), generic subprograms must be declared with a distinct specification and body.

The body of the generic unit is used to create the bodies of the instances. For example, the above instantiation of ORDER_MAKER with type INTEGER conceptually creates the following body for ORDER:

```
procedure ORDER(I, J : in out INTEGER) is
    TEMP : INTEGER;
begin
    if J ⟨ I then
        TEMP := I;
        I    := J;
        J    := TEMP;
    end if;
end ORDER;
```

An instantiation creates an instance of both the generic specification and body.

5.2 More Formalities

As mentioned above, there are three kinds of generic formal parameters: objects, types, and subprograms. Generic formal parameter declarations resemble other declarations in an Ada program. They define the kinds of actual parameters that can be used with the generic. In Ada terminology, the actual parameters must *match* the generic formal parameters. In general, an actual object matches a generic object, an actual type matches a generic type, and an actual subprogram (or entry, as discussed in Chapter 6) matches a generic subprogram. More specific matching rules are defined; the major ones are discussed in subsequent sections.

Where applicable, Ada defines the semantics of generic formal parameters in terms of the nongeneric counterpart. It is important to keep in mind that, unlike their nongeneric counterparts, generic formal parameters are not particular objects, types, and subprograms. Instead they define the values and operations that are available within the generic declaration and body. Because of the parameter matching rules, these values and operations are available for the corresponding actual parameters supplied in an instantiation.

The words *formal parameter* are used to describe both generic formal parameters and subprogram formal parameters introduced in Chapter 3. In this chapter, we often refer to generic formal parameters as generic parameters.

It is important not to confuse generic formal parameters with subprogram formal parameters. Although both parameterize a given program unit, they are different kinds of entities. Generic parameters can include types and subprograms, as well as objects, and are used in the creation of entirely new program units through instantiation. In contrast, subprogram formal parameters can only be objects and are used to parameterize a particular call of the same subprogram. Conceptually, the substitution of the actual parameters in an instantiation creates a new program unit, whereas the passing of actual parameters in a subprogram call occurs during execution of a program unit.

5.3 Formal Objects

Generic object parameters define constants and variables to be used in the generic. There are two kinds of generic object parameters: **in** and **in out**. The declarations have the same form as the corresponding subprogram formal parameter declarations. Unlike subprogram formal parameters, a generic formal object parameter cannot have mode **out**. Several examples of generic object parameters are shown below:

```
generic
    SIZE              : POSITIVE := 200;    -- default value is 200
    INFLATION_RATE : in      FLOAT;        -- no default given
    TOTALS            : in out DOLLAR;
procedure G;
```

A generic **in** parameter defines a constant. If no parameter mode is given, as in the case of SIZE above, the mode **in** is assumed. Like subprogram **in** parameters, the generic **in** parameter is a constant and therefore cannot be changed within the generic program unit. The value supplied in an instantiation can be any value that matches the type of the generic object parameter.

A generic **in** parameter can have a default value. If no corresponding actual parameter is provided in the instantiation, the default value is used.

For example, consider the following generic declaration and two instantiations:

```
generic
      SIZE : POSITIVE    := 200;        -- default size for queue
        type ELEMENT_TYPE is private; -- a generic type declaration
      package QUEUE_MAKER is

        ...

      end QUEUE_MAKER;

      package CUSTOMER_QUEUE is new QUEUE_MAKER(
          ELEMENT_TYPE => CUSTOMER);
      package ACTOR_QUEUE      is new QUEUE_MAKER(
          ELEMENT_TYPE => AUDITIONER,
          SIZE         => 10);
```

where CUSTOMER and AUDITIONER are visible types declared earlier. The instantiation that declares CUSTOMER_QUEUE provides no value for SIZE, so the default value in the generic parameter declaration is used. Hence, the length of queues in package CUSTOMER_QUEUE is 200. ACTOR_QUEUE, however, gives an explicit value for SIZE, specifying its queues to have length 10.

A generic **in out** parameter defines a variable. Within the generic, this variable can be used in any way that other variables of that same type can be used. An instantiation of the generic provides the actual variable used within the resulting instance. Unlike generic **in** parameters, **in out** parameters cannot be given a default.

5.4 Formal Types

Generic type parameters give generics much of their power and flexibility. A generic formal type defines the values and operations that must be available for the actual type supplied in an instantiation. The matching rules for types ensure that the actual type has the needed operations.

Generic formal types can be scalars (i.e., integer, enumeration, floating, and fixed point types), array types, access types, and private types. Each generic formal type has an associated set of operations appropriate for its type. For an array formal parameter, for example, indexing is available for objects of the type, and for an integer formal parameter, the predefined arithmetic operations are available. These operations can be used within the generic specification and body, and the matching rules ensure that they will be meaningful for the actual types used in instantiations. The generic formal types and the matching of corresponding actual types are discussed below.

The following declaration illustrates the generic scalar formal parameters.

```
generic
    type FORMAL_DISCRETE is (<>);
    type FORMAL_INTEGER  is range <>;
    type FORMAL_FIXED    is delta <>;
    type FORMAL_FLOAT    is digits <>;
procedure G;
```

The first formal parameter declares a formal discrete parameter. In an instantiation, a generic formal discrete type is matched by any discrete type, that is, by any integer or enumeration type. Within the generic, the type has the predefined attributes and operations for discrete types. In addition to the predefined operations for discrete types, an integer type also has the predefined arithmetic operations, such as "+", "-", "*", and "/". Similarly, a formal float type is matched by any float type, and a formal fixed type is matched by any fixed type. Like other formal types, formal float and formal fixed types have the associated predefined operations available within the generic.

The following declaration illustrates a generic access type.

```
generic
    type FORMAL_ACCESS is access A_TYPE;
procedure G;
```

A generic access type defines an access type such as those described in Section 2.13. This type has available the same operations as nongeneric access types; that is, assignment, equality, allocation through **new**, and the literal **null**. In an instantiation, a generic access type is matched by any access type, provided that the designated type (which can itself be a generic formal type) also matches.

The following declarations illustrate generic formal array types.

```
generic
    type FORMAL_CONSTRAINED is
        array (INDEX_TYPE) of COMPONENT_TYPE;

    type FORMAL_UNCONSTRAINED is
        array (INDEX_TYPE range <>) of COMPONENT_TYPE;
procedure G;
```

A generic formal array parameter allows passing an array type as an actual parameter to a generic. A generic constrained array type is matched by a constrained array actual type; a generic unconstrained array type is matched by an unconstrained actual array type. To match, the actual type must have the same number and same type of indexes and the same component type.

The most important generic types for building abstract data types are the private and limited private types. Abstractions such as queues, lists, sets, trees, and graphs can be written with the contained data declared as a private or limited private type. ORDER_MAKER and QUEUE_MAKER above illustrated generic private types. The four kinds of private types are shown below:

```
generic
     type FORMAL_PRIVATE          is private;
     type FORMAL_LIMITED          is limited private;
     type DISCRIMINANT_PRIVATE is private        (D : ANY_DISCRETE);
     type DISCRIMINANT_LIMITED is limited private (D : ANY_DISCRETE);
procedure G;
```

Generic private types, like private types declared in packages, have the predefined operations of assignment and comparison for equality available within the generic. A generic private type can be matched by *any* type that has assignment, equality, and inequality defined for it. For example, it can be matched by an integer type, an access type, an array type, or a record type. The following instantiations declare queue packages of INTEGER, TRANSACTION, and PAGE types:

```
package INTEGER_QUEUE         is new QUEUE_MAKER(
     ELEMENT_TYPE =) INTEGER);
package TRANSACTION_QUEUE is new QUEUE_MAKER(
     ELEMENT_TYPE =) TRANSACTION);
package PAGE_QUEUE            is new QUEUE_MAKER(
     ELEMENT_TYPE =) PAGE,
     SIZE             =) 64);
```

Limited private types, again like their package counterparts, have no operations predefined for them. Any operations to be performed within the generic on objects of limited private type must be passed as additional subprogram parameters to the generic. A generic limited private is matched by any type. Because they require no operations of the corresponding actual type, formal limited private types are the most general of the generic type parameters.

Although the syntax is the same and the allowed operations are the same, generic private types and nongeneric privates differ in several important ways. The full declaration for a nongeneric private type must be given in the package private part. The details of this full declaration (such as whether it is an array or record) are available within the package private part and body. In contrast, a generic private type does not have a corresponding full declaration within the generic. Thus the details of the type are unavailable within the generic declaration *and* within the body. Only predefined assignment, equality, and inequality are available. The full type is given by the corresponding actual parameter in an instantiation. Neither the generic declaration nor the body have access to the internal structure of the private type. In short, generic private types are similar to ordinary private types because they have the same predefined operations; however, they differ in that the generic does not give a full declaration for the type.

5.5 Formal Subprograms

Subprograms are the third kind of generic parameter and are used to parameterize a generic by a procedure or function. The reader should be careful to note the difference between "generic formal subprogram parameter" and a "subprogram formal parameter." The first is a generic formal parameter that *is* a subprogram; the latter is an ordinary formal parameter *of* a subprogram.

As is true of other kinds of generic parameters, the actual subprogram given in an instantiation must match the generic formal subprogram parameter. An actual subprogram matches a formal subprogram if the parameter and result type profile (see Section 3.6), as well as the parameter modes, are the same.[1]

We saw an example of a generic formal subprogram parameter in the ORDER_ MAKER procedure. It is reproduced below:

```
generic
     type ITEM is private;
     with function "<"(LEFT, RIGHT : ITEM) return BOOLEAN is <>;
procedure ORDER_MAKER(I, J : in out ITEM);
```

As the declaration shows, a generic formal subprogram parameter—in this case the "<" function—looks like an ordinary subprogram declaration preceded by the reserved word **with**. The important point to note is that the generic formal subprogram parameter gives a full specification of subprogram parameter and result types. The specification enables full compiler checking of the matching actual subprogram parameters and full checking of calls to the subprogram parameter within the generic declaration and body. Hence, it is impossible to violate the type security by passing an inappropriate subprogram to "<".

Notice that the "<" function is followed by the **is** <>. This phrase defines a default parameter for instantiations of ORDER_MAKER. A default parameter allows an instantiation to omit the parameter, provided that a "<" function exists for the actual parameter given for ITEM. If an instantiation omits the function, and if a matching function named "<" is defined for the actual type, this function is used by default. The actual function is determined in the context of the instantiation, not the context of the generic declaration. If no matching function named "<" is defined, the instantiation is illegal without an explicit actual parameter.

For example, in the following instantiation

---

[1] In addition to procedures and functions, task entries (discussed in Chapter 6) and enumeration literals also can be used as actual parameters in an instantiation. As Chapter 6 describes, task entries are similar to procedures. Enumeration literals can be considered parameterless functions whose return value is the literal itself.

procedure INTEGER_ORDER **is new** ORDER_MAKER(ITEM =〉 INTEGER);

which omits the "〈" parameter, the compiler uses the "〈" for INTEGERs; that is, the compiler looks for a function with the following specification:

function "〈"(LEFT, RIGHT : INTEGER) **return** BOOLEAN;

Since this specification is the predefined INTEGER "〈", the instantiation is legal. The names of the formal parameters, LEFT and RIGHT, are not significant but, as mentioned earlier, the parameter modes are significant.

Default parameters also can be given in a form using an identifier (or operator symbol). For example, a previously-declared function RANDOM could be used as a default:

with function NEXT **return** FLOAT **is** RANDOM;

As before, RANDOM is used if no actual function is given explicitly for NEXT in an instantiation. Named defaults are less useful than the "〈〉" form, however, because the default name is determined at the point of the generic declaration, not at the point of instantiation. For this reason, named defaults generally are not useful if the subprogram has a parameter of a generic formal type. To illustrate, the following ORDER_MAKER is illegal:

```
generic
      type ITEM is private;
      with function "〈"(LEFT, RIGHT : ITEM) return BOOLEAN is IS_LESS;
            -- illegal because no IS_LESS is defined for ITEM
procedure ORDER_MAKER(I, J : in out ITEM);
```

because IS_LESS must refer to a function with the specification:

function IS_LESS(LEFT, RIGHT : ITEM) **return** BOOLEAN;

Since no IS_LESS function is declared for the formal type ITEM, the default name is illegal. (The only way IS_LESS for ITEM could be declared is as a formal subprogram parameter of ORDER_MAKER.) Thus the "〈〉" form is more flexible than named defaults.

5.6 Queues Revisited

In the earlier formulations of a queue, we specified the type of the elements that the queue holds. In accordance with strong typing, the queue can hold only one type of element. Because of type checking, the compiler can ensure that we do not attempt to place other types of elements in the queue and perhaps thereby corrupt the queue.

An abstract definition of a queue, however, mentions nothing about the type of the elements in the queue. In Chapter 3 a queue was defined as a data structure in which data elements are entered and removed first-in-first-out. This definition places no restrictions on the type of the elements placed in the queue. The operations of a queue are meaningful regardless of the types of elements in the queue. This description suggests formulation of the queue as a generic package. A possible declaration for a generic queue package is given below.

```
generic

    SIZE : POSITIVE := 200;   -- a generic object declaration
    type ELEMENT_TYPE is private; -- a generic type declaration

package QUEUE_MAKER is

    type KIND is limited private;

    function  IS_EMPTY(Q : in KIND) return BOOLEAN;
    function  IS_FULL  (Q : in KIND) return BOOLEAN;

    procedure ENTER (Q : in out KIND; ITEM : in  ELEMENT_TYPE);
    QUEUE_IS_FULL : exception;

    procedure REMOVE (Q : in out KIND; ITEM : out ELEMENT_TYPE);
    QUEUE_IS_EMPTY : exception;

private

    subtype INDEX is INTEGER range 1 .. SIZE;
    type SPACE is array (INDEX) of ELEMENT_TYPE;
    type KIND is record
        ITEMS  : SPACE;
        HEAD   : INDEX := 1;
        TAIL   : INDEX := 1;
        COUNT : INTEGER range 0..SIZE := 0;
    end record;

end QUEUE_MAKER;
```

The queue package is a data type abstraction (as discussed in Section 3.12) for a queue. It is more general than the queue package presented in Chapter 3, however, because it can be instantiated with other types to create other queue packages. Each of these instances is a data type abstraction for a queue of objects of the given type.

QUEUE_MAKER illustrates the difference between a generic formal private type and a nongeneric private type. It has a formal private type parameter and it declares a nongeneric limited private type in its specification. ELEMENT_TYPE is a formal parameter and therefore has no full declaration. Because the declaration of KIND is in the package specification, and not in the generic formal part, it requires a corresponding full type declaration in the private part.

The type is named KIND so that, by careful choice of an instance name, declarations using this name in expanded form will be meaningful. For example, the following declaration uses an appropriate package name to make declarations of transaction queues readable.

```
package TRANSACTION_QUEUE is new QUEUE_MAKER(
    SIZE            = > 100,
    ELEMENT_TYPE = > TRANSACTION);

INCOMING : TRANSACTION_QUEUE.KIND;
...

TRANSACTION_QUEUE.ENTER(Q      = > INCOMING,
                        ITEM = > GET_TRANSACTION);
```

The instantiation declares a new package TRANSACTION_QUEUE operating on 100-element queues of TRANSACTIONs.

TRANSACTION_QUEUE is an ordinary package with a type KIND and subprograms IS_FULL, IS_EMPTY, ENTER, and REMOVE visible in its specification. This fragment declares a queue variable called INCOMING, using the type KIND made available within the TRANSACTION_QUEUE package. Later in the program, the ENTER subprogram is called to enter the result of GET_TRANSACTION in the INCOMING queue.

A body for the QUEUE_MAKER package is given below. It uses the same circular array algorithm as previous examples.

```
package body QUEUE_MAKER is

    function   IS_EMPTY(Q : in KIND) return BOOLEAN is
    begin
        return Q.COUNT = 0;
    end IS_EMPTY;

    function   IS_FULL (Q : in KIND) return BOOLEAN is
    begin
        return Q.COUNT = SIZE;
    end IS_FULL;
```

```
    procedure ENTER (Q : in out KIND; ITEM : in  ELEMENT_TYPE) is
    begin
        if Q.COUNT = SIZE then      -- the formal object SIZE
            raise QUEUE_IS_FULL;
        end if;
        Q.ITEMS(Q.TAIL) := ITEM;
        Q.TAIL          := (Q.TAIL rem SIZE) + 1;
        Q.COUNT         := Q.COUNT + 1;
    end ENTER;

    procedure REMOVE (Q : in out KIND; ITEM : out ELEMENT_TYPE) is
    begin
        if Q.COUNT = 0 then
            raise QUEUE_IS_EMPTY;
        end if;
        ITEM     := Q.ITEMS(Q.HEAD);
        Q.HEAD   := (Q.HEAD rem SIZE) + 1;
        Q.COUNT := Q.COUNT - 1;
    end REMOVE;

end QUEUE_MAKER;
```

Although it is wise to hide implementation details, in general it is impossible to ignore implementation considerations. In the case of QUEUE_MAKER, the circular queue implementation requires assignment for the generic type, and thus a formal private type parameter is required rather than a formal limited private type.

5.7 An Associative Table

As another illustration of generics, consider a table that manages associations between pairs of objects. One of the objects is considered the key of the pair; the other is the value associated with the key. Pairs can be inserted into the table; the value associated with a key subsequently can be retrieved by supplying the key. A value can be inserted more than once for a given key. A retrieve operation returns the most recent value inserted for that key. A data structure to manage associations is sometimes called an *associative table*.

Notice that in our description of the data structure no mention is made of the types of the objects of the pairs. Such a description suggests that the associative table be specified as a generic. A possible specification for a generic associative table is given below:

```
generic
    type KEY   is private;
    type VALUE is private;
    SIZE : POSITIVE := 100;
package TABLE_MAKER is
```

```
procedure INSERT   (ITEM : KEY; GETS : VALUE);
TABLE_IS_FULL     : exception;

function RETRIEVE (ITEM : KEY) return VALUE;
ITEM_NOT_FOUND : exception;

end TABLE_MAKER;
```

The generic has three formal parameters: a type for the key, a type for the value, and an object of subtype POSITIVE. The object SIZE gives the size of the associative table.

A possible body to implement this specification is given below:

```
package body TABLE_MAKER is
    type PAIR is record
        A_KEY      : KEY;
        ITS_VALUE : VALUE;
    end record;

    subtype INDEX  is INTEGER range 1 .. SIZE;
    subtype COUNT is INTEGER range INDEX'FIRST-1 .. SIZE;
    SPACE : array (INDEX) of PAIR;
    CURRENT_INDEX : COUNT := COUNT'FIRST;

    procedure INSERT   (ITEM : KEY; GETS : VALUE) is
    begin
        if CURRENT_INDEX = SIZE then
            raise TABLE_IS_FULL;
        end if;
        CURRENT_INDEX := CURRENT_INDEX + 1;
        SPACE(CURRENT_INDEX).A_KEY := ITEM;
        SPACE(CURRENT_INDEX).ITS_VALUE := GETS;
    end INSERT;

    function RETRIEVE (ITEM : KEY) return VALUE is
    begin
        -- Search SPACE backwards linearly.
        for I in reverse INDEX'FIRST .. CURRENT_INDEX loop
            if SPACE(I).A_KEY = ITEM then
                return SPACE(I).ITS_VALUE;
            end if;
        end loop;
        raise ITEM_NOT_FOUND;
    end RETRIEVE;

end TABLE_MAKER;
```

The implementation simply stores the pairs linearly in an array. INSERT increments the CURRENT_INDEX into the table and places a new pair at this index. RETRIEVE searches the array backwards for the first key value that matches the given key. Thus for a given key, the most recently inserted is found by RETRIEVE.

Examples of instantiations and uses of the generic are illustrated below:

```
subtype        NAME     is STRING(1..20);
type           HEIGHT   is range 6 .. 100; -- Inches
type           DOLLAR   is delta 0.01 range 0.0..1.0e8;
VERY_TALL : BOOLEAN;
IS_BROKE  : BOOLEAN;

package HEIGHT_TABLE is new TABLE_MAKER(
    KEY     => NAME,
    VALUE   => HEIGHT);

package CUSTOMER_TABLE is new TABLE_MAKER(
    KEY     => NAME,
    VALUE   => DOLLAR);

...

HEIGHT_TABLE.INSERT      (ITEM   => "FLORINOY KROPOTKIN   ",
                          VALUE  => 59);
CUSTOMER_TABLE.INSERT(ITEM       => "BEULAH BELLE BAKUNIN",
                          VALUE  => 100.00);

VERY_TALL := HEIGHT_TABLE.RETRIEVE    ("FLORINOY KROPOTKIN   ")
                > 80;
IS_BROKE  := CUSTOMER_TABLE.RETRIEVE("BEULAH BELLE BAKUNIN")
                = 0.0;
```

5.8 A Sort Procedure

A common problem that often results in reinvented solutions is sorting. Algorithms of varying efficiency for sorting are well-known. The main features of a sort are a list of elements and an ordering relation between elements. The following specification is a generic formulation of a sorting subprogram.

```
generic
    type ELEMENT_TYPE is private;
    type INDEX_TYPE     is (<>);
    type ARRAY_TYPE     is array (INDEX_TYPE range <>)
                              of ELEMENT_TYPE;
    with function "<"(LEFT, RIGHT : ELEMENT_TYPE) return BOOLEAN
        is <>;

procedure SORT_MAKER(UNSORTED : in out ARRAY_TYPE);
```

In this generic, we represent the element as a private type (ELEMENT_TYPE) and the list as an unconstrained array (ARRAY_TYPE) of elements. To make the generic as general as possible, the index type (INDEX_TYPE) of the array also is declared as a formal type parameter. The ordering relation is given by the generic parameter "<", which is an operator that takes two elements and returns a BOOLEAN value indicating whether the first parameter is less than the second. The body of SORT_MAKER is given below:

```
with ORDER_MAKER;
procedure SORT_MAKER(UNSORTED : in out ARRAY_TYPE) is
    procedure ORDER_ELEMENTS is new ORDER_MAKER(
        ITEM => ELEMENT_TYPE);
begin
    if UNSORTED'LENGTH <= 1 then      -- Nothing to do.
        return;
    end if;

    for I in UNSORTED'FIRST .. INDEX_TYPE'PRED(UNSORTED'LAST)
    loop
        for J in INDEX_TYPE'SUCC(I) .. UNSORTED'LAST loop
            ORDER_ELEMENTS(UNSORTED(I), UNSORTED(J));
        end loop;
    end loop;
end SORT_MAKER;
```

The body declares an instance of ORDER_MAKER (from Section 5.1) named ORDER_ELEMENTS, which is used to arrange the two array components so that the smaller one is placed at the lower index.

Our SORT_MAKER body uses an inefficient but simple algorithm, called "straight selection" (Wirth, 1976): The outer loop begins at the first index position and iterates up to the next-to-last index. The inner loop iterates from one more than the current value of the outer index to the last index. Note the use of attributes to express the bounds of the two loops. The expression

INDEX_TYPE'PRED(UNSORTED'LAST)

uses the attribute 'PRED of the formal discrete parameter INDEX_TYPE. Its argument is the attribute 'LAST of the array object being sorted. This expression specifies the upper limit of I to be one less than the upper bound of UNSORTED. The attribute 'SUCC similarly is used with the current value of I to define the lower bound of J.

The declaration of ORDER_ELEMENTS illustrates an interesting use of default formal subprograms. The instantiation does not supply an actual parameter for the "<" formal subprogram parameter of ORDER_MAKER. Because the formal subprogram has a default of **is** <>, the "<" function for ELEMENT_TYPE is used, which in this case is the formal parameter of SORT_MAKER. Thus ultimately the

"⟨" used in ORDER_MAKER is the same one supplied in the instantiation of SORT_MAKER.

5.9 A List Package

In Section 2.13, we saw an example of an access type used to create linked lists of TRANSACTION_NODE. The list was threaded through the NEXT_TRANSACTION component of the TRANSACTION_NODE type. A different approach to list management is to encapsulate the list operations in a package to hide the list implementation. The details of the list operations are hidden in the body of the package, so that the list implementation can be changed without affecting program units that use the lists. In this section, we illustrate this approach using a generic package for list management. Like queues, lists are an example of a common data structure that does not depend on the data type contained within it, which again suggests specification as a generic program unit.

A list is defined recursively as a data structure that is either empty or consists of an element and a list that is the remainder. A specification for a generic list package is given below:

```
generic
    type ELEMENT_TYPE is private;
package LIST_MAKER is

    type KIND is private;

    function MAKE                       return KIND;
    function IS_EMPTY(L : in KIND) return BOOLEAN;

    function HEAD(L : in KIND) return ELEMENT_TYPE;
      -- The first element.
    function TAIL (L : in KIND) return KIND;
      -- Second through last
      -- elements.
    LIST_IS_EMPTY   : exception;

    procedure INSERT (L : in out KIND; E : in ELEMENT_TYPE);
    procedure APPEND(L : in out KIND; E : in ELEMENT_TYPE);

private
    type INTERNAL_RECORD;
    type KIND is access INTERNAL_RECORD;

end LIST_MAKER;
```

This package provides a data type for the list and operations for constructing a list, testing whether a list is empty, taking the head element off a list, taking the tail of a list, inserting at the beginning of a list, and appending to the end of a list. This set of operations is minimal; a general package for list management would include many more operations, such as ones to iterate over the elements of a list, to delete an element of a list, and to destroy a list.

A point unrelated to generics is noteworthy about this specification. LIST_MAKER illustrates a unique aspect of incomplete types declared in package private parts (INTERNAL_RECORD in this example). Recall from Section 2.13 that an incomplete type requires a later full declaration in the same declarative part, yet LIST_MAKER gives no full declaration in the private part. It is permissible to defer the full declaration until the package body if the incomplete type is declared in a package private part. The ability to defer the full declaration until the body results in additional independence (uncoupling) of the package specification and the units that use it, which avoids unnecessary recompilations if the full declaration changes. Chapter 9 describes further the dependence relationships between compilation units and the recompilation rules.

A body for LIST_MAKER is given below.

```
package body LIST_MAKER is
    EMPTY_LIST : constant KIND := null;
    type INTERNAL_RECORD is record       -- full declaration here
        ITEM : ELEMENT_TYPE;
        NEXT : KIND;
    end record;

    function MAKE return KIND is
    begin
        return EMPTY_LIST;
    end;

    function IS_EMPTY(L : in KIND) return BOOLEAN is
    begin
        return L = EMPTY_LIST;
    end;

    function HEAD(L : in KIND) return ELEMENT_TYPE is
    begin
        return L.ITEM;
    exception
        when CONSTRAINT_ERROR => raise LIST_IS_EMPTY;
    end;

    function TAIL(L : in KIND) return KIND is
    begin
        return L.NEXT;
    exception
        when CONSTRAINT_ERROR => raise LIST_IS_EMPTY;
    end;
```

```
    procedure INSERT(L : in out KIND; E : in ELEMENT_TYPE) is
    begin
        L := new INTERNAL_RECORD'(ITEM => E, NEXT => L);
    end;

    procedure APPEND(L : in out KIND; E : in ELEMENT_TYPE) is
    begin
        if L = EMPTY_LIST then
            L := new INTERNAL_RECORD'(ITEM => E,
                                        NEXT => EMPTY_LIST);
        else
            declare
                TEMP : KIND := L;
            begin
                while TEMP.NEXT /= EMPTY_LIST loop
                    TEMP := TEMP.NEXT;
                end loop;
                TEMP.NEXT := new INTERNAL_RECORD'(ITEM => E,
                                        NEXT => EMPTY_LIST);
            end;
        end if;
    end;
end LIST_MAKER;
```

The body supplies the full definition for INTERNAL_RECORD and implements the operations declared in the specification. INTERNAL_RECORD consists of an element and an access variable which links to the next element in the list.

Several points unrelated to generics are noteworthy concerning the body of LIST_MAKER. The constant EMPTY_LIST is declared so that if the implementation changes (e.g., by storing the elements in an array and using indexes as the links), only the definition of the constant must change—not all the places (e.g., the operation APPEND) that need to refer to an empty list.

Note also that the operation HEAD provides an exception handler for CONSTRAINT_ERROR. As described in Chapter 2, an attempt to access the designated object of a null access variable raises the exception CONSTRAINT_ERROR. If an empty list is passed to HEAD, the selection of the ITEM component of L will raise CONSTRAINT_ERROR. HEAD provides a handler for CONSTRAINT_ERROR, which raises LIST_IS_EMPTY, a more meaningful exception to the units that call HEAD.

One final point about the implementation of LIST_MAKER is important. The specification provides operations for creating lists but no operation for destroying them. In practice, an operation to destroy a list often is required to assure that storage occupied by unneeded lists can be reclaimed. A technique for recovering unneeded space occupied by objects allocated through **new** is available by means of the predefined generic UNCHECKED_DEALLOCATION, discussed further in Chapter 8.

5.10 A Stack Package

Given the specification for LIST_MAKER, we can build other data structures upon it. For example, a *stack* is a data structure that stores elements, which can be removed in last-in-first-out order. Elements are added to the stack by a *push* operation and are removed from the stack by a *pop* operation. A pop removes the most recently pushed element.

One implementation of a stack is to use a list to store the stack elements. Using a list, a push operation is an insert operation on the list. A pop operation is the removal of the most recently inserted element. Thus the INSERT and HEAD operations of LIST_MAKER are suitable for the PUSH and POP functions of a stack. The following stack specification builds upon the LIST_MAKER package.

```
generic
    type ELEMENT_TYPE is private;
package STACK_MAKER is

    procedure PUSH(E : in  ELEMENT_TYPE);
    STACK_IS_FULL   : exception;

    procedure POP (E : out ELEMENT_TYPE);
    STACK_IS_EMPTY : exception;

end STACK_MAKER;
```

STACK_MAKER is a generic data object abstraction that contains a hidden implementation for a stack object and provides operations for pushing and popping the stack. The generic formal type parameter, ELEMENT_TYPE, defines the type of the elements placed in the stack. A body for STACK_MAKER is given below:

```
with LIST_MAKER;
package body STACK_MAKER is

    package STACK_LIST is new LIST_MAKER(ELEMENT_TYPE);
    use STACK_LIST;

    THE_STACK : STACK_LIST.KIND := MAKE;

    procedure PUSH(E : in  ELEMENT_TYPE) is
    begin
        INSERT(THE_STACK, E);
    end;
```

```
procedure POP (E : out ELEMENT_TYPE) is
begin
    E := HEAD(THE_STACK);
    THE_STACK := TAIL(THE_STACK);
exception
    when LIST_IS_EMPTY => raise STACK_IS_EMPTY;
end;

end STACK_MAKER;
```

The **with** clause makes the generic package LIST_MAKER available for instantiation within STACK_MAKER. Because we use the LIST_MAKER package as the basis for the stack, we must instantiate LIST_MAKER with the type that the stack is to hold. Within the body of STACK_MAKER, STACK_LIST is created to hold the elements of the stack. It is an instance of LIST_MAKER with the same actual parameter as that given to STACK_MAKER when it is instantiated. An instantiation of STACK_MAKER results in STACK_MAKER instantiating LIST_MAKER; that is, the actual parameter to STACK_MAKER is passed on to LIST_MAKER to create a list of that type. At the point of instantiation of STACK_LIST, ELEMENT_TYPE is a formal parameter of STACK_MAKER and an actual parameter of LIST_MAKER.

After the instantiation that creates STACK_LIST, an object of the list type is declared and initialized. This object holds the elements of the stack. PUSH is simply an INSERT operation on the list. POP returns the HEAD of the list and sets the stack to the TAIL of the list.

5.11 A Binary Tree Package

A *binary tree* is a data structure often used to hold sorted data. A binary tree is defined recursively as a data structure that is either empty or consists of a root node which contains application-defined information, a left subtree, and a right subtree. When a binary tree is used to store sorted information, the usual convention is that objects less than a node are stored in the left subtree of the node, and objects greater than a node are stored in the right subtree. The ordering relation "less than" depends on the type; for example, for STRINGs, the ordering relation could be lexicographic order. Figure 5.3 illustrates a sorted binary tree structure whose information is a string, and shows the effect of an insertion.

Visiting the nodes of a tree (e.g., to set information in each node) is called *traversing* the tree. Binary trees can be traversed in a number of ways; a common order is *inorder* traversal. A recursive description of inorder traversal is as follows: inorder traverse the left subtree, visit the node itself, and then inorder traverse the right subtree. For sorted binary trees, an inorder traversal visits the nodes in ascending order.

The following generic BINARY_TREE_MAKER shows a simple tree abstraction.

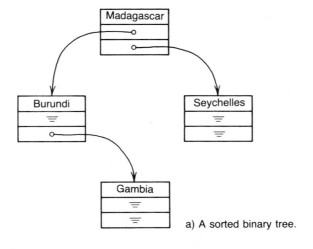

a) A sorted binary tree.

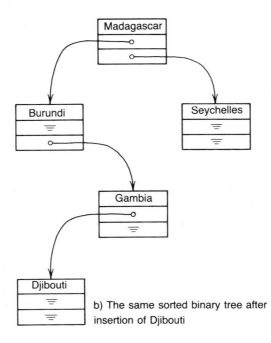

b) The same sorted binary tree after insertion of Djibouti

Figure 5.3 Sorted Binary Trees

BINARY_TREE_MAKER has three generic formal parameters: a type for the key of the information contained in a node, a type for the information associated with a key, and a function "⟨" to determine if one key is less than another key. The package specification makes available a type KIND for the tree, and subprograms to

```
generic
    type KEY_TYPE      is private;
    type ELEMENT_TYPE is private;
    with function "<"(LEFT, RIGHT : KEY_TYPE) return BOOLEAN is <>;

package BINARY_TREE_MAKER is

    type KIND is private;

    function   MAKE return KIND;
    function   IS_EMPTY(T : KIND) return BOOLEAN;
    procedure INSERT    (T : in out KIND;
                         K : KEY_TYPE;
                         E : ELEMENT_TYPE);
    function   RETRIEVE(T : KIND;
                         K : KEY_TYPE) return ELEMENT_TYPE;
    KEY_NOT_FOUND : exception;

    generic
        with procedure OPERATION(K : KEY_TYPE;
                                  E : ELEMENT_TYPE);
    procedure INORDER_TRAVERSE(THE_TREE : in KIND);

private
    type INTERNAL_RECORD;
    type KIND is access INTERNAL_RECORD;

end BINARY_TREE_MAKER;
```

determine if a tree is empty, to insert a new key and its associated information, and to retrieve the information associated with a key. RETRIEVE raises the exception KEY_NOT_FOUND if the key is not contained in the tree. Because BINARY_TREE_MAKER provides a type for declaring trees, instances of this package are data type abstractions. Program units that instantiate BINARY_TREE_MAKER can use the tree package instance to declare as many binary trees as needed. Notice that again we defer until the package body the full declaration of the incomplete type declared in the private part.

An interesting feature of BINARY_TREE_MAKER is that it declares a generic procedure, INORDER_TRAVERSE, nested inside the package specification. IN-ORDER_TRAVERSE has a formal subprogram parameter, OPERATION, which is an operation on a tree node. When a program unit instantiates BINARY_TREE_MAKER, the resulting instance contains a generic procedure INORDER_TRAV-ERSE. Instantiation of BINARY_TREE_MAKER does *not* also instantiate IN-ORDER_TRAVERSE; it merely creates an instance that contains the generic procedure INORDER_TRAVERSE. INORDER_TRAVERSE then can be instantiated with an operation on the nodes of the tree. This second instance is a procedure that, when called, performs an inorder traversal on a tree passed in the parameter THE_TREE.

To illustrate, the following package is a simple employee data base, based upon the BINARY_TREE_MAKER.

```
with BINARY_TREE_MAKER;
package EMPLOYEE_DATA_BASE is

    NAME_LENGTH        : constant := 40;
    subtype NAME_TYPE is STRING(1 .. NAME_LENGTH);
    type    DOLLAR     is delta 0.01 range 0.0..1.0e8;
    type    AGE_TYPE   is range 0 .. 150;
    type    YEAR_TYPE  is range 1900..2100;

    type EMPLOYEE_INFO  is record
        SALARY : DOLLAR;
        AGE    : AGE_TYPE;
        HIRED  : YEAR_TYPE;
    end record;

    package EMPLOYEE_TREE is new BINARY_TREE_MAKER(
        KEY_TYPE     => NAME_TYPE,
        ELEMENT_TYPE => EMPLOYEE_INFO);

    ROOT_NODE : EMPLOYEE_TREE.KIND;

end EMPLOYEE_DATA_BASE;
```

Another program unit can use EMPLOYEE_DATA_BASE to write reports about the records in the data base. For example, a procedure to write separate reports of the salary and the ages of the employees could use EMPLOYEE_DATA_BASE as follows:

```
with EMPLOYEE_DATA_BASE; use EMPLOYEE_DATA_BASE;
with TEXT_IO;            use TEXT_IO;
procedure PRINT_REPORTS  is

    -- Instantiate predefined TEXT_IO generics for IO (see Chapter 7)
    package SALARY_IO is new FIXED_IO   (DOLLAR);
    use SALARY_IO;
    package AGE_IO     is new INTEGER_IO(AGE_TYPE);
    use AGE_IO;

    procedure PRINT_SALARY(
        KEY  : NAME_TYPE;
        INFO : EMPLOYEE_INFO) is
    begin
        PUT_LINE ("Employee: " & KEY);
        PUT      ("Salary: ");
        PUT      (INFO.SALARY);
        NEW_LINE(SPACING => 2);
    end;
```

```
procedure PRINT_AGE    (
   KEY  : NAME_TYPE;
   INFO : EMPLOYEE_INFO) is
begin
   PUT_LINE ("Employee: " & KEY);
   PUT      ("Age: ");
   PUT      (INFO.AGE);
   NEW_LINE(SPACING => 2);
end;

procedure REPORT_SALARIES is new
   EMPLOYEE_TREE.INORDER_TRAVERSE(
   OPERATION => PRINT_SALARY);
procedure REPORT_AGES      is new
   EMPLOYEE_TREE.INORDER_TRAVERSE(
   OPERATION => PRINT_AGE);

begin
   PUT_LINE("Salary Report");
   REPORT_SALARIES(ROOT_NODE);
   NEW_LINE;
   PUT_LINE("Age Report");
   REPORT_AGES(ROOT_NODE);
end PRINT_REPORTS;
```

This procedure declares two procedures—PRINT_SALARY and PRINT_AGE—and then instantiates two new procedures, REPORT_SALARIES and REPORT_AGES, with the first two procedures. When called, REPORT_SALARIES prints the salaries of all employees contained in the data base. Similarly, REPORT_AGES prints the ages of all employees in the data base. The package TEXT_IO and the generic packages FIXED_IO and INTEGER_IO nested in TEXT_IO are necessary for input-output in this example; they are described further in Section 7.4.

Returning to BINARY_TREE_MAKER, a body for BINARY_TREE_MAKER is given below.

```
package body BINARY_TREE_MAKER is

   EMPTY_TREE : constant KIND := null;
   type INTERNAL_RECORD is record
       KEY         : KEY_TYPE;
       ELEMENT     : ELEMENT_TYPE;
       LEFT, RIGHT : KIND;
   end record;

   function MAKE return KIND is
   begin
       return EMPTY_TREE;
   end;
```

```
function IS_EMPTY(T : KIND) return BOOLEAN is
begin
    return T = EMPTY_TREE;
end;


procedure INSERT(T : in out KIND; K : KEY_TYPE;
                    E : ELEMENT_TYPE) is
begin
    if T = EMPTY_TREE then
        T := new INTERNAL_RECORD'(
                KEY           => K,
                ELEMENT       => E,
                LEFT | RIGHT  => EMPTY_TREE);
    elsif K < T.KEY then
        INSERT(T.LEFT, K, E);
    else
        INSERT(T.RIGHT, K, E);
    end if;
end;


function RETRIEVE(T : KIND; K : KEY_TYPE)
  return ELEMENT_TYPE is
begin
    if T = EMPTY_TREE then
        raise KEY_NOT_FOUND;
    elsif K = T.KEY then
        return T.ELEMENT;
    elsif K < T.KEY then
        return RETRIEVE(T.LEFT, K);
    else
        return RETRIEVE(T.RIGHT, K);
    end if;
end;


procedure INORDER_TRAVERSE(THE_TREE : in KIND) is
begin
    if THE_TREE /= EMPTY_TREE then
        INORDER_TRAVERSE (THE_TREE.LEFT);
        OPERATION(THE_TREE.KEY, THE_TREE.ELEMENT);
        INORDER_TRAVERSE (THE_TREE.RIGHT);
    end if;
end;


end BINARY_TREE_MAKER;
```

The body of BINARY_TREE_MAKER declares an internal record type that is a node in the tree. INTERNAL_RECORD contains a KEY which is used to insert and retrieve records in the tree, an ELEMENT which is the information associated with a KEY, and components for the left subtree and right subtree. The INSERT operation has three possible actions at a node. If the tree is empty, it creates a new node, sets the KEY and ELEMENT components from the parameters, and sets the LEFT and RIGHT components to the empty tree. If nonempty, INSERT compares the key values of the parameter and the root of the current tree, using the formal operator "⟨". If the parameter K is less than the current tree key, INSERT calls itself recursively to insert K and E into the left subtree. Otherwise, it recursively inserts K and E into the right subtree.

5.12 Software Engineering and Generics

Generics are a key Ada feature to support software engineering principles. They allow algorithms and data structures to be specified with more abstraction than ordinary program units. The common structures of programs, such as lists, stacks, queues, sets, trees, and graphs, typically can be formulated as generics with types as parameters. Thus they avoid unnecessary overspecification, making the resulting program units more general. Because generics have the same compile-time type security as other program units, this generality is not achieved by sacrificing reliability.

This increased abstraction has obvious benefits for productivity. In the same way that subprogram libraries in previous languages have increased productivity, generics (if carefully specified) promise productivity increases. Using libraries of generic program units, programmers can avoid reinventing the "wheels" (lists, stacks, and so forth) of computer programs and can concentrate instead on *applying* these wheels in the building of more useful vehicles. Perhaps one of the most important effects of generics will be to encourage more careful separation of abstraction and implementation.

In other languages, macro expansion and copying of source programs sometimes is used to achieve an effect similar to Ada generics. Programmers create new program units "outside" the language by copying the source code and editing the copy to make the desired changes (a process that might be termed "manual instantiation"). Creating new program units in this way is inferior to Ada generic instantiation for several reasons. In addition to susceptibility to clerical errors, this technique has no semantics associated with the program creation. The copy and manual edit can lead to substitutions that are incompatible with uses in the original. For example, manual editing could replace an array type identifier with an access type identifier, even though these two types do not have the same set of operations.

In contrast, Ada generics enable the compiler to check the suitability of the actual parameters against the generic formal parameters to ensure that the instantiation is meaningful. For example, the Ada compiler does not allow an array type actual parameter if the generic parameter is an access type, nor does it allow a procedure to be passed to a generic function parameter. Moreover, the creation of program units from generics has advantages for program maintenance. If a programmer improves a generic by implementing a better algorithm or data structure, all the instantiations of the generic benefit from the improvement. For a program created by copying, the copy and edit must be redone for each "manual instantiation."

On a more forward-looking note, generics promise wider results for automated program verification. Although not yet practical, automatic program verifiers hold the possibility of program correctness proofs based on assertions about the effects of subprograms. Assuming automated program verifiers become more practical, a verification of a generic program unit is a more wide-reaching result: all instantiations of the generic also are verified.

Generics are well-suited for rapid prototyping, that is, quick implementation of a minimal program to explore design suitability or performance. Rapid prototyping gives feedback about a proposed system early in the development cycle, thereby allowing adjustments and improvements based upon experience with a working system. Assuming a library of relevant generics, it is possible to construct a prototype by instantiations using the application-defined entities.

Although generics provide a basis for libraries of abstractions, they do not solve the problem of suitable implementations. In general, a catalog of implementations for a given abstraction, each suited to different criteria, such as storage minimization or quick access, is helpful in building a tailored system. The main challenge then is the selection of the most appropriate implementation from those available in the catalog.

A further advantage of generics is that they provide the compiler the opportunity to improve efficiency by sharing executable code among the instantiations of the same generic. Although it is useful for descriptive purposes to say that generic instantiation creates an entirely new program unit, a more space-efficient implementation is possible by sharing some or all of the executable code. Instantiations of the same generic are inherently candidates for code sharing, because they share substantially the same algorithms and data structures. Sharing of executable code among instances illustrates that the increased abstraction of generics does not necessarily imply reduced efficiency.

Generics offer considerable power to reduce the tendency to reinvent solutions to old problems. Appropriate use of generics can boost software productivity. They may be as influential in future software designs as subprograms are in current designs.

5.13 Summary

Generic program units are a key abstraction mechanism of Ada. They are templates, typically parameterized, that are used to create new program units by means of instantiating the generic with actual parameters. The actual parameters of the instantiation must match the formal parameters of the generic declaration. An instantiation creates a new program unit, with each actual parameter substituted in the instance for the corresponding formal parameter in the template.

Generic formal parameters can be objects, types, and subprograms. A formal object can have either mode **in**, which defines a constant, or **in out**, which defines a variable.

Generic formal types can be scalar types, access types, array types, and private types. The formal types define the operations needed within the generic. Because fewer operations are defined for them, private types are the most general; that is, they have a greater range of matching actual types.

Formal subprogram parameters can be functions and procedures, and the actual subprogram parameter must match the formal subprogram. The actual and formal subprograms match if they have the same number and the same type of parameters, and if the modes of corresponding parameters are the same. For functions, the two functions also must have the same result type.

Generics allow factorization that is impossible with nongeneric program units. Because of this additional power to factor properties from algorithms and data structures, generics promote reusable software.

5.14 Exercises

1. Is it possible for a generic subprogram to have a generic formal private type as one of its parameters? Why does a generic formal private type not require a full declaration in a package private part?

2. Instantiate QUEUE_MAKER to declare:
   (a) a 50 element queue of FLOATs,
   (b) a 200 element queue of BOOLEANs,
   (c) a 1000 element queue of COMPLEX (see Section 3.5).

3. Discuss the tradeoffs of the two alternative specifications of ORDER_MAKER below:

```
generic
     type ITEM is private;
     with function "<"(LEFT, RIGHT : ITEM) return BOOLEAN is <>;
procedure ORDER_MAKER(I, J : in out ITEM);
```

```
generic
     type ITEM is (<>);
procedure ORDER_MAKER(I, J : in out ITEM);
```

4. Our generic associative table uses a linear search to find an item in the table. This scheme is simple, but when many items are stored, it is inefficient because the search potentially must look at all items. A scheme that often is used to narrow the search is called *hashing*. A hashing scheme uses a function to convert the given key to an index into the table. Typically the function converts the key into a very large INTEGER and performs a **rem** operation on the number to

obtain the index. Change the declaration of TABLE_MAKER to include a formal subprogram parameter for the hashing function.

5. Add a report to PRINT_REPORTS of Section 5.11 to print a summary of the date of hire for all employees. Assume a procedure PUT that prints a value of type YEAR_TYPE.

Peter Blume. The Rock. *1948. Collection of the Art Institute of Chicago*

C H A P T E R 6

Tasks

A concept of considerable importance in modern software systems is concurrency, the simultaneous execution of more than one logical process. We use the word *process* to mean an activity or a thread of control. A computation may be performed either by a single process or by several cooperating processes. If several processes are active (or potentially active) at a given time, the processes are said to be concurrent.

Sequential processing requires that the steps in a computation or program be done one at a time. To draw an analogy, consider the job of typing a large report. If only one person types, the activity is sequential. If several people type, however, perhaps each typing a separate chapter, the activities are concurrent.

At first glance, it would appear that concurrent programming requires multiple processors, because if there is only one processor, it seems there can be only one process. Truly *overlapped* concurrency is possible only with multiprocessor hardware. Processes are considered to be concurrent, however, if their executions are *interleaved* in time on the same processor. The programming issues are the same, whether execution is overlapped or interleaved. By analogy, whether the typing staff has one or more typewriters is an implementation detail; either way, each person engages in a different logical process which proceeds concurrently with the others. (This implementation detail obviously will affect the total time necessary to accomplish the processing.)

Concurrent programming is important for several reasons. One is economics: It is often faster (and therefore cheaper) to allow several processes to execute concurrently rather than sequentially. For example, if a process spends much time waiting for an "event" to occur, it is more economical to allow other processes to execute between events. In the case of the typewriter, if Chapter 1 must be completely proofread before Chapter 2 can begin, the machine would be idle and poorly utilized. It is more economical to type the first draft of Chapter 2 while the draft of Chapter 1 is being proofread. Another reason for concurrent programming is that activities often have different priorities. In embedded real-time software, typically a noncritical activity must be suspended temporarily to allow a more important activity to execute. A further advantage of concurrency is the modularity in design that results from decomposing a software system into several independently-executing subsystems.

Many programming languages are strictly sequential; that is, a program consists of a sequence of steps to be done one at a time in a fixed order. Other languages, including Ada, allow the programmer to decompose a program into concurrent processes.[1] In concurrent languages, the programmer must be able to control the manner in which concurrent processes interact.

Since the development of multiprocessors and multi-programming operating systems, concurrent programming has been possible, even using traditional nonconcurrent languages. The usual technique is to code the individual processes using conventional programming constructs, compile them, and then "hook" the

---

[1] Languages with facilities for concurrent programming include PL/I, ALGOL 68, CHILL, and Concurrent Pascal.

programs into an underlying executive or software layer that enables them to share the processor(s). These hooks are implementation dependent, which makes it difficult to move the application to a system with a different executive. Moreover, no automatic checking is done to ensure that parameters passed between application and executive are correct. An advantage of Ada for concurrent programming is that there are no "hooks": by using the appropriate constructs, concurrency is achieved automatically. The compiler (not the programmer) takes care of details concerning interface to the underlying layer of software (if any).

6.1 Ada Tasks

In Ada a concurrent process is known as a *task*. Tasks are one of the four kinds of program units (the others are subprograms, packages, and generic program units). Like subprograms and packages, tasks have both a specification and a body. Figure 6.1 distinguishes between a task specification and body. Also like subprograms and packages, the specification defines the external characteristics of the task, and the body provides its implementation. In particular, a task specification indicates how the task can interact with other tasks. The task body contains its executable sequence of statements.

Tasks may be declared in block statements, package specifications, package bodies, subprogram bodies, and even other task bodies. However, unlike subprograms, packages, and generic units, tasks may not be library units; their declaration must always occur textually within some other program unit.

The following procedure skeleton shows a simple example of tasks:

```
procedure CLEAN_HOUSE is
    task CARPET_SWEEPER;
    task DISH_WASHER;

    task body CARPET_SWEEPER is
        -- declarative part
    begin
        -- statements
    end CARPET_SWEEPER;

    task body DISH_WASHER is
        -- declarative part
    begin
        -- statements
    end DISH_WASHER;

begin
    -- statements
end CLEAN_HOUSE;
```

```
task NAME is
   -- Entry declarations
end NAME;
```

```
task body NAME is
   -- Local entities
begin
   statements
   including accept
   statements for entries
end NAME;
```

Figure 6.1 Task Specification and Body

The declarative part of CLEAN_HOUSE contains two tasks—named CARPET_SWEEPER and DISH_WASHER. A task is declared by writing its specification and later its body. In this example, the two tasks have trivial specifications:

```
task CARPET_SWEEPER;
task DISH_WASHER;
```

Note that task bodies are similar to other kinds of bodies; each has a declarative part followed by a sequence of statements. Like declarations made within subprograms, declarations within a task are local to the task and exist only while the task is active. The statements within a task body may be of the ordinary kind, or they may be special constructs (illustrated presently).

In contrast to a subprogram, which begins execution by being called, a task begins by being *activated*. One way for a task to be activated is by the occurrence of a task object declaration in a declarative part. In the above example, when CLEAN_HOUSE is called, its local declarations are elaborated, which includes elaboration of CARPET_SWEEPER and DISH_WASHER. Upon elaboration, the two tasks CARPET_SWEEPER and DISH_WASHER become ready for activation. After *all* declarations of CLEAN_HOUSE have been elaborated and the **begin** is reached, the two tasks are activated, meaning that the declarative part of each task body is elaborated. Note that activation is implicit; that is, no explicit activate statement is provided. After activation, each task begins execution of its statements. CLEAN_HOUSE begins execution of its statements after the activations of CARPET_SWEEPER and DISH_WASHER. At this point, there are three concurrent executions: the procedure and the two tasks.

In an Ada program, the "main" subprogram is the one that begins the program execution. Conceptually, it is called from a task in the environment of the program. If CLEAN_HOUSE is the main subprogram, there are three tasks active during its execution: CARPET_SWEEPER, DISH_WASHER, and the environment task executing CLEAN_HOUSE.

The procedure CLEAN_HOUSE is said to be a *master* of the tasks CARPET_SWEEPER and DISH_WASHER. Conversely, CARPET_SWEEPER and DISH_WASHER are said to *depend* upon the procedure CLEAN_HOUSE.

Every task depends upon at least one master which is an executing subprogram, block statement, library package, or another task. Suppose that CLEAN_HOUSE had been called by another procedure, say, DO_WEEKLY_DUTIES:

```
procedure CLEAN_HOUSE is
    -- declaration of task CARPET_SWEEPER
    -- declaration of task DISH_WASHER
begin
    ...
end;

procedure DO_WEEKLY_DUTIES is
    procedure RELAX is
        ...
    end RELAX;
begin
    ...
    declare
        -- declaration of task BALANCE_BOOKS
    begin
        CLEAN_HOUSE;
    end;
    RELAX;
end DO_WEEKLY_DUTIES;
```

In this example, the procedure DO_WEEKLY_DUTIES enters a block statement which contains a declaration (not shown) for a task called BALANCE_BOOKS. The block statement calls CLEAN_HOUSE which in turn activates the tasks CARPET_SWEEPER and DISH_WASHER. Task dependence may be direct or indirect. During their existence, the two tasks each depend *directly* upon the master CLEAN_HOUSE and *indirectly* upon the block statement and DO_WEEKLY_DUTIES. Further, the task BALANCE_BOOKS depends directly upon the block statement and indirectly upon DO_WEEKLY_DUTIES.

Task dependence affects what happens after a master *completes*. A block statement, subprogram, or task completes when it finishes execution of its statements. Note that completion is not defined for packages. As we describe shortly, a program unit can be complete without being left (i.e., without returning to its caller) immediately. In the above example, the block statement completes when the call to CLEAN_HOUSE returns. Similarly, the procedure DO_WEEKLY_DUTIES completes when the call to RELAX returns.

Once a subprogram body, task, or block statement completes, it then must wait for any dependent tasks to *terminate*. A task can terminate in one of three ways. First, if a task has no dependent tasks (i.e., no further task was activated by the execution of the task), the task terminates when it completes. In our example, if the body of CARPET_SWEEPER activates no dependent tasks, it terminates upon finishing its statements. Second, if a task has dependent tasks, this (master) task terminates when it completes and all its dependents are terminated. Third, a task may terminate by executing a terminate alternative in a selective wait statement. The terminate alternative is discussed later in Section 6.8.

Returning to our example, the procedure CLEAN_HOUSE cannot be left until its two dependent tasks have terminated. Furthermore, the block statement within DO_WEEKLY_DUTIES cannot be left until CLEAN_HOUSE has returned and BAL-ANCE_BOOKS has terminated. If a subprogram did not wait before completing, its dependent tasks could access variables that no longer exist because the subprogram has been left.

6.2 Tasks as Objects

In Ada, a task is actually a special kind of object, which may seem unusual at first, because objects seem more like "nouns" and tasks appear to be more like "verbs." However, an advantage in treating tasks as objects is that each has a type. Consider the following *task type declaration* and its corresponding body:

```
task type SWEEP_CARPET;

task body SWEEP_CARPET is
    -- local declarations
begin
    -- statements
end SWEEP_CARPET;
```

This declaration associates the name SWEEP_CARPET with a task definition. No task is created, only a definition for one. In a similar way one might write

```
task type WASH_DISHES;

task body WASH_DISHES is
    -- local declarations
begin
    -- statements
end WASH_DISHES;
```

Individual objects (i.e., tasks) may then be declared of type SWEEP_CARPET or WASH_DISHES. Declarations of task objects appear like other object declarations. The procedure CLEAN_HOUSE could be rewritten as:

```
procedure CLEAN_HOUSE is
    -- task type declarations for SWEEP_CARPET and WASH_DISHES
    CARPET_SWEEPER    : SWEEP_CARPET;
    DISH_WASHER       : WASH_DISHES;
    -- bodies for SWEEP_CARPET and WASH_DISHES not shown
begin
    -- statements of CLEAN_HOUSE
end CLEAN_HOUSE;
```

This version of CLEAN_HOUSE is nearly identical to the previous one, except that now the two dependent tasks have an explicit type. As the earlier examples show, it is unnecessary to explicitly declare a task type if only one object of the type is needed. When a task object is declared without explicitly declaring a task type, the type is anonymous and thus unavailable elsewhere in the program.

A task type is limited in the same sense as the limited private types introduced in Section 3.12. Therefore, task objects may not be used in assignment statements or in tests for equality and inequality.

The advantage of declaring a task type is that several tasks can be declared of the same type:

```
CARPET_SWEEPER_1, CARPET_SWEEPER_2 : SWEEP_CARPET;
```

Also, as objects, tasks may be the components of records and arrays:

```
TEAM_OF_SWEEPERS : array(1..10) of SWEEP_CARPET;
```

The elaboration of the declarative part that contains TEAM_OF_SWEEPERS is followed by the activation of ten concurrent, identical tasks. Each component in the array is a separate task executing the same computation. Since tasks are objects, subprogram formal parameters can be objects of a task type.[2]

Given a task type, we can declare a corresponding access type,

```
type CARPET_SWEEPER_NAME is access SWEEP_CARPET;
THIS_SWEEPER, THAT_SWEEPER : CARPET_SWEEPER_NAME;
```

and then create task objects by allocation:

```
THIS_SWEEPER := new SWEEP_CARPET; -- create a SWEEP_CARPET
                                  -- task
THAT_SWEEPER := new SWEEP_CARPET; -- and now another
```

Dynamic allocation of a task object creates a new task of the given type and activates it. Aside from declaring a task, allocation is the only other way in which a task can be created. In contrast to task object declarations, a task created by alloca-

---

[2] The mode **out** is not allowed.

tion is activated immediately. A task created by the elaboration of a declaration, as noted, is not activated until all declarations of the same declarative part have been elaborated.

Let us now revise the procedure CLEAN_HOUSE so that the two tasks are created dynamically:

```
procedure CLEAN_HOUSE is
    task type WASH_DISHES;
    task type SWEEP_CARPET;

    type DISH_WASHER_NAME    is access WASH_DISHES;
    type CARPET_SWEEPER_NAME is access SWEEP_CARPET;

    DISH_WASHER    : DISH_WASHER_NAME;
    CARPET_SWEEPER : CARPET_SWEEPER_NAME;

    task body WASH_DISHES is
        -- local declarations
    begin
        -- statements
    end WASH_DISHES;

    task body SWEEP_CARPET is
        -- local declarations
    begin
        -- statements
    end SWEEP_CARPET;
begin
    DISH_WASHER    := new WASH_DISHES;
    CARPET_SWEEPER := new SWEEP_CARPET;
    --
end CLEAN_HOUSE;
```

The declarations of WASH_DISHES and SWEEP_CARPET appear together at the beginning of the declarative part of CLEAN_HOUSE, followed by the type declarations for DISH_WASHER_NAME and CARPET_SWEEPER_NAME, the object declarations for DISH_WASHER and CARPET_SWEEPER, and then the two task bodies.

One may wonder why the two access objects DISH_WASHER and CARPET_SWEEPER were not initialized by their declarations as in:

```
DISH_WASHER    : DISH_WASHER_NAME    := new WASH_DISHES;
                                        -- error!
CARPET_SWEEPER : CARPET_SWEEPER_NAME := new SWEEP_CARPET;
```

Such an initialization would activate the task bodies before they had been elaborated, an error called access-before-elaboration. In general, access to an entity (in

```
task body B is
begin
    ...
    ENTER(TRANSACTION_B);
end B;
```

Recall that ENTER contains the following sequence of actions:

```
QUEUE.ITEMS(QUEUE.TAIL) := T;
QUEUE.TAIL     := (QUEUE.TAIL rem SIZE) + 1;
QUEUE.COUNT := QUEUE.COUNT + 1;
```

If task A and task B each call ENTER concurrently, the result depends on the order in which the tasks execute the statements of ENTER. The result is time-dependent, and therefore unpredictable and probably erroneous. For example, suppose that task A executes the assignment statement

```
QUEUE.ITEMS(QUEUE.TAIL) := T;
```

and before it updates the value of QUEUE.TAIL, task B executes the same assignment statement, "clobbering" the request entered by task A. Many other execution sequences are possible, with similarly incorrect results. Because they are time-dependent and thus cannot be repeated easily, errors caused by incorrect task interaction are extremely difficult to correct.

To avoid such situations, a concurrent language needs a synchronization primitive to allow tasks to communicate, while preventing them from simultaneous access to data. A milestone in solving intertask communication problems was the invention of the *semaphore*. Semaphores are too low-level, however, and therefore Ada does not include them. The communication features of Ada are higher level and are based on cooperative message passing.

Both intertask synchronization and communication are accomplished with *entries*. A task declares its entries in the task specification.

```
task PRINT_PAGE is
    entry SEND(P : in PAGE);
end PRINT_PAGE;
```

An entry declaration appears similar to a procedure declaration. Entry declarations may be placed only in a task specification. Conversely, entry declarations are the only kind of declaration that may appear in a task specification.[3]

The entries of a task are the means by which other tasks may interact with it. Entries are called in a manner similar to procedure calls. For example,

```
PRINT_PAGE.SEND(CURRENT_PAGE);
```

---

[3] As described in Chapter 8, address clauses for an entry also can be given in the task specification.

is a call to the entry SEND of task PRINT_PAGE. Outside the task, dot notation is used to name an entry. Entries may have formal parameters and the rules for calling procedures apply to entry calls: the actual parameters supplied by the calling task must match the formal parameters in number and type. Named association is also valid:

```
PRINT_PAGE.SEND(P  = ⟩  CURRENT_PAGE);
```

An entry call need not occur within a task body. For example, the above call could legally be made from a function or procedure body as well.

For two tasks to interact, the body of the called task must also execute an *accept statement* corresponding to the same entry:

```
accept SEND(P : in PAGE) do
   -- sequence of statements
end SEND;
```

Accept statements may appear only in the sequence of statements within a task body. They may not be placed, for example, within the statements of a procedure nested in the task body. The formal part of the accept statement must conform to the formal part of the entry declaration in the same way that multiple occurrences of subprogram specifications must conform.

After a task has called another task entry, and the called task has reached a corresponding accept statement, a situation called *rendezvous* (depicted in Figure 6.2) takes place. At this point, any **in** or **in out** parameters are passed to the called task. Next, the called task executes its accept statement, and finally any **out** or **in out** parameters are passed back to the caller. During rendezvous, the calling task is suspended while the called task executes the accept statement. After rendezvous, each task continues independently.

Rendezvous cannot take place until after an entry has been called and the called task reaches an accept statement for this entry. If the call is made first, the calling task will be suspended; If the accept statement is reached and the corresponding entry has not yet been called, the owner of this entry will be suspended.

The intertask communication facilities are powerful. In languages lacking the appropriate constructs, intertask communication has often been done via "system calls" to an underlying software layer. In addition to portability problems, the danger here is that the operating system cannot offer the type checking and diagnostics that a language compiler can. A possible error is that data sent to a task may be of a different type than the task expects to receive. This error cannot occur in Ada because the compiler checks that the actual parameters passed to a task entry agree with the formal parameters in the entry declaration.

A task may have more than one entry declared in its specification:

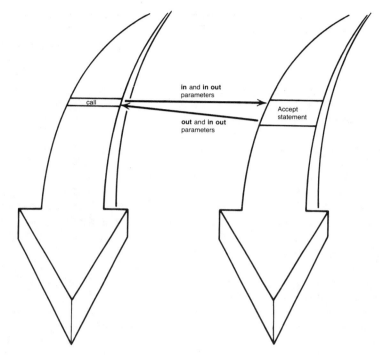

Figure 6.2 Rendezvous

```
task SHARED_DATA is
    entry PUT(X : in   DATA);
    entry GET(X : out DATA);
end SHARED_DATA;
```

For rendezvous to occur, the task must reach an accept statement corresponding to the same entry named by the calling task. Therefore if a task T has called the entry SHARED_DATA.PUT, but the body of SHARED_DATA has reached

```
accept GET(X : out DATA) do
    --
end GET;
```

rendezvous with T will not occur immediately. Instead, rendezvous first must take place with a task calling SHARED_DATA.GET before T can rendezvous.

Several tasks may call the same task entry faster than the called task can execute corresponding accept statements. In this case, the entry calls are queued. Each entry declared in the specification of the called task has an associated queue. When an accept statement corresponding to that entry is reached, a task is taken off the queue so that it can rendezvous.

A task may have more than one accept statement corresponding to the same entry call:

```
accept SEND(P : in PAGE) do
    -- something
end SEND;
...
accept SEND(P : in PAGE) do
    -- something else now
end SEND;
```

Rendezvous terminates normally either because the called task reaches the end of the accept statement or because it executes a return statement. Like return statements within procedure bodies, the return statement in an accept statement may not contain an expression.

```
accept DO_COMMAND(C : in COMMAND; R : out RESULT) do
    if C = SOMETHING then
        -- do something
        return;                       -- rendezvous over
    else
        -- do something else
    end if;
end DO_COMMAND;                        -- rendezvous over
```

In addition to ordinary statements, the statements of an accept body may be further entry calls or accept statements. It follows that if a task makes an entry call (to a third task) from within one of its accept statements, the rendezvous with its original caller will not be complete until rendezvous is completed with the third task. Similarly, if an accept statement is executed within an inner accept statement, rendezvous with the first caller cannot complete until rendezvous completes for the inner accept statement.

Let us now consider a more complete example of intertask communication in Ada:

```
procedure REPORT_WRITER is
    -- declarations for type PAGE
    -- declarations for subprograms GENERATE,
    --      TOP_OF_FORM, PRINT

    task GENERATE_REPORT;          -- the task specifications
    task PRINT_PAGE is             -- declare two tasks
        entry SEND(P : in PAGE);
    end PRINT_PAGE;
```

```
      task body GENERATE_REPORT is-- the corresponding bodies
         CURRENT_PAGE : PAGE;
      begin
         for PAGE_COUNT in 1..100 loop
            GENERATE(CURRENT_PAGE);
            PRINT_PAGE.SEND(CURRENT_PAGE);
         end loop;
      end GENERATE_REPORT;

      task body PRINT_PAGE is
         TEXT_PAGE : PAGE;
      begin
         for PAGE_COUNT in 1..100 loop
            TOP_OF_FORM;
            accept SEND(P : in PAGE) do
               TEXT_PAGE := P;
            end SEND;
            PRINT(TEXT_PAGE);
         end loop;
      end PRINT_PAGE;
   begin
      --
   end REPORT_WRITER;
```

In this example, two tasks—GENERATE_REPORT and PRINT_PAGE—execute concurrently and cooperate in writing a report. This example assumes reports are always 100 pages long. After each page has been generated, the first task calls upon the second task to print it. Note that the accept statement within PRINT_PAGE might have been written so that the call to PRINT is within the accept statement:

```
accept SEND(P : in PAGE) do
   TEXT_PAGE := P;
   PRINT(TEXT_PAGE);
end SEND;
```

which would be correct, but needlessly inefficient because the calling task would be suspended while the page is printing.

An accept statement is not required to have a sequence of statements. For example, we might have:

```
task CARPET_SWEEPER is
   entry FIRE_PLACE_CLEANED;
end CARPET_SWEEPER;
```

```
task body CARPET_SWEEPER is
begin
    SWEEP_BEDROOMS;
    SWEEP_DININGROOM;
    accept FIRE_PLACE_CLEANED;
    SWEEP_LIVINGROOM;
end CARPET_SWEEPER;
```

The task CARPET_SWEEPER sweeps the bedrooms, then the dining room, and finally the living room. For practical reasons, it does not want to sweep the living room until after the fireplace has been cleaned. Presumably, another task cleans the fireplace and calls the entry FIRE_PLACE_CLEANED when finished. The corresponding accept statement has no

do ... end

and so no statements are executed during rendezvous. The rendezvous provides a simple means of synchronization between the calling task and CARPET_SWEEPER.

6.5 Families of Entries

We have seen that a task specification contains entry declarations and the task body contains, among other things, accept statements corresponding to the entries. The task specification may declare a collection of distinct but identical entries called a *family*. A family of entries is indicated by a discrete range or discrete subtype following the entry name in the task specification:

```
type BET is (WIN, PLACE, SHOW);

task BET_TAKER is
    entry WINDOW(BET)(W : in WAGER);
end BET_TAKER;
```

This task specification contains a family of entries named WINDOW indexed over the discrete range WIN..SHOW. Individual entries of this family are named using a notation resembling that of array components:

```
WINDOW(PLACE)
WINDOW(J)
```

Therefore an entry call to the above declared task might look like:

```
BET_TAKER.WINDOW(PLACE)(CURRENT_WAGER);
BET_TAKER.WINDOW(J)(CURRENT_WAGER);
```

Note that in the second example, the specific entry called will depend upon the value of J.

Within the body of BET_TAKER, the accept statements for the family of entries must each indicate the entry by using the indexed notation:

```
accept WINDOW(PLACE)(W : in WAGER) do
    --
end WINDOW;
```

To illustrate further, suppose the task BET_TAKER must service requests from three different groups of user tasks. Suppose also, that the policy of BET_TAKER is to service the groups in the same order. Assume that each group of tasks uses a unique entry when making a call. A possible design for BET_TAKER follows:

```
task body BET_TAKER is
    CURRENT_WAGER : WAGER;
begin
    loop
        for J in BET loop
            accept WINDOW(J)(W : in WAGER) do
                CURRENT_WAGER := W;
            end WINDOW;
            SERVICE(CURRENT_WAGER);
        end loop;
    end loop;
end BET_TAKER;
```

Note that with this implementation, a task calling WINDOW(PLACE) could wait a long time for service if no entry call to WINDOW(WIN) was made.

6.6 Tasks and Scope

As a declared entity, the scope of a task name extends from its declaration to the end of the block or program unit in which it is declared. For example, looking back at procedure REPORT_WRITER, the task PRINT_PAGE is visible following the place of its declaration (i.e., where its specification occurs). The visibility of this name extends to the end of the body of REPORT_WRITER.

The visibility rules for the entry declarations in a task specification are similar to those for packages: The scope of an entry begins with the entry declaration and extends to the end of the scope of the task. Therefore a task entry may be used wherever the task name is visible. Unlike packages, a use clause may not be used with a task name. Entries called from outside the task itself must be prefixed with the name of the task.

Recall that items declared within the body of a task, however, are not visible to the outside. The use of these entities is restricted to the task body.

6.7 Data Encapsulation

Sometimes it is convenient for a collection of tasks to share a common variable. As previously illustrated, it is undesirable to allow tasks to read or write the variable directly. The solution in Ada is to encapsulate the variable using a task. Task entries provide the means to synchronize reading and writing by multiple tasks.

```
task type SAFE_DATA is
    entry PUT(X : in   DATA);
    entry GET(X : out DATA);
end SAFE_DATA;

task body SAFE_DATA is
    BUFFER : DATA;
begin
    loop
        accept PUT(X : in   DATA) do
            BUFFER := X;
        end PUT;
        accept GET(X : out DATA) do
            X := BUFFER;
        end GET;
    end loop;
end SAFE_DATA;
```

The type definition of DATA is irrelevant to synchronization (which suggests that for reusability this task could be encapsulated in a generic package with DATA as a formal private type) and is not shown. The loop statement within SAFE_DATA contains two accept statements, one corresponding to each of its two entries. It is important to put the accept statement for PUT first, because we must guarantee that BUFFER has been written to before it is read. Several tasks may now use a task of type SAFE_DATA as an intermediate buffer in which data are stored.

```
INFO : SAFE_DATA;

task body A is
    D : DATA;
begin
    loop
        -- produce some data
        INFO.PUT(D);
    end loop;
end A;
```

```
task body B is
    D : DATA;
begin
    loop
        INFO.GET(D);
        -- consume some data
    end loop;
end B;
```

In this example there may be several tasks calling INFO.GET and INFO.PUT. Recall that the language guarantees that when entries are flooded with calls, the calling tasks are queued. Therefore the task INFO services calls to a particular entry in the order in which they arrive.

6.8 Selective Waits

A property of the task type SAFE_DATA is that the accept statements which correspond to PUT and GET are always executed in a fixed, alternating sequence; that is, a call to GET is only accepted after accepting a call to PUT, and vice versa. In some applications, this style is appropriate.

Other applications need more flexibility concerning the order that accept statements can be executed. For example, a variable might contain time-dated information (e.g., a formated time of day) that becomes obsolete after a certain time period. In such circumstances we want the variable to be updated whenever there is a new value for it, and we want the variable read whenever a task expresses interest in reading it. We cannot predict in advance the order in which these interactions will take place.

The solution to this problem makes use of a statement called the *selective wait*. Consider the following revision of SAFE_DATA.

```
task type SAFE_DATA is
    entry PUT(X : in   DATA);
    entry GET(X : out DATA);
end SAFE_DATA;

task body SAFE_DATA is
    BUFFER : DATA;
begin
    accept PUT(X : in   DATA) do
        BUFFER := X;
    end PUT;
    loop
        select
            accept PUT(X : in   DATA) do
                BUFFER := X;
            end PUT;
        or
```

```
              accept GET(X : out DATA) do
                  X := BUFFER;
              end GET;
          end select;
      end loop;
  end SAFE_DATA;
```

The body of SAFE_DATA does two things. First, it accepts an entry call to PUT, and second, it repeatedly executes the following selective wait statement:

```
select
    accept PUT(X : in DATA) do
        BUFFER := X;
    end PUT;
or
    accept GET(X : out DATA) do
        X := BUFFER;
    end GET;
end select;
```

This selective wait statement has two *accept alternatives*, separated by the reserved word **or**. Each alternative, in this case, consists of a single accept statement. When SAFE_DATA reaches the beginning of the selective wait, the Ada run-time system will determine if either of the accept statements has any pending entry calls. If there are one or more entry calls awaiting rendezvous, one that corresponds to one of the accept statements will be chosen. It might be that more than one accept alternative is eligible to be chosen; in this case the language does not say which one will be selected. If rendezvous is not immediately possible when SAFE_DATA reaches the beginning of its select statement, it will wait there until one of the accept alternatives can be chosen. In any case, only one alternative of the select statement is executed.

Note that after SAFE_DATA has made the initial accept of PUT, it is impossible to predict the sequence of accept statements which are subsequently executed. Its behavior depends upon the order of entry calls made by other tasks.

A selective wait may have several accept alternatives. Each accept alternative begins with an accept statement, and may have other statements following it. In addition, the selective wait statement may have an else part. If rendezvous cannot immediately occur for one of the accept alternatives, the sequence of statements within the else part then is executed.

```
select
    accept A1(...) do
        --
    end A1;
    -- more statements
or
```

```
        accept A2(...) do
          --
        end A2;
        -- more statements
    or
        accept A3(...) do
          --
        end A3;
        -- more statements
    else                              -- The else part is selected
        -- statements                 -- if rendezvous is not
    end select;                       -- immediately possible.
```

Another form of the selective wait statement includes a *delay alternative*. The delay alternative expresses that the task is willing to wait for an entry call, but only for a given duration. If no accept statement is executed before this duration elapses, the statements (if any) following the delay statement then are executed.

```
    select
        accept KEYBOARD_INPUT(CH : in CHARACTER) do
            INPUT_CHARACTER := CH;
        end KEYBOARD_INPUT;
        -- process character
    or                                -- The delay alternative is chosen
        delay 600.0;                  -- if rendezvous is not possible
        LOGOFF_INACTIVE_USER;         -- within the given time period.
    end select;
```

The delay alternative is chosen only if rendezvous does not occur before the given duration elapses. Note that the choice of the delay alternative means the given delay has already occurred. The delay statement itself, therefore, is not executed.

A delay statement whose duration is negative is treated as if it were zero. In such a case, the delay alternative is selected if there are no pending entry calls. It is interesting to note the equivalence of the two constructs:

```
    select
        accept A ... end A;
    or
        delay 0.0;
        B;
    end select;


    select
        accept A ... end A;
    else
        B;
    end select;
```

It is legal to have more than one delay alternative in a selective wait statement. In this case, the delay statement with the shortest duration is chosen (if any).

Still another form of the selective wait statement involves the *terminate alternative*.

```
select
    accept A1(...) do
        --
    end A1;
        -- more statements
or
    accept A2(...) do
        --
    end A2;
        -- more statements
or                              -- A master has completed and all
    terminate;                  -- dependent tasks have terminated
end select;                     -- or are waiting to terminate.
```

The terminate alternative is selected only under special circumstances. Recall that each task depends on at least one master. As stated earlier, a procedure cannot be left until all its dependent tasks have terminated, which implies that dependent tasks usually determine the lifetime of their masters. There are situations, however, when the dependent task can recognize that its services no longer are needed. The terminate alternative is a way for dependent tasks to terminate gracefully. In particular, the terminate alternative of a selective wait statement is chosen if the task depends upon a master that already has completed, and all dependent tasks of the master either have terminated or also are waiting at a terminate alternative in a select statement. These dependent tasks then terminate together. Consider the following revision of REPORT_WRITER:

```
procedure REPORT_WRITER is
    -- declarations for type PAGE
    -- declarations for subprograms GENERATE,
    --      TOP_OF_FORM, PRINT

    task GENERATE_REPORT;

    task PRINT_PAGE is
        entry SEND(P : in PAGE);
    end PRINT_PAGE;

    task body GENERATE_REPORT is
        CURRENT_PAGE : PAGE;
    begin
        for PAGE_COUNT in 1..100 loop
            GENERATE(CURRENT_PAGE);
            PRINT_PAGE.SEND(CURRENT_PAGE);
        end loop;
    end GENERATE_REPORT;
```

```
    task body PRINT_PAGE is
        TEXT_PAGE : PAGE;
    begin
        loop
            TOP_OF_FORM;
            select
                accept SEND(P : in PAGE) do
                    TEXT_PAGE := P;
                end SEND;
            or
                terminate;
            end select;
                PRINT(TEXT_PAGE);
        end loop;
    end PRINT_PAGE;
begin
    ...
end REPORT_WRITER;
```

In the previous version of REPORT_WRITER, the two dependent tasks GENER-ATE_REPORT and PRINT_PAGE each completed and terminated after they processed 100 pages. In this version, GENERATE_REPORT still uses a for loop, but PRINT_PAGE does not. Instead, a selective wait statement within PRINT_PAGE is used with a terminate alternative. The terminate alternative allows PRINT_PAGE to terminate automatically when REPORT_WRITER has completed and the other dependent tasks of REPORT_WRITER (in this case GENERATE_REPORT) have terminated. PRINT_PAGE has no further use at this point because there is no longer an active task that can call its entry.

From a software engineering viewpoint, the use of the terminate alternative allows decoupling of the two tasks. The task PRINT_PAGE is concerned only with printing pages without having to detect the end of a report. By using the terminate alternative, it agrees to terminate when its services no longer can be used.

In this section we have examined several alternate forms of the selective wait statement. Each selective wait statement must have at least one accept alternative. In addition, it may have an else part, delay alternatives, or a terminate alternative. These three options are mutually exclusive. In the next section we further examine the selective wait statement.

6.9 Safety in Queues

Consider the problem of allowing several tasks access to a queue. Following previous examples we can encapsulate the queue with a task whose sole purpose is to manage the data structure. The queue task will contain entries called PUT and GET which can be called to enter and retrieve information. Because the queue cannot predict the order in which requests will be made, it uses a selective wait statement so that it can service requests as soon as they arrive. An initial attempt to design the queue task might be:

```
task QUEUE_TASK is
    entry PUT(T : in   TRANSACTION);
    entry GET(T : out TRANSACTION);
end QUEUE_TASK;

task body QUEUE_TASK is
    ...
    QUEUE : QUEUE_TYPE;                     -- See Section 3.7
begin
    loop
        select
            accept PUT(T : in TRANSACTION) do
                QUEUE.ITEMS(QUEUE.TAIL) :=  T;
            end PUT;
            -- adjust QUEUE.TAIL and QUEUE.COUNT
        or
            accept GET(T : out TRANSACTION) do
                T := QUEUE.ITEMS(QUEUE.HEAD);
            end GET;
            -- adjust QUEUE.HEAD and QUEUE.COUNT
        or
            terminate;
        end select;
    end loop;
end QUEUE_TASK;
```

Using this approach, the queue task still needs a way to prevent the caller from entering an item into a full queue or removing one from an empty queue. One way in which this problem was solved earlier was to provide functions IS_FULL and IS_EMPTY and allow the user of the queue to check that the ensuing call will be safe. If the queue is accessed concurrently, however, such a solution will not work: Because a queue is determined to be not full, there is no guarantee that it will not become full a moment later because of some other task making an insertion.

A better approach is to suspend a caller that tries to enter an item in a full queue or to remove one from an empty queue. In this way, the queue never appears full to the task entering information and never appears empty to the task removing information. This policy requires *when conditions* to guard the select alternatives of the selective wait statement. Consider the following fragment:

```
loop
    select
        when QUEUE.COUNT /= SIZE =>            -- when not FULL
            accept PUT(T : in TRANSACTION) do
                QUEUE.ITEMS(QUEUE.TAIL) := T;
            end PUT;
            -- adjust QUEUE.TAIL and QUEUE.COUNT
    or
        when QUEUE.COUNT /= 0 =>               -- when not EMPTY
            accept GET(T : out TRANSACTION) do
                T := QUEUE.ITEMS(QUEUE.HEAD);
            end GET;
            -- adjust QUEUE.HEAD and QUEUE.COUNT
    or
        terminate;
    end select;
end loop;
```

In general, each select alternative (an accept alternative, a delay alternative, or a terminate alternative) may be preceded by a when condition. (An else part, however, may not have a when condition.) When the selective wait statement is first encountered, each select alternative is evaluated to be either *open* or *closed*. A select alternative is open if it does not have a when clause or if it has a when clause whose condition is TRUE. A select alternative that is not open is said to be closed. Only open select alternatives are eligible to be selected.

In the above selective wait statement there are three select alternatives: two accept alternatives and a terminate alternative. The first accept alternative is open if the queue is not full. The second alternative is open if the queue is not empty. The third alternative, terminate, is always open because it is not preceded by a when condition.

The when conditions are evaluated only once—at the beginning of the select statement. Therefore once a select alternative is determined to be closed, the alternative cannot be selected for the current execution of the selective wait statement.

We can now describe the complete set of rules for the selective wait statement. The selective wait must contain at least one accept alternative. The statement begins by determining the open select alternatives. There must either be at least one open alternative or the statement must have an else part; otherwise, the predefined exception PROGRAM_ERROR is raised.

If rendezvous is immediately possible with a task calling one of the entries corresponding to an open accept alternative, such an alternative is selected. The execution of the statements within the accept alternative completes the execution of the selective wait statement.

If rendezvous is not immediately possible within an open accept alternative, there are four mutually exclusive possibilities:

1. *The statement has an else part.* The else part is then executed.

2. *There is an open delay alternative.* In this case the task waits at the top of the select statement until either rendezvous can occur or the delay period elapses. Whichever occurs first will determine whether an accept alternative or delay alternative completes the execution of the accept statement.

3. *There is an open terminate alternative.* In this case the task waits at the top of the select alternative until either an accept alternative can be be selected or the conditions for the terminate alternative become satisfied. These conditions are: the task depends on some master who has completed, and further, all tasks that depend on the master have either terminated or are also waiting upon an open terminate alternative within a select statement.

4. *There is no else part, open delay alternative, nor open terminate alternative.* In this case the task waits until rendezvous is possible.

Following is the complete version of the queue task:

```
task QUEUE_TASK is
    entry PUT(T :    in TRANSACTION);
    entry GET(T : out TRANSACTION);
end QUEUE_TASK;

task body QUEUE_TASK is
    SIZE : constant POSITIVE := 10;
    subtype INDEX is INTEGER range 1..SIZE;
    type SPACE is array(INDEX) of TRANSACTION;
    type QUEUE_TYPE is record
        ITEMS   : SPACE;
        HEAD    : INDEX := 1;       -- next value to be removed
        TAIL    : INDEX := 1;       -- next available slot
        COUNT : INTEGER range 0..SIZE := 0;
    end record;
    QUEUE   : QUEUE_TYPE;
begin
    loop
        select
            when QUEUE.COUNT /= SIZE =>
                accept PUT(T : in TRANSACTION) do
                    QUEUE.ITEMS(QUEUE.TAIL) := T;
                end PUT;
                QUEUE.TAIL    := (QUEUE.TAIL rem SIZE) + 1;
                QUEUE.COUNT := QUEUE.COUNT + 1;
            or
            when QUEUE.COUNT /= 0 =>
                accept GET(T : out TRANSACTION) do
                    T := QUEUE.ITEMS(QUEUE.HEAD);
                end GET;
                QUEUE.HEAD    := (QUEUE.HEAD rem SIZE) + 1;
                QUEUE.COUNT := QUEUE.COUNT - 1;
```

```
      or
          terminate;
      end select;
   end loop;
end QUEUE_TASK;
```

As noted earlier, tasks cannot be library units; they must be declared within some other program unit or block. To allow the queue task to be accessible to other program units, we place it in a package. The package specification appears similar to the previous queue packages; it declares procedures ENTER and RE-MOVE. The package body, however, contains a task to synchronize access to the queue. The bodies of ENTER and REMOVE call the entries of this task to access the queue.

```
package QUEUE_PACKAGE is
   procedure ENTER (T : in  TRANSACTION);
   procedure REMOVE(T : out TRANSACTION);
end QUEUE_PACKAGE;

package body QUEUE_PACKAGE is
   task QUEUE_TASK is
      entry PUT(T : in  TRANSACTION);
      entry GET(T : out TRANSACTION);
   end QUEUE_TASK;

   task body QUEUE_TASK is
      -- as above
   end QUEUE_TASK;

   procedure ENTER(T : in TRANSACTION) is
   begin
      QUEUE_TASK.PUT(T);
   end ENTER;

   procedure REMOVE(T : out TRANSACTION) is
   begin
      QUEUE_TASK.GET(T);
   end REMOVE;
end QUEUE_PACKAGE;
```

When called, the procedures QUEUE_PACKAGE.ENTER and QUEUE_PACK-AGE.REMOVE must rendezvous with QUEUE_TASK before they can return.

As the most general example of a queue, let us define a generic version of the above package. The generic package SAFE_QUEUE has two generic formal parameters. The parameter SIZE is supplied so that the user of the generic can control the size of the underlying data structure when SAFE_QUEUE is instantiated. The second parameter, ELEMENT, allows the user of SAFE_QUEUE to indicate the type of objects the queue will contain. This generic formal parameter is declared to be private. Therefore the user may choose any nonlimited type as a corresponding actual parameter.

```ada
generic
    SIZE : POSITIVE;
    type ELEMENT is private;
package SAFE_QUEUE is
    procedure ENTER (ITEM : in    ELEMENT);
    procedure REMOVE(ITEM : out ELEMENT);
end SAFE_QUEUE;

package body SAFE_QUEUE is
    task QUEUE_TASK is
        entry PUT(E : in    ELEMENT);
        entry GET(E : out ELEMENT);
    end QUEUE_TASK;

    task body QUEUE_TASK is
        subtype INDEX is INTEGER range 1..SIZE;
        type SPACE is array(INDEX) of ELEMENT;
        type QUEUE_TYPE is record
                ITEMS  : SPACE;
                HEAD   : INDEX := 1;        -- next value to leave
                TAIL   : INDEX := 1;        -- next available slot
                COUNT : INTEGER range 0..SIZE := 0;
        end record;
        QUEUE   : QUEUE_TYPE;
    begin
        loop
            select
                when QUEUE.COUNT /= SIZE =>  -- when not FULL
                    accept PUT(E : in ELEMENT) do
                        QUEUE.ITEMS(QUEUE.TAIL) := E;
                    end PUT;
                    QUEUE.TAIL   := (QUEUE.TAIL rem SIZE) + 1;
                    QUEUE.COUNT := QUEUE.COUNT + 1;
            or
                when QUEUE.COUNT /= 0  =>      -- when not EMPTY
                    accept GET(E : out ELEMENT) do
                        E := QUEUE.ITEMS(HEAD);
                    end GET;
                    QUEUE.HEAD   := (QUEUE.HEAD rem SIZE) + 1;
                    QUEUE.COUNT := QUEUE.COUNT - 1;
            or
                    terminate;
            end select;
        end loop;
    end QUEUE_TASK;
```

```
    procedure ENTER(ITEM : in ELEMENT) is
    begin
        QUEUE_TASK.PUT(ITEM);
    end ENTER;

    procedure REMOVE(ITEM : out ELEMENT) is
    begin
        QUEUE_TASK.GET(ITEM);
    end REMOVE;
end SAFE_QUEUE;
```

6.10 A Real-Time Example with Queues

Using the generic package SAFE_QUEUE, we design a task to monitor a mechanical keyboard device and detect valid keystrokes. Each key is associated with an ASCII character. Thus each keystroke produces a value of type CHARACTER. The task monitoring the keyboard enters each valid incoming character into a queue named KEY_QUEUE, an instantiation of SAFE_QUEUE. A function NEXT_KEY allows other program units to remove characters from the queue. The queue, then, serves as a buffer between the task that produces characters and the program units that consume them.

Let us assume each mechanical key rests on a tiny spring. When the key is first depressed, or when it is later released, it tends to "bounce" between the two states of depressed and open. This bouncing always ceases within 5 milliseconds, after which the key reaches a stable state of either depressed or open. A detected key closure is a valid input only if the same key closure is again detected 5 milliseconds later. Once a keystroke is detected as valid, it must be released before any other key may be accepted.

The following package, KEY_BOARD_SCAN, makes visible only the function NEXT_KEY. The polling and queue manipulation are done in the package body. The body uses an auxiliary function (not shown) which determines if a key for a given character is depressed or open. The specification of this function is:

```
    function DEPRESSED(CH : CHARACTER) return BOOLEAN;
```

The KEY_BOARD_SCAN package follows:

```
    package KEY_BOARD_SCAN is
        function NEXT_KEY return CHARACTER;
    end KEY_BOARD_SCAN;

    with SAFE_QUEUE;
    with DEPRESSED;
    package body KEY_BOARD_SCAN is
        package KEY_QUEUE is new SAFE_QUEUE(SIZE    = > 80,
                                            ELEMENT = > CHARACTER);
```

```
task SCAN;

procedure WAIT_TIL_RELEASED(CH : CHARACTER) is
begin
   while not DEPRESSED(CH) loop
      delay 0.01;                -- delay 10 milliseconds
   end loop;
end WAIT_TIL_RELEASED;

task body SCAN is
begin
   for CH in CHARACTER loop
      if DEPRESSED(CH) then
         delay 0.005;                -- finish bouncing
         if DEPRESSED(CH) then   -- still depressed so its valid
            KEY_QUEUE.ENTER(CH);
            WAIT_TIL_RELEASED(CH);
         end if;
      end if;
   end loop;
end SCAN;

function NEXT_KEY return CHARACTER is
   CHAR : CHARACTER;
begin
   KEY_QUEUE.REMOVE(CHAR);
   return CHAR;
end NEXT_KEY;

end KEY_BOARD_SCAN;
```

In this example, the task SCAN constantly monitors the keyboard and never voluntarily "gives up" the processor until it detects a key closure. This polling could waste processor time unless either the underlying Ada run-time system preempts tasks at regular intervals or the task SCAN executes on its own dedicated processor. Another alternative (illustrated in Chapter 8) is to use hardware interrupts to alert the monitoring task that a new datum has arrived.

A final point concerns the size of durations used in this example. Ada requires that the smallest positive representable duration be less than or equal to 20 milliseconds. (The language recommends, however, that durations as small as 50 microseconds be represented.) Therefore the values .01 and .005 could be converted to 0.0 in some implementations.

6.11 A Data Base Example

Previous sections have emphasized that tasks typically must have exclusive access to shared variables. Using an additional task to encapsulate or monitor shared data, other tasks can synchronize to avoid mutual interference. In some situations, however, such precautions are unnecessary. If tasks need to read a data structure, but not modify it, it is safe to allow simultaneous read operations. This policy is appropriate if the read operations are lengthy or if there is heavy demand to read the data. In this section we illustrate how several "reading" tasks can access data simultaneously, while "writing" tasks still are granted exclusive access to the data. This classical problem, known as the "readers and writers" problem, is important in many concurrent applications.

Consider the automatic banking center application described in Section 3.7. To begin a transaction, a customer must supply both an account number and a password. To validate customer passwords, the application must have a data structure that contains all account numbers and corresponding passwords. One possibility for this data structure is a binary tree in which the key to each node is a customer account number. Given the subtypes ACCOUNT_ID and PASSWORD_TYPE from Chapter 2 and the generic package BINARY_TREE_MAKER (Section 5.11), the binary tree can be created by the following instantiation and object declaration:

```
package PASSWORD_TREE is new BINARY_TREE_MAKER(
                      KEY_TYPE      => ACCOUNT_ID,
                      ELEMENT_TYPE => PASSWORD_TYPE);
PASSWORDS : PASSWORD_TREE.KIND := PASSWORD_TREE.MAKE;
```

Next, we design a package named PASSWORD_DATA_BASE, which allows user tasks to access the binary tree. Two operations are provided. The first, READ_PASSWORD, retrieves a customer password using a given account number. The other operation, INSERT_NEW, inserts a new account number-password node into the tree. (In practice, other operations such as changing passwords or deleting accounts also would be implemented.) The package specification is:

```
package PASSWORD_DATA_BASE is
    procedure READ_PASSWORD(CUSTOMER : ACCOUNT_ID;
                            PASSWORD : out PASSWORD_TYPE);
    CUSTOMER_NOT_FOUND : exception;    -- raised by
                                       -- READ_PASSWORD
    procedure INSERT_NEW(CUSTOMER : ACCOUNT_ID;
                         PASSWORD : PASSWORD_TYPE);
end PASSWORD_DATA_BASE;
```

The body of PASSWORD_DATA_BASE allows several tasks simultaneously to perform the READ_PASSWORD operation. Tasks that call INSERT_NEW, however, are blocked until they have exclusive access to the tree. In this example, we make a simplifying but realistic assumption: Reading tasks have priority over writing tasks. This policy is reasonable because the banking system must respond quickly to customers and validate their passwords. Establishing new customers, (i.e., inserting new nodes in the tree) is less frequent and less urgent and can be delayed during peak hours.

The body of PASSWORD_DATA_BASE follows:

```
with BINARY_TREE_MAKER;              -- See Section 5.11
package body PASSWORD_DATA_BASE is
    package PASSWORD_TREE is new BINARY_TREE_MAKER(
                                   KEY_TYPE       => ACCOUNT_ID,
                                   ELEMENT_TYPE => PASSWORD_TYPE);
    PASSWORDS : PASSWORD_TREE.KIND := PASSWORD_TREE.MAKE;

    task TREE_MONITOR is
        entry START_READING;     -- Must be called before reading
        entry FINISH_READING;    -- Must be called after reading
        entry INSERT(ACC : ACCOUNT_ID;  PASS : PASSWORD_TYPE);
    end TREE_MONITOR;

    task body TREE_MONITOR is
        READ_COUNT : NATURAL := 0;
    begin
        loop
            select
                accept START_READING
                do READ_COUNT := READ_COUNT + 1; end;
            or
                accept FINISH_READING
                do READ_COUNT := READ_COUNT - 1; end;
            or
                when READ_COUNT = 0 =>
                    accept INSERT(ACC : ACCOUNT_ID;
                                  PASS : PASSWORD_TYPE) do
                    PASSWORD_TREE.INSERT(PASSWORDS, ACC, PASS);
                    end;
            end select;
        end loop;
    end TREE_MONITOR;


    procedure READ_PASSWORD(CUSTOMER : ACCOUNT_ID;
                            PASSWORD : out PASSWORD_TYPE) is
    begin
        TREE_MONITOR.START_READING;
        begin
            PASSWORD := PASSWORD_TREE.RETRIEVE(PASSWORDS,
                                               CUSTOMER);
        exception
            when PASSWORD_TREE.KEY_NOT_FOUND =>
                TREE_MONITOR.FINISH_READING;
                raise CUSTOMER_NOT_FOUND;
            when others  =>
                TREE_MONITOR.FINISH_READING;
                raise;
        end;
        TREE_MONITOR.FINISH_READING;
    end READ_PASSWORD;
```

This attribute must be used with caution. For example, a program fragment such as

```
if not ENGINE_CONTROLLER'TERMINATED then
    -- dangerous
end if;
```

is not reliable because ENGINE_CONTROLLER could terminate between the evaluation of the attribute and the subsequent action.

Ordinarily, a task becomes completed by finishing its statements. As we have seen, a task may also complete by executing a statement that raises an exception. Another way a task may become complete is by being named in an *abort statement:*

```
abort CARPET_SWEEPER, DISH_WASHER;
```

The execution of an abort statement causes the named tasks to become abnormal; an abnormal task completes prematurely.[4] Once aborted, a task can no longer communicate with other tasks. If a task calls an entry of an aborted task, TASK-ING_ERROR is raised in the calling task at the point of the call. The **abort** statement should be not be used as a substitute for a careful design in which tasks complete normally; it should be used only in severe circumstances.

6.14 Priorities

If the number of "runnable" tasks exceeds the number of available processors in a system, a scheduling decision must be made about which tasks to execute. Scheduling decisions ordinarily are not made by the programmer. The programmer may influence the scheduling decision, however, by associating a degree of "urgency" to tasks using the PRIORITY pragma. The pragma is placed in the specification of the task:

```
task A is
    pragma PRIORITY (5);
    -- entry declarations
end A;

task B is
    pragma PRIORITY (10);
    -- entry declarations
end B;
```

---

[4] The aborted task might not complete immediately. The rules governing when task completion occurs are explained in (Ada, 1983) Section 9.10.

The expression given by the pragma defines the relative urgency of the task: higher numbers indicate higher priorities. Its value is of the implementation-dependent INTEGER subtype PRIORITY whose definition occurs in the library package SYSTEM (see Chapter 8). The expression in a PRIORITY pragma must be static; it is evaluated at compilation time. The pragma PRIORITY is optional, but if used, it may be given only once within a task specification. It may also be used within a library subprogram. If a task is not explicitly given a priority, its priority is undefined by the language.

A higher priority task cannot be waiting while a lower priority task executes. In the above example, the programmer states that task B has higher priority than task A. Therefore if there is a scheduling decision to be made and tasks A and B are runnable, task B will be executed. If two tasks with explicit priorities are engaged in rendezvous, the rendezvous is executed with the higher of the two priorities. If only one task has an explicit priority, the rendezvous is executed with at least that priority.

6.15 Summary

Tasks are one of the four program units which comprise Ada programs and are independent threads of control that execute in parallel, except at synchronization points. A task has both a specification and a body. Task types can be declared, and a task type is limited in the same sense as limited private types.

A task specification can contain entry declarations, which are the means by which tasks communicate. Entries can be called by other program units, and the entry is accepted by the called task. An entry can have parameters, which allow tasks to exchange data (pass messages).

The body of the task can contain local declarations, executable statements, and exception handlers. The body of a task also may have accept statements corresponding to its entries. Rendezvous occurs when a task calls an entry and the called task reaches an accept statement corresponding to the entry. During rendezvous, tasks are synchronized.

The selective wait statement allows a task to select an accept statement from more than one alternative. The selective wait statement may include, in addition to accept alternatives, delay alternatives, a terminate alternative, or an else part. These three possibilities are mutually exclusive.

The conditional and timed entry calls allow a task to make an entry call and then cancel it. The conditional entry call cancels the call if rendezvous is not immediately possible. The timed entry call cancels the call if a time limit expires.

Exceptions raised within a task body, but not immediately within an accept statement, can be handled at the end of the task. After executing the handler, the task completes. If there is no handler, the exception causes the task to complete immediately. An exception occurring during rendezvous is raised again outside the accept statement and is also raised at the point at which the entry call was made.

Scheduling decisions may be influenced through the use of the pragma PRIOR-ITY.

6.16 Exercises

1. Explain the notion of intertask communication and rendezvous.

2. Explain the rules of the selective wait statement.

3. Consider two tasks A and B, each using the same instance of the generic package SAFE_QUEUE (see Section 6.9). If A and B each call the procedure ENTER at about the same time:
   (a) Is there any danger of one task's actual parameter "overwriting" an actual parameter passed by the other task?
   (b) What will take place if the queue has only one free slot before both calls are made?

4. Consider the following synchronization problem: Task A cannot begin a critical part of its execution until task B finishes a certain critical part of its execution. Illustrate how this can be solved in Ada.

5. Design a simple command interpreter that receives characters, parses them into commands, and invokes other tasks to process the commands. Assume characters are obtained from KEY_BOARD_SCAN.NEXT_KEY of Section 6.10.

6. Consider the problem of finding the largest number in a large array of integers. Suggest how two tasks each could search half of the array at the same time.

7. Design an Ada function that adopts the strategy of the previous problem. In a single processor computer will the function execute any faster than an ordinary linear search? What if the computer architecture is multiprocessor?

8. In Ada it is legal for a task to call one of its own entries. What must result from such an action?

9. In the procedure REPORT_WRITER illustrated in Section 6.8, suppose an exception was raised by the execution of a statement within the accept statement of PRINT_PAGE. Explain what effect this will have upon the two tasks GEN-ERATE_REPORT and PRINT_PAGE, and upon the procedure REPORT_WRITER.

10. When using languages without facilities for intertask communication, the programmer is sometimes forced to make "system calls" to an operating system or some other layer of software to allow tasks to exchange data. Explain the advantage of using a strongly typed language with built-in facilities with which tasks can communicate.

11. Describe the effect of each of the following statements:

```
select
    accept PUT(E : in ELEMENT) do
        ...
    end PUT;
else
    delay 60.0;
end select;

select
    accept PUT(E : in ELEMENT) do
        ...
    end PUT;
or
    delay 60.0;
end select;

select
    A.PUT(E);
or
    delay 60.0;
end select;

select
    A.PUT(E);
else
    delay 60.0;
end select;
```

12. Consider a restaurant with tables that seat up to four people. Parties smaller than four can still be seated at their own table, but parties larger than four must be split into separate tables. An entire party, however, must always be seated at the same time even though they may be split. Design a table scheduling package which makes visible two procedures:

    procedure SEAT(SIZE : **in** POSITIVE; ASSIGNED : **out** TABLES);
    procedure UNSEAT(ASSIGNED : **in** TABLES);

    This is an example of a resource allocation problem. The package body must ensure that when a request is made, the caller eventually is allocated tables, even though it may take some time.

13. In the appropriate context, could the following text be a legal Ada statement? Explain.

    T(I).E(J)(A(K));

14. Write a procedure named WAIT_TIL_THE_HOUR which delays itself until the beginning of the next hour.

15. Modify PASSWORD_DATA_BASE of Section 6.11 so that a writing task will not get overtaken and "blocked" by a reading task arriving after it.

Patrick Hughes. Inside Out. © *Patrick Hughes*

CHAPTER 7

Input-Output

Input-output is concerned with communicating data between an executing program and its environment. Depending on the application, an Ada program may need to communicate with interactive users, external files, external sensors and other specialized devices, or some combination of the above.

Ada input-output is well-integrated within the language. Many languages are a problem because they either define no input-output at all within the language or they define special semantics, such as allowing a varying number of parameters to a subprogram *only* in the case of input-output subprograms. The first approach hinders transportability; the second compromises uniformity and consistency of subprograms.

By contrast, Ada defines no special rules for input-output subprograms, which have the same syntax and semantics as those of user-defined subprograms. Moreover, the more novel Ada constructs that support software engineering, such as overloading, packages, generics, and exceptions, are integral parts of the input-output facilities.

7.1 Overall Organization

Ada input-output facilities consist of four predefined packages: TEXT_IO, SEQUENTIAL_IO, DIRECT_IO, and LOW_LEVEL_IO. Each of these packages is a library unit. (Library units were introduced in Chapter 3, and Chapter 9 discusses them further.)

The structure of the TEXT_IO, SEQUENTIAL_IO, and DIRECT_IO packages is similar. All three are file-oriented; that is, they provide objects, types, and operations for manipulating external files.

TEXT_IO is for input-output of values in human-readable form, as ordinary text. Text is a convenient form for people to read; a text file consists of elements organized into lines and pages. The elements may represent numeric values (integer, float, and fixed numbers), characters, strings, and enumeration literals. TEXT_IO is a single library unit which contains character and string input-output operations and nested generic packages for numeric and enumeration input-output.

SEQUENTIAL_IO and DIRECT_IO are generic packages for input-output of values of any nonlimited type, including composite types such as arrays and records. These packages must be instantiated with a type for the values to be input and output. The files processed by instances of these packages generally are formated by Ada output operations, and the formatting is intended for efficient machine reading, rather than human reading. Typically, such files will be in binary format.

LOW_LEVEL_IO is for input-output to physical devices. The procedures in LOW_LEVEL_IO are device and machine dependent. In addition to these four main packages, which contain the input-output operations, a supporting package, IO_EXCEPTIONS, groups together the exceptions that can be raised within the main packages.

The common structure of the file-oriented packages is discussed below, followed by a description of the features unique to each. The structure of LOW_LEVEL_IO is different than the other three and is discussed after them.

7.2 File-oriented Input-Output

As we mentioned above, input-output is concerned with communication of values between an executing program and its environment. In the case of file-oriented I-O, data in the environment are contained within external files. An external file is something in the environment of the program from which a value can be read or to which a value can be written. It may reside in secondary storage, or it may be a high-level interface to a hardware device in a system that treats devices as files.

The general structure of the file-oriented packages (using TEXT_IO as an example) is given below:

```
with IO_EXCEPTIONS;
package TEXT_IO is

        type FILE_TYPE is limited private;

        -- other declarations to define file characteristics

        -- File management operations

        -- Input-output and control operations

        -- Input-output exceptions

    private

        -- Implementation defined

    end TEXT_IO;
```

The packages also make available operations to manage files of the given type, operations to perform input-output to files, and exceptions to notify users of errors that may occur during I-O operations. The overall organization of this package may appear familiar: it is similar to the abstract data type formulation of queues in Section 3.12.

Each package declares a type for the kinds of files it manages. To process an external file, an Ada program must declare an object of the corresponding file type. The input-output operations themselves are conducted using this file object. For example, to declare a file object which later will be associated with an external text file, the following declaration can be used:

```
with TEXT_IO;
...
TRACE_FILE : TEXT_IO.FILE_TYPE;
```

This declaration specifies that the variable TRACE_FILE will be used with text files, but it does not associate TRACE_FILE with any external file. Note the **with** clause to make the library unit TEXT_IO available.

7.3 File Management

To associate a file object with an external file, and to inquire about the status and characteristics of the external file, Ada provides several operations. The following excerpt from TEXT_IO illustrates the file management operations:

```
with IO_EXCEPTIONS;
package TEXT_IO is

        type FILE_TYPE is limited private;

        type FILE_MODE is (IN_FILE, OUT_FILE);

        -- File Management

        procedure CREATE (FILE  : in out FILE_TYPE;
                          MODE : in FILE_MODE := OUT_FILE;
                          NAME : in STRING     := "";
                          FORM : in STRING     := "");

        procedure OPEN    (FILE  : in out FILE_TYPE;
                          MODE : in FILE_MODE;
                          NAME : in STRING;
                          FORM : in STRING := "");

        procedure CLOSE   (FILE  : in out FILE_TYPE);
        procedure DELETE  (FILE  : in out FILE_TYPE);
        procedure RESET   (FILE  : in out FILE_TYPE;
                          MODE : in FILE_MODE);
        procedure RESET   (FILE  : in out FILE_TYPE);

        function   MODE    (FILE  : in FILE_TYPE) return FILE_MODE;
        function   NAME    (FILE  : in FILE_TYPE) return STRING;
        function   FORM    (FILE  : in FILE_TYPE) return STRING;

        function   IS_OPEN(FILE  : in FILE_TYPE) return BOOLEAN;
```

```
        -- Other operations

private
        -- implementation-dependent
end TEXT_IO;
```

The names aptly indicate the corresponding actions. Before describing the operations, we look at an example of using the package:

```
with TEXT_IO; use TEXT_IO;
procedure REGROUP is
      PHONE_LIST_FILE : FILE_TYPE;
      A_DIPLOMAT      : STRING(1..80);
      LAST            : NATURAL;
begin
      OPEN( FILE   => PHONE_LIST_FILE,
            MODE  => IN_FILE,
            NAME  => "RETIRED_DIPLOMATS");

      while not END_OF_FILE(PHONE_LIST_FILE) loop
            GET_LINE(PHONE_LIST_FILE, A_DIPLOMAT, LAST);
            ... Process the line
      end loop;

      CLOSE(PHONE_LIST_FILE);
end REGROUP;
```

This procedure opens an external file called RETIRED_DIPLOMATS and associates it with the file object PHONE_LIST_FILE, then loops over each line in the file. The while loop that controls each cycle tests the function END_OF_FILE, which becomes TRUE when no more items can be read from the file. GET_LINE returns the next line from the PHONE_LIST_FILE to the **out** parameter A_DIPLOMAT and also returns in the parameter LAST the index of the last character read. If the STRING begins at index 1, which is the case in this example, LAST is also the number of characters read. Finally, the CLOSE operation disconnects the object PHONE_LIST_FILE from the external file named "RETIRED_DIPLOMATS".

The FILE_MODE type gives values for the modes of access to an external file. The literal IN_FILE indicates the file is to be accessed in read-only. OUT_FILE indicates the file is to be accessed in write-only mode. Notice the analogy of the file modes to the semantics of parameter modes for subprograms (discussed in Chapter 3). In the case of DIRECT_IO, an additional literal, INOUT_FILE, is provided, and it indicates the file will be accessed in both read and write modes. The access mode of a file object can be changed.

The CREATE operation creates a new external file and makes it ready for processing. The parameter FILE is an Ada file object that is associated with the created file. This file object is left open by the CREATE operation. The string given by NAME is used to identify the external file in the environment. Notice that the NAME parameter has a null STRING default value. Use of the default value indicates that the created file is temporary and will be discarded by the environment when the program completes.

Because systems differ in the interpretation of file names, the string NAME is implementation dependent. Many systems place restrictions on file names, for example allowing only file names that are upper case alphanumeric characters or allowing only those less than a given maximum length.

After CREATE, further manipulation of the external file will be with regard to the value returned for FILE. The file is opened for access according to the MODE parameter. FORM is a system-dependent string which defines further characteristics of the external file, such as its physical organization. A null FORM indicates that the default file characteristics are to be used. By careful selection of the default forms for files, an Ada implementation can avoid many potential problems which can arise from the system-dependence of this string. Use of the default in programs is no guarantee that the program will be transportable without change, but it improves the chances.

The OPEN operation is similar to CREATE, except that NAME must identify an existing external file. The exception NAME_ERROR is raised if the external file is nonexistent. For both CREATE and OPEN, the exception STATUS_ERROR is raised if the given file object is already open; that is, the following sequence of calls would cause STATUS_ERROR to be raised

```
with TEXT_IO; use TEXT_IO;
...                          .
A_FILE : FILE_TYPE;
...
CREATE(A_FILE, NAME = > "Secret_Treaties");
OPEN   (A_FILE, NAME = > "Secret_Treaties"); -- raises STATUS_ERROR
```

because the file *object* A_FILE is already open as a result of the CREATE when the OPEN operation is attempted. It is important to note that the exception is raised because the file object is already open, not because the external file is already open.

Returning to the remaining file manipulation operations, the CLOSE operation disconnects the file object from its associated external file. No further input-output is possible with respect to the file object unless a subsequent CREATE or OPEN is performed using it. The DELETE operation closes the file object and deletes the external file associated with it from the environment. If the file cannot be deleted in the environment, perhaps because of the access rights permitted to the program attempting the DELETE, the exception USE_ERROR is raised. The RESET operation positions the external file so that the next read or write will take place at the beginning of the file. The first form of the RESET operation above takes a second parameter which specifies the file mode after the RESET. For example, a file can be written sequentially and then read in again by the following operations:

```
...
CREATE(FILE   => SCRATCH_FILE,
        MODE  => OUT_FILE);

... process items into SCRATCH_FILE

RESET(FILE    => SCRATCH_FILE,
       MODE   => IN_FILE);
```

The RESET specifies that the mode of the file is to be IN_FILE, so that the items can be read. Notice that the CREATE does not specify the name of the file, which defaults to the null string. As mentioned earlier, such a file is temporary and ceases to exist when the program completes.

The three functions MODE, NAME, and FORM return the corresponding attributes of the file object given as their parameter. MODE returns the current mode (one of IN_FILE, OUT_FILE, or INOUT_FILE) of the file object. NAME returns the unique identification within the environment of the external file associated with the given file object. If the environment allows a file name to be specified in a number of ways (e.g., using an abbreviation), the string returned by NAME is the full unique identification of the external file (not the abbreviation). FORM returns the form string, which gives system dependent characteristics, for the external file associated with the given parameter. Like the NAME function, it returns the full specification for the form of the external file, including all the default characteristics of the file, even if the corresponding OPEN or CREATE statement chose defaults. Excluding OPEN and CREATE, each of the subprograms discussed above expects the given file to be open already; otherwise it is an error to perform these operations. For this reason, the subprograms raise STATUS_ERROR if the given file object is not open. Finally, the function IS_OPEN returns a BOOLEAN value, indicating whether the file object given as a parameter currently has an external file associated with it. If so, the function returns TRUE, otherwise FALSE.

7.4 Text Input-Output

The package TEXT_IO is a predefined package for input-output of values in a readable form. It provides subprograms for input-output of character, string, integer, real, and enumeration types. Values are read or written sequentially to text files.

The overall layout of a text file is based on an analogy with text in printed form. A TEXT_IO file is structured as sequences of lines, which themselves form sequences of pages. The end of a line is marked by a line terminator, the end of a page by a page terminator, and the end of a text file by a file terminator. The form of the terminators themselves is not specified by the language and generally is unnecessary to know in an application. Operations are provided to manipulate lines and pages of text.

The overall structure of TEXT_IO is as follows:

```
with IO_EXCEPTIONS;
package TEXT_IO is

    -- Declarations of types, subtypes, and constants

    -- File management as discussed above

    -- Control of default input and output files

    -- Line and page control operations

    -- Character input-output

    -- String input-output

    -- Generic package for input-output of integer types

    -- Generic packages for input-output of real types

    -- Generic package for input-output of enumeration types

    -- Exceptions

private
    -- implementation-dependent
end TEXT_IO;
```

In addition to the declarations for FILE_TYPE, FILE_MODE, and the file management operations that we saw earlier in Section 7.3, TEXT_IO contains nested subprograms and packages for input-output of values in text form and for the control of formatting and files.

The subprograms for character and string values are nested directly within TEXT_IO. Those for integers, reals, and enumeration values are declared in generic packages nested within TEXT_IO. These packages must be instantiated for the type that is to be input-output.

The basic subprograms available in TEXT_IO are called GET and PUT. These subprograms are overloaded on each type. Generally, two GET and PUT operations are defined for a given type, one that takes an explicit file object as a parameter and one that has no file parameter. A default input and a default output file are associated with TEXT_IO. If no file parameter is given to a GET, the operation uses the default input file. Similarly, a call to PUT without a file parameter uses the default output file.

When a program that uses TEXT_IO begins execution, it automatically has two files implicitly associated with it. These two files are called the standard input and standard output files and have modes IN_FILE and OUT_FILE, respectively. They are open implicitly at the beginning of execution and are made the default input and output files. The external files connected to the standard input and standard output files are defined by the implementation. For example, they could be connected to the keyboard and video display of a user terminal or they could be connected to disk files determined by a naming convention. Subprograms are provided to change the default files.

Using the default files, a simple program to copy its standard input to its standard output can be written as follows:

```
with TEXT_IO; use TEXT_IO;
procedure COPY_FILE is
    CH : CHARACTER;
begin
    while not END_OF_FILE loop
        GET(CH);
        PUT(CH);
    end loop;
end COPY_FILE;
```

Because TEXT_IO is a library unit, like library units supplied by the programmer, it must be mentioned in a **with** clause to make it available. This program is simpler than our example in Section 7.3 because it uses the default files, rather than declaring another file object and explicitly opening and closing it. This program writes the characters of the input file as a stream of characters and does not necessarily preserve the line and page structure of the input.

A program to copy a text file as lines of at most 80 characters, again using the standard input and output as the default files, can be written as follows:

```
with TEXT_IO; use TEXT_IO;
procedure COPY_LINES is
    A_STRING : STRING(1..80);
    LAST     : NATURAL;
begin
    while not END_OF_FILE loop
        GET_LINE(A_STRING, LAST);
        PUT_LINE(A_STRING(A_STRING'FIRST .. LAST));
    end loop;
end COPY_LINES;
```

We saw GET_LINE in our example in Section 7.3. GET_LINE has the effect of calling successive GETs on characters until a line terminator is reached or the end of the string given as its parameter is reached. If the line terminator is reached first, the characters after the last position read are undefined. For this reason, the parameter LAST is needed to determine the index of the last valid character. The value of LAST is then used in the PUT_LINE as the last index of the string.

PUT_LINE must receive only the number of characters that are valid in A_STRING. Therefore we must be able to extract a subarray of A_STRING in case the number of characters read does not equal the size of A_STRING. This subarray is extracted by the slice operation, which takes the portion of A_STRING bounded by the 'FIRST attribute and the value of LAST, which is set by the preceding GET_LINE.

Input-output of integers, reals, and enumerations is similar to that for characters and strings, except that the subprograms for these types are defined within generic packages. Below is an outline of the generic package INTEGER_IO. The packages for the other types are similar.

```
generic
    type NUM is range <>;
package INTEGER_IO is

    DEFAULT_WIDTH : FIELD := NUM'WIDTH;
    DEFAULT_BASE  : NUMBER_BASE := 10;

    procedure GET(ITEM : out NUM; WIDTH : in FIELD := 0);

    procedure PUT(ITEM   : in NUM;
                  WIDTH : in FIELD := DEFAULT_WIDTH;
                  BASE  : in NUMBER_BASE := DEFAULT_BASE);

    -- Other GET and PUT operations

end INTEGER_IO;
```

Recall from Chapter 5 that the declaration

```
    type NUM is range <>;
```

defines a generic formal integer type. Any integer type can be given in an instantiation to this generic formal type. To perform input-output of an integer type, it is first necessary to instantiate this generic package with the integer type as the actual parameter. The following program illustrates input-output for the predefined type INTEGER by adding the INTEGERs in a file:

```
    with TEXT_IO; use TEXT_IO;
    procedure ADD_INTEGERS is
        package IO_OF_INTEGERS is new INTEGER_IO(NUM => INTEGER);
        SUM            : INTEGER := 0;
        LINE_NUMBER : NATURAL := NATURAL'FIRST;
        use            IO_OF_INTEGERS;
```

```
begin
    while not END_OF_FILE loop
        declare
            AN_INTEGER   : INTEGER;
        begin
            LINE_NUMBER := LINE_NUMBER + 1;
            GET(AN_INTEGER);
            SUM := SUM + AN_INTEGER;
        exception
            when DATA_ERROR =>
                PUT("Bad format for the integer on line ");
                PUT(LINE_NUMBER);
                NEW_LINE;
        end;
    end loop;
    PUT("The sum of the integers is ");
    PUT(SUM);
    NEW_LINE;
end ADD_INTEGERS;
```

The package IO_OF_INTEGERS is created by the instantiation, and then the GET and PUT procedures of IO_OF_INTEGERS are used. The subprogram does not OPEN and CLOSE the input and output files because it uses the standard files (which also are the default files). The overloading of the PUT operation makes the calls to output the literal strings and the INTEGERs uniform, even though different subprograms are called. This uniformity follows naturally from overloading, rather than from special rules that allow the input-output subprograms to take parameters of different types.

As a final word about this example, notice the use of a block statement to introduce an exception handler for bad input data. In general, the exception DATA_ERROR is raised by the input operations whenever the format of the input data does not conform to the type and the subtype of the object to be input.

Input-output of real and enumeration values follows the same model as that for integer values. Enumeration input-output is a notable feature in that it allows enumeration values to be input and output as text. If a language includes enumeration types but does not allow input-output of values, it is less convenient to use them. In developing a program, it is rare to define a data structure that never needs to be input and output, even if for no reason other than debugging. Without enumeration input-output, the programmer must convert a textual encoding, such as a string or integer, of the enumeration literal into the internal representation used by the compiler. (The attributes 'IMAGE and 'VALUE make this conversion easier in Ada than it otherwise would be.) Ada relieves the programmer of the job of performing explicit conversions by defining a generic package for input-output of enumerations.

The ENUMERATION_IO package has the following outline:

```
generic
    type ENUM is (<>);
package ENUMERATION_IO is

    ...

end ENUMERATION_IO;
```

The ENUM generic formal parameter matches any discrete type passed in an instantiation. For example, the following subprogram illustrates the use of enumeration input-output to communicate with an interactive user.

```
with TEXT_IO; use TEXT_IO;
procedure SCHEDULE is
    type      RESPONSE is (QUIT, DATA_STRUCTURES,
                                ALGORITHMS, HUMAN_FACTORS);
    subtype COURSES  is RESPONSE
        range RESPONSE'SUCC(RESPONSE'FIRST) .. RESPONSE'LAST;
    package RESPONSE_IO is new ENUMERATION_IO(ENUM
                                                    => RESPONSE);
    package COUNT_IO      is new INTEGER_IO      (NUM
                                                    => INTEGER);
    CHOICE       : RESPONSE;
    ENROLLMENT : array (COURSES) of INTEGER := (0, 0, 0);
    use       RESPONSE_IO, COUNT_IO;
begin
    loop
        begin
            PUT_LINE("What course would you like to enroll in? ");
            GET(CHOICE);
            exit when CHOICE = RESPONSE'FIRST;
            ENROLLMENT(CHOICE) := ENROLLMENT(CHOICE) + 1;
            PUT_LINE("Fine choice, one of our better courses.");
            NEW_LINE;
        exception
            when DATA_ERROR =>
                PUT       ("Sorry, we don't offer that one. ");
                PUT_LINE("Please choose another.");
            when END_ERROR  =>
                    exit;
        end;
    end loop;
    NEW_LINE; PUT_LINE("Enrollment totals:");
    COUNT_IO.DEFAULT_WIDTH := 4;
    for I in COURSES loop
        PUT(I); SET_COL(17); PUT(":"); PUT(ENROLLMENT(I));
        NEW_LINE;
    end loop;
end SCHEDULE;
```

Although not a model of user interface design nor curriculum variety, this subprogram illustrates several points. A type RESPONSE is defined, and the first value, QUIT, is reserved to indicate the end of input. The subtype COURSES is defined to be the range beginning at the second value of RESPONSE and extending to the last value of RESPONSE. The second value of RESPONSE is obtained without references to any of its literal values by the expression RESPONSE'SUCC(RESPONSE'FIRST), which takes the successor of the first value of the type RESPONSE. Using attributes in this way makes the program easier to modify, for example, by adding more courses or changing the names of existing courses (although the first value is always reserved to indicate end of input).

A hapless student faced with this program can type in one of the three course offerings. If anything else is typed, the exception DATA_ERROR is raised, the exception handler is executed to complete the block, and control flows back to the top of the loop. A handler also is provided for END_ERROR, which is raised if the GET operation encounters a file terminator. The handler simply exits the enclosing loop, causing control to flow to the statements following the loop. Thus the loop can be exited by either typing the QUIT command or by generating the file terminator. (Generating the file terminator in an interactive session is implementation-dependent.)

The subprogram keeps an array, initialized to zeros, of the count of students enrolled in a given class. For example, a user could have the following interaction with the program (user typing indicated by italics):

```
What course would you like to enroll in?
DATA_STRUTCURES
Sorry, we don't offer that one. Please choose another.
What course would you like to enroll in?
DATA_STRUCTURES
Fine choice, one of our better courses.

What course would you like to enroll in?
QUIT

Enrollment Totals:
DATA_STRUCTURES :    1
ALGORITHMS       :    0
HUMAN_FACTORS    :    0
```

In the first response the word "STRUCTURE" is misspelled, which causes DATA_ERROR to be raised. (The program is about as unforgiving of typing errors as the course selection is limited.) The second response is accepted by the program. The user then types the QUIT response, causing the enrollment summary to be printed.

Before printing the enrollment summary, the variable COUNT_IO.DEFAULT_WIDTH is set to the width of the field that governs output of integer values. Field positions not occupied by digits in the output value are blank filled to the left. The subprogram SET_COL positions the output device to the column given by the parameter.

Generic program units are used to define input-output for the numeric and enumeration types, because the full range of user-defined types cannot be anticipated. The basic logic for input-output of these types, however, is the same. The reason is especially apparent in the case of enumeration types. Each enumeration type defines its own set of enumeration literals. The programmer defines these literals, so it is impossible to define an input-output package for it unless the type, and its corresponding set of literals, is already defined. Clearly, such an input-output package cannot be *predefined* in the language, because the type itself is defined by the programmer. The basic specification, however, can be predefined as a generic with a formal type parameter for the type. As we saw in Chapter 5, generic program units provide the ability to pass types as parameters to be used to create a program unit.

7.5 Binary Input-Output

Binary input-output is concerned with efficient machine reading and writing of data. Like the numeric and enumeration type packages in TEXT_IO, the packages for binary input-output must deal with programmer-defined data types. For this reason, the two packages for binary input-output also are generic packages, which must be instantiated with a type by the application. Unlike the numeric and enumeration packages, the binary input-output packages provide for input-output of a wider variety of types, including array and record types.

For binary input-output, an external file contains values of a given type; but only one type is associated with a given file. For example, a file can contain values of type INTEGER, or values of type TRANSACTION, but it cannot contain a mixture of values of both types.

The two binary input-output packages are called SEQUENTIAL_IO and DIRECT_IO. As the name implies, SEQUENTIAL_IO provides the ability to read and write the elements of a file in sequence, starting from the beginning of the file and continuing to the end without skipping elements. The file is a sequence of values of the element type, which must be processed in the order in which the values appear in the sequence.

The outline of SEQUENTIAL_IO is given below:

```
with IO_EXCEPTIONS;
generic
    type ELEMENT_TYPE is private;
package SEQUENTIAL_IO is
```

```
type FILE_TYPE is limited private;

type FILE_MODE is (IN_FILE, OUT_FILE);


-- File management as described above

-- Input and output operations

procedure READ  (FILE : in FILE_TYPE;
                 ITEM : out ELEMENT_TYPE);
procedure WRITE (FILE : in FILE_TYPE; ITEM : in ELEMENT_TYPE);

function END_OF_FILE(FILE : in FILE_TYPE) return BOOLEAN;

-- Exceptions

private
     -- implementation-dependent
end SEQUENTIAL_IO;
```

An example of an instantiation of SEQUENTIAL_IO is given below:

```
package TRANSACTION_IO is new SEQUENTIAL_IO(
    ELEMENT_TYPE => TRANSACTION
    );
```

which declares a new package called TRANSACTION_IO, giving the type TRANS-ACTION as the actual parameter.

The main operations provided by SEQUENTIAL_IO are the READ and WRITE subprograms. READ operates on a file of mode IN_FILE and returns the next element from the external file. We saw an example of using this package in Chapter 4, without fully explaining it. We repeat the example below:

```
with TEXT_IO;            -- predefined package for text input-output
with TRANSACTIONS;       -- application-defined package
                         -- with type TRANSACTION
with TRANSACTION_IO;     -- application-defined transaction file input-output
with REPORT;             -- application-defined subprogram

procedure DAILY_REPORT is
    use TRANSACTIONS;
    use TRANSACTION_IO; -- makes declarations directly visible
    TRANSACTION_FILE  : FILE_TYPE;
    NEXT_TRANSACTION : TRANSACTION;
```

```
begin
    OPEN(FILE   => TRANSACTION_FILE,
         MODE   => IN_FILE,
         NAME   => "TODAYS_TRANSACTIONS");

    while not END_OF_FILE(TRANSACTION_FILE) loop
        READ(TRANSACTION_FILE, NEXT_TRANSACTION);
        REPORT(NEXT_TRANSACTION);
    end loop;

exception
    when NAME_ERROR    => -- can be raised by OPEN
        TEXT_IO.PUT_LINE("Could not open transaction file");
    when STATUS_ERROR => -- can be raised by OPEN
        TEXT_IO.PUT_LINE("Transaction file already open");
    when DATA_ERROR    => -- can be raised by READ
        TEXT_IO.PUT_LINE("Input format error");
        TEXT_IO.PUT_LINE("Check TODAYS_TRANSACTIONS file");
end DAILY_REPORT;
```

We now explain in more detail the input-output operations in this example. The TRANSACTION_IO package is a library unit that is an instantiation of the SEQUENTIAL_IO package. A file object, TRANSACTION_FILE, is declared and associated with an external file identified as "TODAYS_TRANSACTIONS". Elements of the TRANSACTION_FILE are then read sequentially by the call to READ and processed by the library unit REPORT. Processing completes when no more elements can be read from TRANSACTION_FILE, as a result of END_OF_FILE returning TRUE. As before, exception handlers provide for handling and recovery of errors during input-output.

In the case of DIRECT_IO, the elements of a file need not be read sequentially, but instead can be directly addressed within the file by means of an index. Each element of the file has an index position associated with it. The first element of the file has index position one, the second has index position two, and so on. A file in which the elements are obtained by index position is called a direct access file. When opened, a direct access file has a current index, initialized to one, associated with it. An excerpt of DIRECT_IO is given below:

```
with IO_EXCEPTIONS;
generic
    type ELEMENT_TYPE is private;
package DIRECT_IO is
    type FILE_TYPE is limited private;
    type FILE_MODE is (IN_FILE, INOUT_FILE, OUT_FILE);

    type   COUNT           is range 0 .. implementation_defined;
    subtype POSITIVE_COUNT is COUNT range 1..COUNT'LAST;
```

-- Input and output operations

```
procedure READ   (FILE  : in FILE_TYPE;
                  ITEM  : out ELEMENT_TYPE;
                  FROM : POSITIVE_COUNT);
procedure READ   (FILE  : in FILE_TYPE;
                  ITEM  : out ELEMENT_TYPE);
procedure WRITE( FILE  : in FILE_TYPE;
                 ITEM  : in  ELEMENT_TYPE;
                 TO : POSITIVE_COUNT);
procedure WRITE( FILE  : in FILE_TYPE;
                 ITEM  : in ELEMENT_TYPE);
procedure SET_INDEX(FILE : in FILE_TYPE;
                    TO : in POSITIVE_COUNT);
function INDEX(FILE : in FILE_TYPE) return POSITIVE_COUNT;
function SIZE  (FILE : in FILE_TYPE) return COUNT;
```

-- Exceptions

```
private
    -- implementation-dependent
end DIRECT_IO;
```

Unlike files in TEXT_IO and SEQUENTIAL_IO, DIRECT_IO files can have mode INOUT_FILE, which allows both reading and writing of elements in the file. The file position where the next value is input or output is given by a current index of type COUNT. Two varieties of READ and WRITE are provided: one has a parameter used to set the current index before the operation and one has no parameter. Both varieties increment the value of the current index following the operation. The procedure SET_INDEX sets the current index for the file object to the value given by the parameter TO. The function INDEX returns the current index associated with the file, and SIZE returns the current size of the file.

DIRECT_IO files can be used to access an element efficiently without having to read all the preceding elements in the file, as would be necessary using SEQUENTIAL_IO. This kind of file typically would be used in applications that require fast access to a large amount of data in an external file. More complicated access methods, such as index-sequential or B-tree, can be built efficiently using DIRECT_IO.

7.6 Low-Level Input-Output

The LOW_LEVEL_IO package provides operations to interface directly with physical devices. As such, the operations are implementation and device dependent. The outline of the package is given below:

```
package LOW_LEVEL_IO is
   -- declarations of the possible types for DEVICE and DATA;
   -- declarations of overloaded procedures for these types:
   procedure SEND_CONTROL     (DEVICE : DEVICE_TYPE;
                               DATA : in out DATA_TYPE);
   procedure RECEIVE_CONTROL (DEVICE : DEVICE_TYPE;
                               DATA : in out DATA_TYPE);
end;
```

The declarations for DEVICE_TYPE and DATA_TYPE are implementation dependent. For example, assume a terminal device has an output buffer located in memory location 100 octal. An implementation could provide the following declarations in LOW_LEVEL_IO:

```
-- addresses of device registers
subtype TERMINAL_REGISTER is    NATURAL range 8#10# .. 8#1000#;
TERMINAL_OUT_BUFFER : constant TERMINAL_REGISTER := 8#100#;

procedure SEND_CONTROL     (DEVICE : TERMINAL_REGISTER;
                            DATA : in out CHARACTER);
```

To send the character value contained in a variable A_CHARACTER to the output buffer using these declarations, the following subprogram call could be used:

```
SEND_CONTROL(TERMINAL_OUT_BUFFER, A_CHARACTER);
```

This call places the value of the character A_CHARACTER in memory location 100 octal. The LOW_LEVEL_IO package is available for direct interface to physical devices, allowing system programming and interface to specialized devices to be uniform with the rest of the language.

7.7 Summary

Ada input-output is a complete, standard definition of input-output. Four predefined packages are provided: TEXT_IO, SEQUENTIAL_IO, DIRECT_IO, and LOW_LEVEL_IO. The first three packages are concerned with input-output for external files; the last package is concerned with low-level device operations. The file-oriented packages define largely portable operations, and the LOW_LEVEL_IO package provides access to hardware-level device handling.

An external file is an object in the environment that can provide or receive a value. A program accesses an external file by declaring an internal file object and connecting it to an external file using an OPEN procedure. The CLOSE procedure disconnects an internal file from its associated external file.

TEXT_IO provides operations for input-output in human-readable format. The data types that can be input-output using TEXT_IO are characters, strings, enumerations, and numerics (integer, float, and fixed numbers). TEXT_IO has two files—standard input and standard output—implicitly associated with it, and these files are automatically opened and closed by the implementation. Internal file objects for text files also may be explicitly declared and manipulated. The TEXT_IO operations have two forms: one with an explicit file parameter and one using the default input and output files. The default input and output files are set initially to the standard input and output files respectively. Input-output of enumerations and numerics is provided by generic packages nested within TEXT_IO. These packages can be instantiated with the actual types used in an application.

The SEQUENTIAL_IO and DIRECT_IO packages provide input-output in binary format. These packages are generic and can be instantiated with any nonlimited type as the actual parameter. SEQUENTIAL_IO reads and writes values in sequence, whereas DIRECT_IO allows reading and writing arbitrary elements within a file using an index to locate the element.

The LOW_LEVEL_IO package provides implementation-dependent access to physical devices. For a given implementation, operations are available to access directly the buffers and status register of peripherals. This package can be used for low-level device handling.

7.8 Exercises

1. Write a subprogram using TEXT_IO to read a file of integers from the default input file and to write them to the default output file.

2. Write a subprogram using SEQUENTIAL_IO to read a file of integers from the external file given by its first parameter and write them to the external file given by its second parameter. The specification for the procedure is given below:

   procedure COPY_INTEGERS(INPUT_FILE, OUTPUT_FILE : STRING);

3. Change the implementation of the generic BINARY_TREE_MAKER (Section 5.11) to store the tree nodes in an external file, rather than internally. Use the DIRECT_IO package to access the nodes of the tree. Must the specification of BINARY_TREE_MAKER change? To use the new version, must program units that used the earlier version of BINARY_TREE_MAKER change?

Gerald Murphy. Watch. *Dallas Museum of Art, Foundation for the Arts Collection, gift of the artist*

CHAPTER 8

Specifying Representation

As we have seen, a central goal of Ada is to promote abstraction. Abstraction means in part that the programmer is able to avoid low level and unnecessary detail. For example, an Ada programmer ordinarily is unconcerned with how an object of a record type is mapped onto the underlying physical storage. That is, the number of bits each record component will occupy, and the physical address at which the record object will reside, are decisions usually made by the compiler rather than the programmer.

By contrast, an assembly language programmer must make this sort of low level decision for every object in the program. Because the amount of information a programmer can remember at a time is small in comparison with the amount of information inherent in a large program, the Ada programmer has a great advantage over the assembly language programmer. The Ada compiler handles many details that the assembly language programmer must explicitly remember and manage.

This sort of abstraction makes the program more representation independent, which has advantages for transportability. Ada programs can be compiled and run on different machines, if Ada compilers exist for the machines. If an Ada program is written carefully, it usually can be run without modification.

Some applications, however, require explicit mapping onto the underlying hardware. Programs such as operating systems, which manage hardware resources, must access specialized registers and memory locations. Embedded computer systems often require interfacing to specialized devices. These applications require detailed control over the machine-level representation of the program. Such needs obviously hinder transportability, but it is important to be able to apply Ada to these applications also.

The need for representation control has been met in the past by using assembly language where necessary. This approach, however, can force large portions of a system to be in assembly language if the data structures involved are accessed frequently. Ada provides an alternative to assembly language, called *representation clauses*. A representation clause is a directive written by the programmer, instructing the compiler how to map an Ada entity onto the underlying machine. The way the entity is used within other Ada constructs is unchanged by the representation clause. That is, the representation clause in general does not change the meaning of the entity; it merely affects the compiler representation of it. Objects given explicit representation clauses by the programmer are used in the same way as if the programmer had let the compiler determine the representations.

8.1 Package SYSTEM

A difficulty in allowing control over representation is that the Ada language has no built-in understanding of any particular target hardware, memory address requirements, or machine word length. Indeed, the machine-dependent nature of specifying representation makes it difficult to provide general rules for every machine. This difficulty is overcome by requiring each Ada compiler to provide a predefined library package named SYSTEM. The specification of this package includes declarations that describe the underlying target environment. Let us illustrate some of these declarations that might describe a hypothetical target computer.

```
package SYSTEM is
    type ADDRESS is range 0..16_777_215;      -- 24 bit addresses
    STORAGE_UNIT : constant := 8;             -- 8 bits per storage unit
    MEMORY_SIZE  : constant :=  16_777_216;
    subtype PRIORITY is INTEGER range 1..50;
    --
    --
end SYSTEM;
```

The entities ADDRESS, STORAGE_UNIT, MEMORY_SIZE, and PRIORITY must be declared within SYSTEM. In addition, other declarations must also be provided (see Ada, 1983, Section 13.7). These declarations describe the environment to which the compiler is targeted. For different compilers, of course, the definitions of these entities will vary. Each compiler is required to give the specification of SYSTEM in a special section of the compiler reference manual, "Appendix F."

Given that each compiler provides a package SYSTEM, let us now see how programmers may specify representation. Two major forms of representation clauses give the programmer control over the mapping from Ada to the target machine. These are called, respectively, *type representation clauses* and *address clauses*.

8.2 Type Representation Clauses

Type representation clauses allow the programmer to specify how a type is to be represented at the bit level. Consider the following Ada text:

```
package SOLAR_SYSTEM is
    type PLANET is (MERCURY, VENUS, EARTH,
                    MARS, JUPITER, SATURN,
                    URANUS, NEPTUNE, PLUTO);
    for PLANET'SIZE use 8;

    subtype TERRESTRIAL_PLANET is PLANET range MERCURY..MARS;
    -- other declarations
end SOLAR_SYSTEM;
```

The clause

```
for PLANET'SIZE use 8;
```

is known as a *length clause*. Its purpose is to instruct the compiler to use a maximum number of bits (in this case 8) to represent all objects of the given type. Of course, the number of bits given in the length clause must be adequate to represent all values of the specified type. Because 8 bits is more than sufficient to represent 9 values, the clause is legal.

Before illustrating more examples of type representation clauses, let us first make some general comments. First, representation clauses (type representation and address clauses) are said to *apply* to entities such as types, objects and subprograms declared within the Ada program. Next, both the declared entity and the corresponding representation clause must occur within some declarative part, package specification, or task specification; for example, the type representation clause shown above applies to the declaration for PLANET. Both the declaration and the clause occur within the package specification for SOLAR_SYSTEM. Further, the representation clause must occur after the declaration to which it applies.

Because representation clauses are implementation dependent, the rules governing them will vary somewhat between implementations. Some representation clauses may be rejected by the compiler if they cannot be handled in a simple way. In any case, the conventions governing them must be explained in Appendix F of the compiler reference manual.

As mentioned previously, type representation clauses are one of the two major forms of specifying representation. Each type representation clause has the general form:

for ... **use** ...;

The three kinds of type representation clauses are:

1. Length clauses

2. Enumeration representation clauses

3. Record representation clauses

Above, we saw an example of a length clause which specified the maximum number of bits for representing objects of a given type. Another form of the length clause specifies the number of storage units to be reserved for the dynamic allocation of objects designated by values of a certain access type. Here, "storage unit" is the unit of memory whose size in bits is defined in the package SYSTEM. Consider the following length clause:

```
type TRANSACTION_NAME is access TRANSACTION;
for TRANSACTION_NAME'STORAGE_SIZE use 1000;
```

Assuming that SYSTEM.STORAGE_UNIT has been defined to be 8, this length clause instructs the compiler to set aside at least 1000 bytes of storage for objects designated by values of type TRANSACTION_NAME. For example, if each object of type TRANSACTION requires 16 bytes, the above length clause reserves enough storage for about 62 (1000/16) (dynamically) allocated objects. Some of the 1000 bytes may be used for internal tables and addresses, so this calculation is only approximate.

There are two other forms of length clauses. One allows the programmer to specify the amount of internal storage to be used with tasks of a given type. The other allows the programmer extra control in the representation of fixed point types.

The enumeration representation clause is used to indicate the internal values the compiler will use to represent the abstract literal values of an enumeration type. The general form is

for *type_name* **use** *aggregate*;

For example,

```
package SOLAR_SYSTEM is
    type PLANET is (MERCURY, VENUS, EARTH,
                    MARS, JUPITER, SATURN,
                    URANUS, NEPTUNE, PLUTO);
    for PLANET use (MERCURY =〉 1,  VENUS    =〉 5,  EARTH   =〉 6,
                    MARS     =〉 8,  JUPITER  =〉 9,  SATURN  =〉 13,
                    URANUS   =〉 33, NEPTUNE  =〉 89, PLUTO   =〉 100);
    -- other declarations
end SOLAR_SYSTEM;
```

Note that this enumeration representation clause uses named association notation. It states the internal values that are to be used for values of type PLANET. Like all representation clauses, the enumeration clause does not affect the meaning of a program. Values of type PLANET will still be manipulated in the same way as if there were no representation clause.

The third kind of type representation clause is known as the record representation clause. This clause applies to record declarations and is used to specify the size and order of the bit fields corresponding to record components. To illustrate, suppose that in implementing a processor-management kernel we need to store copies of the status register of the MC68000 microprocessor, depicted in Figure 8.1.[1] This figure shows the programmer's model of this status register.

To represent the status register abstractly we might make the following declarations:

---

[1] MC68000 is a trademark of Motorola, Inc.

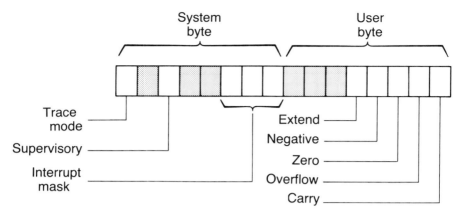

Figure 8.1 The MC68000 Status Register

```
type FLAGS is (CARRY, OVERFLOW, ZERO, NEGATIVE, EXTEND);
type USER_FLAGS is (FLAGS) of BOOLEAN;
type STATUS_REGISTER is
   record
      TRACE_BIT       : BOOLEAN;
      SUPERVISORY_BIT : BOOLEAN;
      INTERRUPT_MASK  : INTEGER range 0..7;
      USER_STATE      : USER_FLAGS;
   end record;
```

We would like to make sure that the components TRACE_BIT and SUPERVI-SORY_BIT are each represented as a single bit. Further, we want INTERRUPT_MASK to be represented as 3 bits, and USER_STATE to be an array of 5 contiguous bits. Moreover, we want the order and position of the components to be identical to Figure 8.1. The following record representation clause accomplishes this.

```
for STATUS_REGISTER use
   record at mod 2;
      TRACE_BIT          at 0 range 7..7;
      SUPERVISORY_BIT    at 0 range 5..5;
      INTERRUPT_MASK     at 0 range 0..2;
      USER_STATE         at 1 range 0..4;
   end record;
```

Several observations should be made about this representation clause. First, the subclause containing **at mod** is called an *alignment clause*. It specifies that objects of the type must be located in memory at an address which is divisible by the integer in the expression. In this case, objects of type STATUS_REGISTER will be placed on even byte boundaries. Next, note that the components of STATUS_REGISTER are named in subclauses such as

USER_STATE **at** 1 **range** 0..4;

This clause specifies the position and size of the component USER_STATE. The integer following the reserved word **at** is an offset (in storage units) from the beginning of the object. The component begins at STORAGE_UNIT 1 and occupies bits 0 through 4. The first storage unit of the object is considered to have offset 0. The range always describes a set of contiguous bits relative to the storage unit.

In some implementations, bits may be numbered from left to right, and in other implementations the reverse applies. In the present example, we assume bits are labeled from right to left.

8.3 Address Clauses

Address clauses are used to specify the address for an entity. There are three uses of address clauses. They may be used to:

1. Specify the address of a variable or constant.
2. Specify the address of the machine code corresponding to the body of a subprogram, task, or package.
3. Specify the address of a hardware interrupt with which a task entry is to be identified.

The general format of an address clause is

for some_name **use at** some_expression;

One use of address clauses is to associate objects with special memory addresses that control external devices. Consider a type called INPUT_DEVICE and an object of this type that must be located at address (hexadecimal) 1000. The following declaration and address clause specify these requirements.

DV : INPUT_DEVICE;
for DV **use at** 16#1000#;

The code for a body of a subprogram, package, or task also may be located at a particular address in the following way:

package I_O_HANDLERS **is**
   procedure KEYBOARD_HANDLER;
   for KEYBOARD_HANDLER **use at** 1024;
   --
end I_O_HANDLERS;

Because representation clauses must always apply to entities declared within a declarative part, package specification, or block statement, it is impossible to give an address clause that applies to a library unit.

Hardware interrupts in Ada are viewed as entry calls made by some task outside the system. The programmer may specify a task entry to receive the interrupt by associating the entry with the hardware interrupt address. For example, the following task specification declares a single entry named FULL. The address clause associates FULL with the interrupt whose vector is at address (hex) 80. Therefore FULL is "called" whenever this hardware interrupt occurs.

```
task DEVICE_MONITOR is
    entry FULL;
        for FULL use at 16#80#;
end DEVICE_MONITOR;
```

Entries that have been given address clauses may have formal **in** parameters, but not parameters of mode **out** or **in out**.

With some processors, hardware interrupts are queued; with others, interrupts not serviced immediately are lost. Ada entries are compatible with both these situations, because the first kind of interrupt can be considered an ordinary entry call and the second a conditional entry call.

8.4 Escaping the Language

The Ada rules about explicit declarations and strong typing help detect programming errors by preventing meaningless operations. The compiler does not allow an oversight or clerical error by the programmer (such as using an access variable as an integer) to remain undetected. Certain applications, however, require the ability to convert a value from one type to another type. For example, an operating system may need to treat addresses as integers to perform address arithmetic.

In such cases, Ada allows the programmer to convert explicitly between the two types. The conversion is done by instantiating the predefined generic function UNCHECKED_CONVERSION with the two types. The specification of UNCHECKED_CONVERSION is given below:

```
generic
    type SOURCE is limited private;
    type TARGET is limited private;
function UNCHECKED_CONVERSION(S : SOURCE) return TARGET;
```

An instantiation of this generic creates a function to convert a value from one type to another type. The block statement that follows illustrates its use:

```
declare
    BUFFER : BYTE;
    CH      : CHARACTER;
    function TO_CHARACTER is
        new UNCHECKED_CONVERSION(SOURCE = > BYTE,
                                 TARGET = > CHARACTER);
begin
    ...
    CH := TO_CHARACTER(BUFFER);
end;
```

The return value of a function that is an instance of UNCHECKED_CONVERSION is the identical bit pattern passed as the source value. Therefore the expression

```
TO_CHARACTER(BUFFER)
```

has the same bit pattern at the machine level as BUFFER. However, the call to TO_CHARACTER makes the value have type CHARACTER rather than type BYTE. An implementation may place restrictions on the use of UNCHECKED_ CONVERSION; for example, the types used in the instantiation of UN-CHECKED_CONVERSION may be required to have compatible machine repre-sentations.

In an application where efficiency is the highest priority, it is sometimes neces-sary to code a subprogram body in machine language. Although use of the capa-bility should be rare, because it forsakes the benefits of the language, Ada allows a subprogram body to be coded completely in machine instructions. Each machine instruction is represented textually as a special record aggregate whose type is de-clared in a predefined (and implementation-dependent) package named MA-CHINE_CODE. Machine instructions and ordinary Ada statements cannot be inter-mixed, and hence a subprogram that has machine instructions can have no other kinds of statements.

To shorten initial development time in some cases, existing subprograms writ-ten in other languages can be applied advantageously until Ada versions become available. Ada provides a way to specify that the body of a subprogram is written in a "foreign" language. To use such a foreign language subprogram, the programmer writes an Ada subprogram specification for the subprogram, fol-lowed by the pragma INTERFACE, which has the following form:

pragma INTERFACE (*language_name, subprogram_name*);

The pragma is placed in a package specification or in a declarative part after a subprogram declaration. It specifies that the subprogram is written in a different language.

```
function SQRT(X : FLOAT) return FLOAT;

pragma INTERFACE(FORTRAN, SQRT);
```

The only form of communication allowable with a foreign language subprogram is through parameters and function results; the foreign subprogram cannot access other declarations in the Ada program.

8.5 Unchecked Deallocation

Often variables allocated by means of access variables are no longer needed after they have been processed. It is desirable to reclaim the storage occupied by unneeded objects, so that memory is not consumed by such objects. The run-time system may reclaim objects that are no longer accessible through any path of existing access variables, a process called garbage collection.

Because garbage collection involves searching through the existing data structures accessible through all access variables, it can be expensive during execution, and other processing may be delayed. Such unpredictable delays could be harmful in a real-time application, and for this reason, Ada does not require (nor prohibit) garbage collection. Ada provides as an alternative the predefined generic procedure UNCHECKED_DEALLOCATION, which allows the programmer to explicitly release storage for an accessed object that no longer is needed.

The specification for UNCHECKED_DEALLOCATION and a use of it is given below:

```
generic
      type OBJECT is limited private;
      type NAME   is access OBJECT;
procedure UNCHECKED_DEALLOCATION(X : in out NAME);

with UNCHECKED_DEALLOCATION;
procedure P is
      type TRANSACTION           is record ... end record;
      type TRANSACTION_NAME is access TRANSACTION;
      THIS_TRANSACTION : TRANSACTION_NAME;

      procedure FREE is new UNCHECKED_DEALLOCATION(
                            OBJECT => TRANSACTION,
                            NAME   => TRANSACTION_NAME);

begin
      -- Create and process THIS_TRANSACTION
      -- ...

      FREE(THIS_TRANSACTION);
end;
```

After executing FREE, THIS_TRANSACTION has the value **null** and the storage occupied by the designated object is reclaimed. If THIS_TRANSACTION was **null** already, FREE has no effect. As Section 2.13 described, UNCHECKED_DEALLO-CATION is dangerous if more than one access variable designates the object whose storage is reclaimed. The nonexistent object still can be accessed through these other access variables, which can cause elusive errors.

8.6 An Input-output Chip Example

Several semiconductor manufacturers provide standard I/O interface chips which are designed to simplify software/hardware interfaces. The chip is the interface between the software and the actual hardware that the software must control. The hardware engineer assures that the chip is configured properly to the device. To the software engineer, the interface chip appears as special memory locations that provide a window to the hardware device.

Let us design the interface to a simple hypothetical input chip containing two hardware registers: a buffer and a control register. Figure 8.2 illustrates the programmer's model of this chip.

The buffer is capable of storing an incoming 8-bit datum. The control register has 3 bits that may be used to reset the device, detect when the buffer contains a new datum, and detect hardware errors.

Input devices such as the one described are usually used in either of two ways. One approach is for a hardware *interrupt* to occur whenever the buffer becomes full with a new input value. When the hardware interrupt occurs, control is transferred to a portion of the program that services the interrupt by reading the contents of the input buffer.

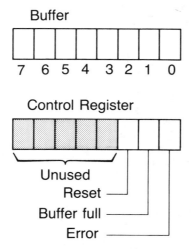

Figure 8.2 A Hypothetical Input Device

A second way in which an input device can be serviced is called *polling*. In this method, the program periodically checks the device for a new datum. In our current example, the check is done by inspecting bit 1 of the control register.

The input chip is used as follows: it first must be initialized by giving a value to bit 2 of the control register. If bit 2 has the value 1, a hardware interrupt will occur when a new datum arrives; if it has the value 0, interrupts are disabled, and the device must be serviced by polling.

After the device is initialized, a program can receive input values by reading the buffer. If interrupts are enabled, the program reads the buffer after each interrupt. Otherwise, it must detect the change in the buffer state by polling.

The following package contains declarations for the hardware-level data types used to control the input chip.

```
package INPUT_DEVICE_TYPES is

    type BIT is new BOOLEAN;
    for  BIT'SIZE use 1;
    for  BIT use (FALSE = > 0, TRUE = > 1);

    type BYTE is array(0..7) of BIT;
    for  BYTE'SIZE use 8;

    type CONTROL_BITS is (INTERRUPTS, FULL, ERROR);
    type CONTROL       is array(CONTROL_BITS) of BIT;
    for  CONTROL'SIZE use 3;

    type INPUT_DEVICE is          -- the record declaration
        record
                DATA : BYTE;
                CTRL : CONTROL;
        end record;

    for  INPUT_DEVICE use          -- the record representation
        record at mod 2
                DATA at 0 range 0..7;
                CTRL at 1 range 0..2;
        end record;
    for  INPUT_DEVICE'SIZE use 16;

end INPUT_DEVICE_TYPES;
```

We now declare a package that hides the hardware details, allowing other program units to use the input chip as an abstract object. The package specification of INPUT_DEVICE_HANDLER makes visible a single procedure named RECEIVE which can be called to receive the next input character.

```
package INPUT_DEVICE_HANDLER is
   procedure RECEIVE(CH : out CHARACTER);
end INPUT_DEVICE_HANDLER;
```

In designing the body of INPUT_DEVICE_HANDLER, a queue named IN_Q is used to store incoming characters temporarily until they are consumed. The queue is created by instantiating the generic package SAFE_QUEUE from Section 6.9 to be a queue of CHARACTERs.

Incoming bytes of data may have arbitrary 8-bit values. Because we wish to use these values as characters, the high order bit must first be cleared in order to assure that the value falls in the range of ASCII characters. In addition, it is necessary to be able to translate these values to type CHARACTER to enter them into the queue. To do this the generic function UNCHECKED_CONVERSION is used.

In the current version of the package, the interrupt method of servicing the device is used. Interrupt entry calls signal a monitor task to read data from the buffer, convert it, and enter it in the queue.

```
with SAFE_QUEUE, UNCHECKED_CONVERSION, INPUT_DEVICE_TYPES;
use INPUT_DEVICE_TYPES;
package body INPUT_DEVICE_HANDLER is
   DV : INPUT_DEVICE;
   for DV use at 16#1000#;

   package IN_Q is new SAFE_QUEUE(
                        SIZE    => 100,
                        ELEMENT => CHARACTER);
   use IN_Q;

   function TO_CHARACTER is new UNCHECKED_CONVERSION(
                        SOURCE => BYTE,
                        TARGET => CHARACTER);

   task DEVICE_MONITOR is           -- interrupt approach
      entry FULL;
      for FULL use at 16#80#;
   end DEVICE_MONITOR;

   task body DEVICE_MONITOR is
      B : BYTE;
      MASK : constant BYTE :=
            (FALSE, TRUE, TRUE, TRUE, TRUE, TRUE, TRUE, TRUE);
   begin
      loop
         accept FULL;                     -- buffer now full
         B := DV.DATA and MASK;           -- zero high order bit
         IN_Q.ENTER(TO_CHARACTER(B));     -- make it a character
      end loop;
   end DEVICE_MONITOR;
```

```
    procedure RECEIVE(CH : out CHARACTER) is
    begin
        IN_Q.REMOVE(CH);
    end RECEIVE;

begin
        DV.CTRL(INTERRUPTS) := TRUE; -- initialize & enable interrupts
    end INPUT_DEVICE_HANDLER;
```

Note the use of the logical operator **and** in the body of DEVICE_MONITOR. It is applied to two operands of the same boolean array type by applying the operator to each pair of corresponding components. The operators **not**, **or**, and **xor** also are allowed for boolean arrays. These operators may be applied to one-dimensional boolean arrays. With the binary operators (**and**, **or**, and **xor**) both operands must have the same type and size.

8.7 More Pragmas

In this chapter we have seen how representation clauses allow the programmer to specify low-level representation information to the compiler that the programmer otherwise could not control. Another way for the programmer to influence the compiler is by using pragmas. Pragmas allow the programmer to set criteria the compiler is to use when compiling a program unit.

The pragma PACK can be used to tell the compiler that storage minimization should be the main criterion when selecting a representation for a record or array type. The pragma is used by supplying the name of the type. For example,

```
    type BIG_ARRAY is array(1..1000) of BOOLEAN;
    pragma PACK(BIG_ARRAY);
```

This pragma means that memory gaps that occur between components of the array or record should be minimized. The pragma does not necessarily affect the size of the components themselves. The size of the components, however, can also be controlled either by another PACK pragma or by a representation clause.

Another pragma that influences the size of a program is OPTIMIZE. This pragma is concerned with executable code size, however, rather than the size of objects. The pragma may be used with one of two arguments—TIME or SPACE. The pragma is used to tell the compiler which of these two criteria should be most important for optimization. For example,

```
    procedure QUICKSORT(...) is
        pragma OPTIMIZE(TIME);
    begin
    --
    end QUICKSORT;
```

This pragma is allowed only within a declarative part. It affects the statements of the associated block or body. Therefore in the above example, the OPTIMIZE pragma affects the statements of the procedure QUICKSORT.

Structured programming and data abstraction encourage writing layers of relatively short, single-purpose subprograms. A subprogram that is short and simple is more likely to be correct and to be readily understood by someone reading it, such as the developer or maintainer.

With some processors, the overhead incurred by a subprogram call can be expensive during execution. A call to a short subprogram could consume processing time that is out of proportion with the work accomplished by the subprogram. For applications that are time-critical and cannot tolerate such overhead, the programmer can use the pragma INLINE. This pragma takes arguments that are subprogram identifiers, as illustrated below.

pragma INLINE(ENTER);

INLINE directs the compiler not to use the normal subprogram call for ENTER, but instead to insert the body of ENTER wherever ENTER is called. The pragma is placed after the declaration of ENTER in the same package specification or declarative part. The statements of ENTER are inserted inline, if possible, at the point of a call. The inline insertion may not be possible if the subprogram is recursive (directly or indirectly) or if the body is compiled separately (as discussed in Chapter 9) and has not been submitted yet to the compiler. The INLINE pragma achieves the same effect as if the programmer had written the statements directly, rather than called a procedure. Using INLINE, the overhead of a procedure call is avoided.

8.8 Summary

Each compiler implementation provides a machine-dependent package named SYSTEM, which contains declarations describing its intended target computer. For example, one such entity declared in SYSTEM is ADDRESS, whose definition indicates the range of memory addresses.

A representation clause can be placed after a declaration to force the compiler to translate a declaration in a certain way. There are two kinds of representation clauses—type representation clauses and address clauses.

Type representation clauses apply to all objects of a certain type and are used to indicate representation details of those objects. For example, one kind of type representation clause is used to tell the compiler the maximum number of bits it may use for objects of that type.

Address clauses may be used to place an object or program unit at a particular address. An address clause also can associate a task entry with a hardware interrupt, which means that the occurrence of the interrupt causes an entry call on the task. The address appearing in an address clause must be of the subtype ADDRESS given in the package SYSTEM.

The predefined generic function UNCHECKED_CONVERSION can be used to create functions that convert a value of one type to another type. This function must be used with caution. Ada allows the programmer to make use of assembly language by means of a package called MACHINE_CODE and to make calls to subprograms written in other languages, using a pragma named INTERFACE.

The pragma PACK can be used to tell the compiler to minimize the gaps of memory between adjacent array or record components. The pragma OPTIMIZE can be used to indicate whether code execution speed or code size is the most important criterion for generating code.

8.9 Exercises

1. Rewrite the INPUT_DEVICE_HANDLER so that it uses the "polling" method of servicing its device. (Hint: Consider using the delay statement.)

2. A 25 line, 80 column CRT device can display characters in red, blue, green, or a combination. The computer memory is addressed in bytes, and each of the 2000 locations on the display screen is mapped to a 16-bit word in the address range of 1024 through 3022. Bits 0 to 6 of each word indicate the character to be displayed. Bits 8, 9, and 10 indicate if the character will have the attributes red, blue, or green, respectively. All other bits are ignored by the CRT hardware. Describe the CRT in Ada as an array of records that contains the necessary display information. Use representation clauses so that the array object conforms to the physical requirements described above.

3. Given the declarations from Section 2.13:

```
type TRANSACTION_NODE;
type NODE_POINTER       is access TRANSACTION_NODE;
type TRANSACTION_NODE is record

    ...
    NEXT_TRANSACTION : NODE_POINTER;
end record;
```

write a package which makes visible the procedure declaration shown below. The procedure deallocates all records in a linked list of TRANSACTION_NODEs. The parameter passed is an access value which designates the head of the list.

procedure FREE_LIST(HEAD : **in out** NODE_POINTER);

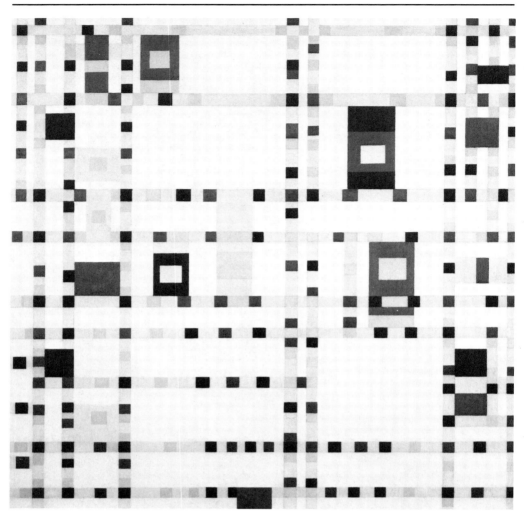

Piet Mondrian. Broadway Boogie Woogie. *1942-43. Oil on canvas. 50 × 50 in. Collection of the Museum of Modern Art, New York*

CHAPTER 9

Compilation: The Big Picture

Although we have presented the various program units in Ada, we have not fully described how these pieces are put together to make an Ada program. This chapter discusses the overall structure of an Ada program, the visibility of names, and the facilities for separate compilation. Before describing the Ada facilities, we briefly survey the overall problem and several past approaches to its solution.

9.1 Physical Modularity

An important feature in any language is the ability to compile a program as physically separate modules. The term *module* is used in this discussion when referring to languages in general; it refers to a portion of a program that can be submitted as a unit to the compiler. In many languages, a module by this definition is a subprogram. As discussed further below, a module is called a *compilation unit* in Ada and is a specification or body of a package or subprogram, or a task body.

Physical modularity can be helpful for small programs, but it is not essential. For large programs, however, physical modularity is central to development and enhancement. A large program typically is partitioned into logical pieces, and each major piece is assigned to one or more programmers. For programmers to be able to develop their assignments independently, the program must be physically as well as logically partitioned. Physical modularity can promote logical modularity.

Although they can be developed independently, the modules of a large program in general are not fully independent. If module A uses declarations given in module B, A is said to *depend upon* B. Typically modules depend upon others because they use objects, types, and subprograms declared in these other modules.

The ability to compile a program in pieces with full compiler checking is called *separate compilation*. In contrast, physical modularity with no compiler checking of module interfaces is called *independent compilation*. Prior to Ada, most common languages supported only independent compilation; that is, they sacrificed compiler checking across module boundaries. Full compiler checking, as noted previously, is important for reliability and early error detection, since module interfaces are a frequent source of errors.

To illustrate, FORTRAN allows subroutines and functions to be submitted as units to a compiler. With the majority of FORTRAN compilers, no checking is performed across different compilations. Thus a subroutine can be called with the wrong number of parameters and with the wrong type of parameters. No compiler diagnostic indicates that the subroutine has been used inappropriately. The way in which such errors are detected (if at all) is dependent on the run-time environment of the application program. At best, the programmer must face a run-time diagnostic that bears no obvious relation to the incorrect call of the subroutine. At worst, the program executes without apparent error and without correct results.

FORTRAN achieves sharing among different modules by the use of "common" blocks. A subroutine shares data with other subroutines by naming a common block in which these data reside. Each subroutine must repeat the declaration of the objects in the common block. As with sharing through subroutine parameters, most FORTRAN compilers do not check that subroutines agree on the order and types of objects in the common block.

Pascal does not support physical modularity. A Pascal program must be compiled as a single, monolithic program, and this restriction clearly is impractical for development of very large programs. Most Pascal implementations therefore define an extension to allow physical modularity. Because compiler implementors often are an opinionated lot, most implementations define physical modularity differently, with the result that programs written for one compiler will not be processed readily by a different compiler. Often the definition sacrifices compiler checking across modules, leaving a wide hole in the Pascal seal of compiler-enforced security.

The C programming language allows an arbitrary group of data and function declarations to be submitted as a unit to the compiler. No checking is performed across different submissions to the compiler. To enable sharing of declarations, C has an "include" directive that is processed before compilation. The "include" directive names a file containing declarations, and this file is copied into the source text of the module that contains the include directive. The declarations in the included file are written once and included in the source files that depend upon them. This technique often is used also with FORTRAN, Pascal, and many assembly languages.

The "include" technique enables sharing and compiler checking, but it can be a problem if a programmer changes the include file, because the modules that depend upon it are not invalidated. Modules compiled with the old include file can continue to be used, although the new version may differ substantially from the old one. An executable program built from such an out-of-date module is likely to contain elusive errors.

With C, this problem is often ameliorated, but not solved, by the use of other tools (such as the "make" utility on UNIX[1]) that determine when a module must be recompiled. To use such tools, the programmer must observe unchecked conventions in developing the program, or must write the tool input, which restates in another form information already available in the program. The fundamental problem is that the validity of the compilation unit is not checked automatically based upon information available directly in the program. Instead, validity is checked by auxiliary tools that rely ultimately on programmer consistency.

One of the main reasons for the inadequacy of prior approaches to physical modularity is that the goal of reliability was sacrificed to the goal of easier, and therefore simpler, compiler implementation. Language designs have been restricted because of compiler technology; in the case of Pascal, one of its stated design goals was a simple compiler. If a compiler is to check consistency between separate compilations, it must retain information about previously compiled modules, so that it may check, for example, the types and number of parameters in a subprogram call. This information must persist across compilations and therefore must reside on secondary storage in the environment of the compiler.

---

[1] UNIX is a trademark of AT&T Bell Laboratories.

Not retaining information about previous compilations makes the compiler simpler, an especially worthy goal when compiler technology was less mature, but it passes the inherent complexity of the problem to the programmer or to other auxiliary tools. Therefore solutions are reinvented with each implementation and more tools are introduced into the development activity to substitute for the compiler shortcoming. Several Pascal implementations, however, have shown that practical implementations of separate compilation are possible.

Ada requires full compiler checking of compilation units, including determining if a compilation unit needs recompilation because a depended-upon unit has changed. *Thus an Ada program developed as several compilation units receives the same compiler checking as one developed as a single compilation unit.* Because separate compilation is defined in the language, a program in multiple compilation units can be compiled readily on any Ada compiler. This portability of the source program is more difficult in a language that does not require separate compilation. Because of the reliability and earlier error detection benefits, separate compilation is a key Ada feature.

9.2 Library Units

An Ada program is divided into compilation units. A compilation unit is one of the following:

1. a package declaration,

2. a subprogram declaration,

3. a generic declaration,

4. a generic instantiation,

5. a package body,

6. a subprogram body, or

7. a task body.

A submission to the compiler is called a compilation and consists of one or more compilation units. These compilations occur in relation to a *program library*. A successful compilation updates the program library with the results of compilation. The program library contains necessary information so that compilation units can use compilation units that have been compiled previously. Using this information, the compiler can check for errors in uses of library units just as it checks a single compilation unit. Only legal compilation units are allowed in the program library: unsuccessful compilation units do not update the library. Conceptually, a program library is a single Ada program or application (although an implementation may achieve sharing of program units among several logically distinct program libraries).

Consider a package specification that contains declarations to be used by several other program units in an automatic teller application.

```
with  CALENDAR;
package  TRANSACTIONS  is

    PASSWORD_LENGTH : constant := 12;

    subtype  ACCOUNT_ID        is  POSITIVE  range  1..1e9;
    subtype  PASSWORD_TYPE  is  STRING  (1  ..  PASSWORD_LENGTH);
    type      DOLLAR            is  delta  0.01  range  0.0..1.0e8;

    DAILY_LIMIT : constant  DOLLAR := 1000.00;

    type  ACTION  is  (CHECKING_DEPOSIT,      SAVINGS_DEPOSIT,
                       CHECKING_WITHDRAWAL,  SAVINGS_WITHDRAWAL,
                       CHECKING_BALANCE,      SAVINGS_BALANCE,
                       SAVINGS_TO_CHECKING,  CHECKING_TO_SAVINGS);

    type  RESULT_TYPE  is  (OKAY, BAD_ACCOUNT, BAD_PASSWORD,
                       INSUFFICIENT_FUNDS, DAILY_LIMIT_EXCEEDED,
                       SYSTEM_ERROR);

    type  TRANSACTION  is  record
        ACCOUNT   : ACCOUNT_ID;
        PASSWORD : PASSWORD_TYPE;
        DATE       : CALENDAR.TIME;
        KIND       : ACTION;
        AMOUNT    : DOLLAR;
        RESULT    : RESULT_TYPE;
    end  record;

end  TRANSACTIONS;
```

If this package specification is compiled, the library is updated to include the results of this compilation. (The details of invoking the compiler and associating the appropriate program library are not defined by the language and therefore depend upon the environment of the compiler.) A package specification such as TRANSACTIONS is called a *library unit*. A library unit occurs at the outermost textual level of the program. A library unit can be a subprogram declaration, a package declaration, a generic declaration, a generic instantiation, or a subprogram body. As discussed below, not all compilation units are library units.

A library unit is available in the program library for use by other compilation units of this program. A compilation unit using TRANSACTIONS is given below:

```
with  TRANSACTIONS;  use  TRANSACTIONS;
package  CUSTOMER_INTERFACE  is
    type  WINDOW  is  limited  private;

    procedure  OPEN  (THE_WINDOW : in out  WINDOW);
    procedure  CLOSE(THE_WINDOW : in out  WINDOW);
```

```
        procedure GET_REQUEST(FROM : in WINDOW;
                                REQUEST : out TRANSACTION);
        procedure GIVE_REPLY  (TO    : in WINDOW;
                                REPLY    : in    TRANSACTION);

    private
            ...
    end CUSTOMER_INTERFACE;
```

To make TRANSACTIONS available, CUSTOMER_INTERFACE mentions it in a *with clause*. The portion of the program preceding the word **package** is called the *context clause*, because it specifies the library units that are available to the compilation unit (i.e., its context). Only the names of library units may appear in a context clause. The context determines the objects, types, and other entities that this compilation unit can reference. CUSTOMER_INTERFACE is said to *depend upon* TRANSACTIONS because it uses declarations given in TRANSACTIONS (e.g., the type TRANSACTION). Although Ada defines no term for the depended-upon units, for clarity we call TRANSACTIONS an *antecedent* of CUSTOMER_INTERFACE.

Because CUSTOMER_INTERFACE uses declarations given in TRANSACTIONS, the specification of TRANSACTIONS must be compiled before CUSTOMER_IN-TERFACE. This order is required so that the compiler has the information necessary to check that CUSTOMER_INTERFACE correctly uses the declarations made available in TRANSACTIONS. Moreover, without prior compilation of TRANSAC-TIONS, the compiler would be unable to generate efficient executable code, because it would have no information about, for example, the size of the type TRANSACTION.

Any number of antecedents may be given in the context clause of a compilation unit, as illustrated below:

```
    with GENERIC_TABLE_MANAGER, ACCOUNTING_TYPES;
    procedure MANAGE_RESTAURANT;

    with APPLICATION_CONSTANTS;
    with PRIMITIVE_TYPES;
    generic
        with function MANAGEMENT_DECISION return BOOLEAN;
    procedure APPLICATION_GENERATOR;
```

Note that the **with** reserved word has a different meaning, depending on where it appears. In the generic formal part shown above, the **with** introduces the specification of a generic formal subprogram parameter; in the context clause, it indicates antecedents.

The CUSTOMER_INTERFACE package specification declares four subprograms that must have bodies supplied for them. These subprogram bodies are given in the package body for CUSTOMER_INTERFACE. Because it implements the declarations in the specification, a package body must be compiled after its specification. Because it is a compilation unit, a package body may have its own context clause. The units named in the body context clause are in addition to those named in the specification context clause.

```
with LOW_LEVEL_IO;
package body CUSTOMER_INTERFACE is
    -- Declarations in TRANSACTIONS and LOW_LEVEL_IO
    -- are available.
    ...

end CUSTOMER_INTERFACE;
```

The body of CUSTOMER_INTERFACE has access to both the units named in its specification context clause and those named in its own context clause, that is, to TRANSACTIONS and LOW_LEVEL_IO.

To maintain information hiding, when a unit names CUSTOMER_INTERFACE in its context clause, only declarations in the visible part of CUSTOMER_INTER-FACE are available to the unit. The body for a library unit is called a *secondary unit*. A secondary unit must be compiled after its specification, and it cannot be accessed by other program units. Only declarations visible in a specification can be accessed outside of a unit, that is, by other units that name it in their context clause.

Because of the requirement that antecedents must be compiled before a given compilation unit, two specifications cannot depend upon one another; that is, circularity is forbidden among specifications. For example, the relationship among the following two specifications is illegal:

```
with LINES;                          -- Circular dependences
package POINTS is ... end;

with POINTS;                         -- are illegal
package LINES is ... end;
```

Circular dependence among specifications is disallowed because it would require each unit to be compiled before the other. This rule is not especially restrictive, however, because a body also may have a context clause in addition to the one given for its associated specification. The bodies of two compilation units can be mutually dependent on the specification of the other. Thus the following compilation units are legal:

```
package POINTS is ... end;

package LINES is ... end;

with LINES;
package body POINTS is ... end;

with POINTS;
package body LINES is ... end;
```

Because the implementation of LINES is irrelevant to POINTS, the body of LINES need not be compiled before POINTS. In general, the body of a library unit must be compiled after its specification, but can be compiled after uses of its specification by other units. A subprogram body alone can be a library unit, in which case the body defines both the specification and the body.

9.3 Subunits

Thus far, we have described the rules governing separate compilation of specifications and bodies. We have seen that specifications are library units and the corresponding bodies are secondary units. In general, the body of a subprogram or package can be so large that compiling it as a single compilation unit is inconvenient.

To enable decomposition of a body into smaller compilation units, the bodies within it can be *subunits*, which can be compiled separately. Within the containing compilation unit, a placeholder, called the *body stub*, stands for the subunit. The compilation unit that contains the body stub is called the *parent* unit.

Three examples of body stub declarations are given below:

```
procedure AUTOMATIC_BANKING_CENTER is
   ...
   procedure GET_REQUEST(REQUEST : out TRANSACTION)
                              is separate;
   package body VAULT_INTERFACE is separate;
   task    body TELLER          is separate;
   ...
end AUTOMATIC_BANKING_CENTER;
```

AUTOMATIC_BANKING_CENTER is the parent unit and it declares three body stubs. A body stub declaration specifies that the body is not provided in this compilation unit but instead will be supplied as its own compilation unit. The subunit is logically nested at the point that the stub appears, but it is physically separate. As the above example illustrates, body stubs can be given for the following:

1. a subprogram body

2. a package body

3. a task body

The visibility for subunits is the same as if the *complete* body were given at the point of the stub. Figure 9.1 illustrates the equivalence of using body stubs to stand for the bodies of nested units.

The important fact about the body stub is that the placement of the stub within the parent unit determines the declarations visible to the subunit. For this reason, the subunit must specify the compilation unit that is its parent (i.e., the body that

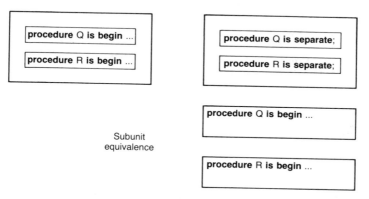

Figure 9.1 Body Stubs and Subunits

contains its stub). The subunit names its parent in a **separate** clause. The separate clause has the general form given below:

separate (PARENT_UNIT_NAME)

For the body stub of GET_REQUEST above, the corresponding subunit has the following form:

separate (AUTOMATIC_BANKING_CENTER)
procedure GET_REQUEST(REQUEST : **out** TRANSACTION) **is**
begin

   ...

end GET_REQUEST;

The corresponding subunits for the stubs of VAULT_INTERFACE and TELLER are similar:

separate (AUTOMATIC_BANKING_CENTER)
package body VAULT_INTERFACE **is**

   ...

end VAULT_INTERFACE;

separate (AUTOMATIC_BANKING_CENTER)
task body TELLER **is**

   ...

end TELLER;

Each of these subunits is submitted separately to the compiler. The separate clause preceding each of these bodies gives the parent compilation unit name.

    The context clause of the subunit also can introduce additional antecedents. For example,

```
with PROCESS;
with TRANSACTIONS;         use TRANSACTIONS;
with CUSTOMER_INTERFACE;  use CUSTOMER_INTERFACE;

separate (AUTOMATIC_BANKING_CENTER)
task body TELLER is
begin
    ...
end TELLER;
```

makes the subunit dependent upon the library units PROCESS, TRANSACTIONS, and CUSTOMER_INTERFACE, in addition to its dependence upon its parent.

Body stubs can be placed in compilation units that are bodies, including subunits. A body stub, however, can only occur immediately within a compilation unit; that is, it cannot be placed within a program unit that is textually nested within a compilation unit.

A potential implementation problem for the program library exists in naming the parent and subunits because of nesting and overloading. Because declarations can nest, the name of a subunit might not be unique in the library. This difficulty can be resolved easily by considering the name of the subunit to be the expanded name of the subunit within the parent. For example,

AUTOMATIC_BANKING_CENTER.TELLER

is the unique identifier of the TELLER subunit. This interpretation of the subunit name resolves the problems for packages and for tasks, because such units with the same name cannot be declared in the same scope.

Overloading remains a problem, however, because the selected name of a subunit also is not unique if the subprogram is overloaded. To resolve this problem, Ada requires that the subunit name of a given compilation unit be unique within that compilation unit. This rule disallows, for example, the following pair of declarations:

```
package body CUSTOMER_INTERFACE is
    ...
    procedure GET_REQUEST(REQUEST : out TRANSACTION)
        is separate;
    procedure GET_REQUEST(REQUEST : out TRANSACTION;
                          FROM : in WINDOW)
        is separate;    -- illegal
    ...
end CUSTOMER_INTERFACE;
```

Although two subprograms with the same name cannot both be subunits of a compilation unit, they can be subunits of different compilation units. For example, both CUSTOMER_INTERFACE and another package body could declare GET_ REQUEST as a subunit.

The relationship among the terms *compilation unit*, *library unit*, *secondary unit*, and *subunit* can be illustrated by the tree diagram in Figure 9.2.

A term in the tree has a descendant when the term includes the concept of the descendant. For example, the term *compilation unit* includes the concepts *library unit* and *secondary unit*.

9.4 Visibility

An important characteristic of a language is the set of places where a name, such as an identifier for a variable, type, or subprogram, can be declared and the places where uses of this name are allowed. As we have noted previously, the places in the program text where a name can be used is called its scope. The name is said to be visible within its scope. A name can be hidden within part of its scope because of nesting. If a name is visible, uses of the name are meaningful. A name is not meaningful, and is therefore illegal, outside of its scope or where it is hidden.

In Ada, the places where declarations can occur are called a *declarative part*. The following Ada entities have declarative parts:

1. a subprogram body

2. a package specification and body

3. a task body

4. a block statement

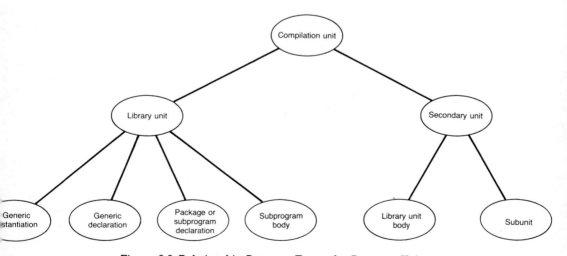

Figure 9.2 Relationship Between Terms for Program Units

A declarative part can contain declarations of other entities, such as constants, variables, subprograms, tasks, and packages.

Like other languages descended from ALGOL 60, Ada allows nesting of scopes, with additional rules concerning overloading and the use of names within other compilation units. Scope nesting means that a program unit may have other program unit declarations nested within it. For example, a subprogram declaration may have a package declaration nested within the declarative part of its body, as the following program fragment illustrates:

```
procedure MAKE_DAILY_REPORT is

    package CUSTOMER_DATA is
        ...
    end CUSTOMER_DATA;

    package TRANSACTION_DATA is
        ...
    end TRANSACTION_DATA;

begin
    ...
end MAKE_DAILY_REPORT;
```

Ada provides several kinds of declarations to simplify use of names. Chapter 3 introduced the use clause. Use clauses permit direct visibility to the names declared within a package. After a use clause within a declarative part, a name declared in the "used" package can be referenced without using the package name as a prefix. For example, the following object declaration uses a type declared in the package CUSTOMER_INTERFACE.

```
MY_CUSTOMER : CUSTOMER_INTERFACE.WINDOW;
```

If a use clause is introduced, the type name need not be prefixed by the package name.

```
use CUSTOMER_INTERFACE;
MY_CUSTOMER : WINDOW;
```

A use clause may also appear in a context clause, in which case the use clause has effect over the entire compilation unit. The only unit names that can appear in a use clause of a context clause are names that also appear in a with clause of the same context clause.

Ada also allows declarations that are renamings of other declarations. Several examples of renaming declarations are given on the following page.

package	FOLKS	**renames** CUSTOMER_INTERFACE;
function	SQRT(X : FLOAT)	
	return FLOAT	**renames** SQUARE_ROOT;
MAX	: DOLLAR	**renames** LARGEST_SO_FAR;
FULL	: **exception**	**renames** QUEUES.QUEUE_IS_FULL;
HANDLE	: NODE_POINTER	**renames** CURRENT.NEXT_TRANSACTION;
		-- See 2.13 for type NODE_POINTER

As these renaming declarations indicate, packages, subprograms, objects, and exceptions may be renamed. In the case of object renaming, the renamed object need not be statically determined. For example, it may be an object designated by an access value, as in the case of HANDLE above. Renaming can be used advantageously to define a shortened name for another declaration. In particular, package renaming is a convenient way to abbreviate a long package name and can be used to ease coding without resorting to the broadly inclusive **use** clause.

9.5 Order of Compilation

The visibility of names imposes an order upon submission of compilation units to the compiler. Ada requires that compilation units be submitted in an order consistent with the context clauses in the units and does not allow a system to be configured if parts of the program are outdated or incomplete.

Units that depend upon a given compilation unit must be compiled *after* the given unit. Without this rule, the declarations in the antecedent would not be available to the dependent unit. For example, the package CUSTOMER_INTERFACE must be compiled after the package TRANSACTIONS, because CUSTOMER_INTERFACE needs to use the type TRANSACTION. Thus the package TRANSACTIONS must already have been compiled into the program library. In general, the library units named in a context clause must already exist in the program library.

Similarly, the body of a library unit must be compiled after its specification. The body contains the implementation for the declarations in the specification, and therefore the specification must be available in the program library before compiling the body. An exception is that a library unit subprogram can be defined by its body alone, without requiring a prior specification. In this case, the body defines the specification. In general, it is good practice to supply an explicit subprogram specification for all library unit subprograms.

A subunit must be compiled after the parent compilation unit that contains the body stub. Because the subunit has visibility to declarations prior to the body stub in the parent unit, the subunit must be compiled after the parent unit; otherwise, names in the subunit that refer to declarations in the parent would be meaningless to the compiler.

The compilation order rules apply to recompilations: If a unit is recompiled, all its dependent units potentially are affected by the recompilation. Thus the dependent units are considered to be outdated and therefore must be recompiled. Similarly, if a parent unit is recompiled, its subunits become outdated and also must be recompiled. (An implementation can avoid the recompilations if it can determine that a potentially-affected unit is not actually affected.)

The Ada rules require the compiler—not the programmer—to keep track of the units made obsolete by a recompilation. *The compiler does not allow an executable program to be made if needed units are outdated*. This automatic detection of errors caused by outdated compilation units greatly simplifies maintenance by eliminating manual tracking, which otherwise would be required.

For example, assume that both TRANSACTIONS and CUSTOMER_INTERFACE have been compiled successfully into a program library. If a programmer changes the declaration of type TRANSACTION (e.g., by adding a component for the customer name) and recompiles TRANSACTIONS, CUSTOMER_INTERFACE becomes outdated. Because it uses a different definition for type TRANSACTION, the previous compilation of CUSTOMER_INTERFACE should not be part of the executable system. In many languages, such outdated units often cause elusive errors. Ada compilation order rules prevent building the executable system with the outdated CUSTOMER_INTERFACE.

9.6 Separate Compilation and Program Design

Program design sometimes is characterized as developing *layers of abstraction* for solving the problem. The highest layers in the program structure are the problem solution in high-level, abstract operations. Lower layers support the higher layers by providing the primitives used to implement the abstract solution. Each layer solves the problem in terms of the operations of a lower-level abstraction. A given layer of abstraction sometimes is called an *abstract machine*. Layers are designed until the required operations are available in the language itself or by simple composition of language operations.

Design methodologies often are characterized by which layers of the abstraction hierarchy they emphasize first. Designing the lower layers first is called "bottom-up" development; designing the higher layers first is called "top-down" development. Note that the order in which components are designed is not necessarily the order in which they must be compiled.

Ada separate compilation allows programs to be developed both bottom-up and top-down as appropriate for the application. Library units directly support bottom-up submission to the compiler. For example, the more basic, lower-level objects and operations are specified as library units, typically as packages. Higher-level units mention the lower-level units in their **with** clause. The specifications for the lower-level units must be compiled before the higher-level abstractions that use them.

Ada subunits permit top-down submissions to the compiler. For example, within a given compilation unit, the bodies of its lower-level abstractions can be specified as body stubs, allowing them to be written and compiled later.

The compilation order rules do not impose a particular design methodology; for example, the dependence among library units does not require that a program be designed bottom-up. Dependence, however, does impose a partial order on the sequence of submission to the compiler.

9.7 Main Programs in Ada

Most programs are composed of many separate subprograms and packages. A program in most languages is defined by a distinguished subprogram, usually called the "main" subprogram. The main subprogram is the one whose execution begins the execution of the entire program. Thus the execution of the main subprogram results in executing the entire program.

In some programming languages, the main subprogram is obvious by inspecting the program. In Pascal, for example, the main subprogram appears textually as the outermost unit in a nested hierarchy of procedures and functions and begins with the keyword "PROGRAM." In the language C, the main function is simply the one named "main."

In Ada, however, the main subprogram is not apparent simply by looking at the program text. Ada programs typically are a collection of compilation units, such as package specifications, package bodies, procedures, and functions. These units are compiled and later linked together to create the complete program. The main program must be a library subprogram, but the rules of Ada do not specify which library subprogram. The main program is identified to the programming environment when making the executable code.

9.8 Programming-in-the-Large

The clear specification of the interconnection of program units in a large software system is crucial to development and enhancement. Prior to Ada, languages provided facilities for building the small units of a large system, but few provided a clear specification of the interconnection between these units. Coding the individual compilation units has been called *programming-in-the-small*. Specifying the interrelationships among these units has been called *programming-in-the-large*.

Historically, the language for programming-in-the-large, if any, has been different than the one used to develop the application itself. This different language is implemented by auxiliary tools, which almost inevitably are reinvented by each development activity and therefore are mutually incompatible. Because the language that expresses the interconnection is not the same as the language in which the program is written, reusability is impaired. Thus to promote reusability and transportability, the interconnection must be *in the source code* and it must be processed by the compiler.

The with clause and the separate clause allow programming-in-the-large in Ada. The dependences are enforced by the compiler, not by auxiliary tools. Because the semantics of the interconnection is defined in the language, Ada programs are more portable and are less likely to contain subtle errors caused by unpublicized or forgotten recompilations. Unlike auxiliary tools, the compiler cannot be bypassed, and therefore the compilation order requirements cannot go unnoticed.

9.9 Package STANDARD

As we have seen, program units can be compiled and placed in the program library. Other units in the library can be accessed by using a **with** clause naming the library unit. The services made available by the named library unit are then available to the using unit. The declarations available within a compilation unit are those either declared directly within the unit itself or those made visible by the context clause or separate clause of the unit.

Compilation units that are library units are considered to be nested immediately within the predefined package STANDARD, which contains the declarations for the predefined types (such as INTEGER), operations (such as "+" for INTEGERs), and exceptions (such as CONSTRAINT_ERROR). Because all compilation units are nested within STANDARD, the declarations for INTEGER, BOOLEAN, and the other predefined entities are directly visible. As with other visible declarations, expanded notation can be used to refer to declarations in STANDARD, as illustrated by the following names:

```
STANDARD.INTEGER
STANDARD.BOOLEAN
STANDARD.CONSTRAINT_ERROR
```

These expanded names are equivalent to using the names INTEGER, BOOLEAN, and CONSTRAINT_ERROR.

9.10 Banking on Ada: Automatic Tellers Revisited

Chapter 3 introduced an automatic banking center, which allows bank customers to deposit and withdraw money, to transfer money between accounts, and to inquire about account balances. Both savings and checking accounts are available. In this section, we develop this application further to illustrate the ideas of Ada program structure. We omit many of the implementation details, such as the low level device interface.

We will refer to the collection of hardware and software that implements the automatic banking center as the ABC. A brief requirements description of the system can be given as follows:

A customer uses the ABC by inserting an identification card into a slot. After the account number encoded on the card is read, the customer is asked to type the password. The ABC then checks that the supplied password agrees with the password stored in its data base (which was illustrated in Section 6.11). Given a valid password, the ABC then asks the user to select a transaction. The available transactions are:

1. Deposit to checking account.
2. Deposit to savings account.
3. Withdraw from checking account.
4. Withdraw from savings account.
5. Inquire about checking balance.
6. Inquire about savings balance.
7. Transfer money from savings to checking.
8. Transfer money from checking to savings.

For a transaction other than a balance inquiry, the customer is prompted for the amount of the transaction. The transaction then is processed by the ABC and a reply given to the customer.

The reply depends upon the transaction. If the transaction is a permissible withdrawal, a money dispenser issues the requested amount. A customer can withdraw a maximum of $1000 within a given 24-hour period. If the transaction is a deposit, the customer inserts an envelope containing the deposit into a deposit slot. The ABC then prints a summary of the transaction.

An Ada program that implements these requirements is composed of four main components. TRANSACTIONS declares the types used by the other components. The procedure PROCESS contains a subprogram to process transactions. The procedure AUTOMATIC_BANKING_CENTER declares a task type, called TELLER, which is the active agent of the system. A package CUSTOMER_INTERFACE provides subprograms to interact directly with the customer by accepting transaction requests and giving replies.

```
-- TRANSACTIONS --------------------------------

with CALENDAR;
package TRANSACTIONS is

    PASSWORD_LENGTH : constant := 12;

    subtype ACCOUNT_ID      is POSITIVE range 1..1e9;
    subtype PASSWORD_TYPE is STRING (1 .. PASSWORD_LENGTH);
    type    DOLLAR          is delta 0.01 range 0.0..1.0e8;

    DAILY_LIMIT : constant DOLLAR := 1000.00;

    type ACTION is (CHECKING_DEPOSIT,     SAVINGS_DEPOSIT,
                    CHECKING_WITHDRAWAL,SAVINGS_WITHDRAWAL,
                    CHECKING_BALANCE,     SAVINGS_BALANCE,
                    SAVINGS_TO_CHECKING, CHECKING_TO_SAVINGS);
```

```ada
type RESULT_TYPE is (OKAY, BAD_ACCOUNT, BAD_PASSWORD,
                     INSUFFICIENT_FUNDS, DAILY_LIMIT_EXCEEDED
                     SYSTEM_ERROR);

type TRANSACTION is record
      ACCOUNT   : ACCOUNT_ID;
      PASSWORD  : PASSWORD_TYPE;
      DATE      : CALENDAR.TIME;
      KIND      : ACTION;
      AMOUNT    : DOLLAR;
      RESULT    : RESULT_TYPE;
end record;

end TRANSACTIONS;
```

The package TRANSACTIONS defines the types and subtypes that are used by other compilation units of the ABC. ACTION enumerates the possible kinds of transactions. RESULT_TYPE is used to indicate the results of transactions. A transaction can be rejected for several reasons, such as a terminated account, insufficient funds, exceeding the daily limit on withdrawals, and because of system errors. TRANSACTION has components for the ACTION and the RESULT_TYPE.

```ada
-- PROCESS --------------------------------------

with TRANSACTIONS; use TRANSACTIONS;
procedure PROCESS(A_TRANSACTION : in out TRANSACTION);
```

The subprogram PROCESS checks A_TRANSACTION for validity and sets the RESULT component of A_TRANSACTION accordingly. It checks for the various conditions that cause a transaction to be rejected.

```ada
-- AUTOMATIC_BANKING_CENTER ---------------------

with TEXT_IO; use TEXT_IO;
procedure AUTOMATIC_BANKING_CENTER is

      task type TELLER is
         entry SHUT_DOWN;
      end TELLER;

      MAXIMUM_TELLER     : constant    :=    10;
      subtype TELLER_RANGE is INTEGER range 1 .. MAXIMUM_TELLER;
      TELLERS   : array (TELLER_RANGE) of TELLER;

      COMMAND : STRING(1..80);
      LAST    : NATURAL;
```

```
    task body TELLER is separate;

begin
    COMMAND_CYCLE:
        loop

            GET_LINE(COMMAND, LAST);
            if COMMAND(1..LAST) = "Shut down tellers." then
                for I in TELLERS'RANGE loop
                    TELLERS(I).SHUT_DOWN;
                end loop;
                exit COMMAND_CYCLE;
            end if;

        end loop COMMAND_CYCLE;

    PUT_LINE("Shut down complete.");

end AUTOMATIC_BANKING_CENTER;
```

AUTOMATIC_BANKING_CENTER is the main program of the entire application. It declares a task type TELLER and an array of 10 TELLERs, which are activated when elaboration of the declarations is completed. The body of AUTOMATIC_BANK-ING_CENTER loops, reading a string from standard input. If it receives the command to shut down the ABC, (e.g., to perform maintenance or repairs) it notifies the TELLERS to shut down when they finish with their customer.

```
    -- CUSTOMER_INTERFACE --------------------------

with TRANSACTIONS; use TRANSACTIONS;
package CUSTOMER_INTERFACE is
    type WINDOW is limited private;

    procedure OPEN (THE_WINDOW : in out WINDOW);
    procedure CLOSE(THE_WINDOW : in out WINDOW);

    procedure GET_REQUEST(FROM : in WINDOW;
                          REQUEST : out TRANSACTION);
    procedure GIVE_REPLY  (TO    : in WINDOW;
                          REPLY   : in   TRANSACTION);
private
    type WINDOW is record
        INTERNAL_VALUE : NATURAL := 0;
    end record;
end CUSTOMER_INTERFACE;
```

```
-- TELLER subunit --------------------------------

with PROCESS;
with TRANSACTIONS;          use TRANSACTIONS;
with CUSTOMER_INTERFACE; use CUSTOMER_INTERFACE;

separate (AUTOMATIC_BANKING_CENTER)
task body TELLER is
    MY_WINDOW : WINDOW;
    REQUEST    : TRANSACTION;
begin
    OPEN(MY_WINDOW);
    loop
        select
            accept SHUT_DOWN do
                CLOSE(MY_WINDOW);
            end SHUT_DOWN;
            exit;
        else
            GET_REQUEST (MY_WINDOW,    REQUEST);
            PROCESS(REQUEST);
            GIVE_REPLY   (MY_WINDOW, REQUEST);
        end select;
    end loop;
exception
    when others = >
        CLOSE(MY_WINDOW);
        accept SHUT_DOWN;
end TELLER;
```

The body of TELLER is a subunit of AUTOMATIC_BANKING_CENTER. It uses the operations provided by CUSTOMER_INTERFACE to interact with the customer. The interaction takes place through a WINDOW, provided by CUSTOMER_INTER-FACE. TELLER first opens its own WINDOW, and then goes into a loop. The loop contains a select statement that either performs a SHUT_DOWN of the TELLER and exits the loop or gets a request from the customer, processes it, and gives a reply.

Below we show only skeletons of the bodies of CUSTOMER_INTERFACE and PROCESS.

```
-- CUSTOMER_INTERFACE body ----------------------

with LOW_LEVEL_IO;
package body CUSTOMER_INTERFACE is

    procedure OPEN (THE_WINDOW : in out WINDOW)
        is ... end;

    procedure CLOSE(THE_WINDOW : in out WINDOW)
        is ... end;
```

```
procedure GET_REQUEST(FROM : in WINDOW;
                             REQUEST : out TRANSACTION)
     is ... end;

procedure GIVE_REPLY  (TO    : in WINDOW;
                             REPLY   : in  TRANSACTION)
     is ... end;

end CUSTOMER_INTERFACE;

-- PROCESS body -------------------------------

  with PASSWORD_DATA_BASE;     -- see Section 6.11
  procedure PROCESS(A_TRANSACTION : in out TRANSACTION) is
     OK_PASSWORD : PASSWORD_TYPE;
     use PASSWORD_DATA_BASE;
  begin
     READ_PASSWORD(CUSTOMER  => A_TRANSACTION.ACCOUNT,
                     PASSWORD  => OK_PASSWORD);
     if A_TRANSACTION.PASSWORD /= OK_PASSWORD then
        A_TRANSACTION.RESULT := BAD_PASSWORD;
     else
           -- Finish processing transaction
           ...
     end if;
  exception
     when CUSTOMER_NOT_FOUND =>
           A_TRANSACTION.RESULT := BAD_ACCOUNT;
  end PROCESS;
```

The relationships among the compilation units are shown in Figure 9.3.

In Figure 9.3, an arc from compilation unit **PROCESS** to **TRANSACTIONS** indicates that **PROCESS** depends upon **TRANSACTIONS**. Dependence diagrams show the relationships among compilation units in an easily understood form.

9.11 Software Components

As we have described, one of the major goals of Ada is to promote reuse of software. Reuse means that previously built program units are applied to a new design; the reinvention of previous work is unnecessary. Reusable components do not automatically follow from the use of Ada; they follow from careful specification and design. Ada, however, provides constructs such as packages, tasks, and generics, to build reusable software more easily. In building program units, designers must place emphasis on providing a complete set of operations in the unit, even if the need for some of these operations initially is not evident. Such generality increases the chances that the unit will be reusable in a subsequent design.

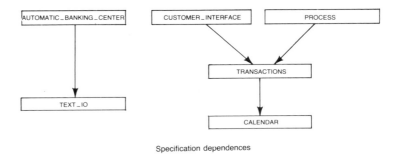

Figure 9.3 Dependence Relationships Among Compilation Units of the Automatic Banking Center

One outcome of reusable software is that libraries of Ada components can be constructed. Software designers can select from a set of standard software components, similar to the way that hardware designers build systems from standard chips. With continuing evolution of VLSI technology and further integration of hardware and software, Ada packages on chips are possible. In this view, Ada package specifications have the role of software chips. Applications can be built from standard Ada components, whether the components themselves are implemented in hardware, software, firmware, or some other technology.

9.12 Summary

Separate compilation refers to the ability to compile a program in different submissions to the compiler with no sacrifice in compiler checking. Separate compilation can be contrasted with independent compilation, which performs no checking across different compiler submissions. Ada separate compilation rules ensure that the compiler fully checks the consistency of separately compiled units and that the compilation units involved are up-to-date.

A submission to the compiler is called a compilation, which is one or more compilation units. A compilation unit is either a specification of a package or subprogram, or the body of a package, subprogram, or task. A compilation that is a specification (or a subprogram body if no prior specification exists) is a library unit. Library units are logically contained in a program library associated with the program. A compilation unit can make available the declarations of an existing library unit by naming the unit in a with clause. The with clauses of a compilation unit define the context of the compilation unit.

The body of a compilation unit can be decomposed further into separately compiled bodies, which are called subunits. Subprogram bodies, package bodies, and task bodies can be subunits. The body (called the parent) declares a body stub for the subunit, indicating that a corresponding subunit is to be supplied later as its own compilation unit. The corresponding subunit body identifies its parent in a **separate** clause. Before the separate clause, the subunit can introduce additional with clauses. These clauses allow further uncoupling of the parent from the additional units needed by the subunit.

The visibility rules define the places in a program where a declared entity (such as an object, type, or subprogram) can be used. Like other languages descended from ALGOL 60, Ada allows nesting of scopes and defines additional visibility rules to account for overloading and context clauses. For nonoverloadable symbols (such as objects, types, and packages), a name in an inner scope hides a name (including overloadable entities) with the same identifier in an outer scope. For overloadable symbols (entries, subprograms, and enumeration literals), an inner name hides an outer name with the same identifier only if the two have the same parameter and result type profiles.

9.13 Exercises

1. If we change the definition of a private type within the private part of a package, must program units that use the previous package specification be recompiled? That is, are the users of the package out-of-date?

2. Reorganize the following procedure to make subunits of Q and F.

```
procedure P is
    procedure Q(I : INTEGER) is
    begin
        ...
    end Q;

    procedure F(I, J : in INTEGER) return INTEGER is
    begin
        ...
    end F;
begin
    ...
end P;
```

Roy Lichtenstein. Drawing for a Modern Painting of New York State. *Leo Castelli Gallery, New York*

CHAPTER 10

Environment:
The Bigger
Picture

A s previous chapters have shown, Ada provides much support for software engineering. A programming language to support software engineering is a foundation for building quality large-scale software. Ada constructs such as packages, exceptions, generics, and tasks are the basis for making reusable software, which can increase productivity and simplify life-cycle maintenance.

Another factor that greatly influences productivity, to a degree at least equal to the programming language, is the programming support environment (PSE). A PSE is the set of software tools used to develop programs in a given language; for Ada, such a set is called an *Ada programming support environment (APSE)*. The purpose of an APSE is life-cycle support. The crucial point is that an APSE supports the entire life cycle, not simply coding, testing, and debugging. The APSE supports software development on the *host computer*, and the developed software executes on the *target computer*. APSE tools use Ada-like concepts, commands, and terminology, rather than requiring awareness of the particular conventions and idiosyncrasies of the host computer.

Traditionally, the tools for building programs have not been well-integrated and have not been designed with the goal of providing full life-cycle support for programming in a single language. Because the tools often support multiple languages, the idea of an *integrated* support environment for a single language has not been widespread in practice. Instead, the tools assume little about the language they support and cannot be considered a PSE, but often are called support software. Typically, support software includes at least an editor for creating programs, a compiler for the development language, and a linker and loader to bind compiled program units into executable code and place it in main memory for execution. Unfortunately, these tools often are the only ones available for program development. Many other tools are useful for life-cycle support, including interactive source language debuggers, pretty printers, and configuration control tools.

The central tool in an APSE is the Ada compiler. The APSE also contains a comprehensive set of tools to support the full life-cycle of large systems. The requirements for an APSE were initially given in a Department of Defense document called "Stoneman" (STONEMAN, 1980).

Ideally, one comprehensive APSE should be used in developing Ada software. Experience with such environments is limited, however, and no consensus has developed about the detailed design of such an APSE. Currently, several APSEs are under development. A single integrated APSE can be expected to emerge from the experience gained from these initial environments. Because APSE technology is evolving, this chapter does not describe specific APSE features but instead emphasizes the overall requirements for an APSE as specified in Stoneman and indicates the common directions of the APSE developments.

10.1 Why Define an APSE?

The reasons for defining an APSE are several:

1. An APSE makes it easier to develop a common set of tools that cooperate and share common assumptions and representations.
2. Programmers can move more easily among projects and development activities.
3. Given an APSE, it is easier to share tools and database objects.
4. An Ada compiler requires interaction with the underlying system for support of separate compilation. The APSE can make the support for separate compilation well suited to the Ada compiler.

10.2 APSE Overview

An APSE is divided into layers, as illustrated in Figure 10.1. The innermost layer is the host computer system. This layer includes the hardware and also may include a host operating system and other support software. The next layer is the kernel APSE (KAPSE) which interfaces with the host system and isolates the remainder of the APSE from the details and idiosyncrasies of the host system. The KAPSE contains a database which is the storage for long-lived information in the

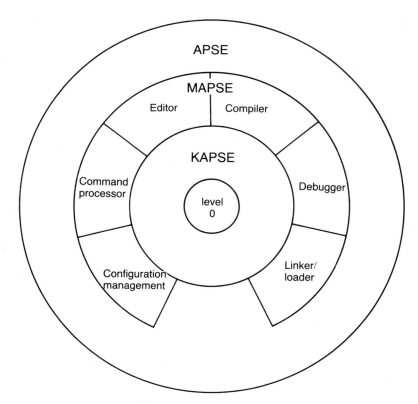

Figure 10.1 Layers of an APSE

APSE. To transport the APSE to another host computer, only the KAPSE must be rehosted; the KAPSE isolates other tools from host dependences.

The minimal APSE (MAPSE) is the collection of tools necessary to build Ada programs. The MAPSE contains support for the entire life cycle, although the support for certain phases, such as requirements analysis, is general-purpose, such as a text editor. The MAPSE includes an Ada compiler (one for the host processor and one for each target processor), an editor, an interactive debugger, a linker, and a command language processor.

10.3 Software Life Cycle

To set the background on the requirements for an APSE, it is helpful to present a brief overview of the software life cycle of large systems. Construction of large software systems usually consists of a blend of different activities, requiring months and often years of effort by a large programming staff. For purposes of abstraction, description, and management control, these activities are divided into phases. The phases of software building are called the *software life cycle*. Most descriptions of the software life cycle, including the simplified sketch presented below, fail to convey adequately the continuous dynamic interplay of activities from all phases. Although actual software building rarely follows the discrete, linear series of events connoted by the term *phases*, the life cycle model nevertheless is useful to characterize the predominant concerns of a given period in the development of a software system.

Descriptions of the software life cycle are similar overall but differ in details. Most include at least the following phases:

1. Requirements Analysis. Experts in the application area consult with computer analysts to identify the functions to be done by the computer. Often hardware engineers are involved cooperatively in designing new hardware.

2. Specification. As an outcome of requirements analysis, analysts develop a specification of the external behavior of the system. The specification gives an external view of the system, without describing how this view is supported internally.

3. Design. A design is developed that provides the behavior described in the specification. The design specifies data structures and algorithms in abstractions appropriate to the application. For Ada, the typical activities of this phase are specifying the subprograms, packages, and tasks that provide the required external view. This phase is sometimes conducted with formal design methodologies and tools. The design may be given in an Ada-based program design language which relaxes Ada rules to allow postponing decisions until the implementation phase.

4. Implementation. The abstractions specified in the design are implemented in Ada. All program unit bodies are coded and compiled successfully.

5. Testing. The implementation is tested in its actual environment or, if the actual environment is impractical, in a simulation of the actual environment.

6. Maintenance and Enhancement. The operational system is improved and corrected as design and implementation inadequacies and errors are exposed in the functioning system. Often the requirements change, and substantial portions of the system must be recoded or completely redesigned and implemented. This phase is often conducted at the operational site rather than at the original host development site.

Each of these phases is often conducted by different teams of personnel. In practice, considerable overlap among phases is characteristic.

Studies have shown that a surprising proportion of the life cycle cost of large embedded systems is in the last phase, maintenance and enhancement. The programming language used to develop the system influences all phases of the life cycle. Ada was developed with the high cost of maintenance and enhancement in mind.

Most support environments have tools to aid implementation, testing, and debugging, even if these tools are not integrated. Few environments, however, contain tools to support the full life cycle, particularly requirements analysis, specification, design, and maintenance and enhancement. These phases have not been, and are not yet, as well understood as the phases directly concerned with coding. Specification and design techniques appropriate to Ada, such as data abstraction, are evolving, and tools to support these techniques will become components of an APSE.

10.4 Host/Target Approach

In discussing development of embedded computer systems, we have distinguished the host system from the target system. The host system is used to develop the embedded computer software and often is a large, time-shared computer that supports many users simultaneously. This system has sufficient resources to enable development of a large software system. These resources include processors, main storage, secondary storage, and peripheral equipment such as terminals and printers.

The host computer can support multiple simultaneous editing sessions, compilations, archiving, and other daily activities of an active project. The reliance on a single, central computer system is being replaced by more distributed computing systems, but the major feature of a host system (i.e., its relatively abundant processing resources) is no different, even if the resources are distributed.

By contrast, the embedded computer, often called the target system because it is the target machine of the compiler, has relatively fewer resources. The term *embedded computer* is used because, in the actual application, the target computer is embedded within a larger, integrated electromechanical system. The larger system typically performs a real-time activity, such as guidance and control for an aircraft.

Because the target system is embedded within a larger system, constraints are imposed on its size, weight, and performance by the larger system. Peripherals often are sensors or other specialized equipment; executable code must be highly optimized to allow processing in real-time and quick response to time-critical events; data commonly must be tightly packed and sometimes must have a format dictated by specialized hardware. Because they must be especially rugged and reliable, embedded computers often are housed within specially-made enclosures, so that they will continue performing in adverse circumstances, such as extreme altitudes and temperatures. The processing resources of the embedded computer generally are well suited to the requirements of the larger system, and as a result the target computer often has little memory and processor power to spare. Due to these factors, the operating environment of the target system often is very different than that of the host system.

In short, the target computer has limited resources and often must respond within microseconds to time-critical events. The host computer, by contrast, has relatively more abundant resources, and its time-critical response merely must satisfy its most impatient users.

The differences between target and host systems sketched above often (but not necessarily) dictate that the two systems have different hardware architectures. In this case the host system must have a cross compiler for the target system. A cross compiler is one that executes on the host system and generates executable code for the target system. The generated code must be transferred by downline loading through a communications link (or by some other means) to the target system for eventual execution. Debugging such code is often complicated by this separation of host and target systems, as discussed below.

10.5 Integrated Environments

Programming environments of interpreted languages historically have been more consistent and integrated than those for compiled languages. As an example, the BASIC programming language has been successful, in part, because it is integrated with a simple programming environment that enables users to edit programs, store files, and execute programs without awareness of a separate file structure, editor, or program linker. The BASIC environment presents the user with a consistent, integrated view of the computer system, albeit a simple one. As a more sophisticated example, several LISP programming environments provide extensive support for LISP programming, including high level debugging, LISP program editors, and typing correction.

10.6 KAPSE

As mentioned above, the KAPSE isolates other APSE tools from the details of the host computer. It contains the support needed to execute Ada programs on the host system. This support is often called the Ada run-time environment; it includes the primitive subprograms defined by the implementation. These primitives vary among implementations, but in many cases include low-level primitives for Ada tasking, exceptions, input/output, and perhaps other basic support.

The KAPSE also provides a database to both APSE users and to executing programs. The database is the central structure in the APSE. It provides long-term storage for project programs and data and is the communications medium among users and tools.

An element in the KAPSE database is termed an *object*.[1] Examples of objects are a requirements document, an Ada source program, tool documentation, and test input data for a tool. An object has contents, which is the information the object holds, and it has attributes, which are meta-information about the object. Attributes convey information to users and to tools, describing both the state of an object and appropriate uses for it. An attribute has a name and an associated value. The KAPSE associates predefined attributes with an object when the object is created. Users also may define attributes and associate them with objects.

The database records relationships among objects. Certain relationships are recorded automatically by tools; others can be established by APSE users. For example, the design, source code, program library, executable code, documentation, and test input data of an Ada program are all related objects. The database maintains the relationships among such objects of an Ada program. The compiler records the relationship between the source program and its program library, and between the program library and the executable code. If the design and the documentation are maintained with the source code, these relationships also can be recorded automatically by tools. In some cases, APSE users may have to establish explicitly the relationships between objects, such as between the executable code and its online help documentation. Relationships may be recorded as attributes of the related objects or they may be recorded structurally within the database.

The three important predefined attributes of objects are:

1. category

2. access control and

3. history

The category attribute indicates the class of objects in which an object belongs. Examples of possible values of the category attribute are "Ada source text," "project schedule," "Ada program library," and "executable tool." The category attribute describes the kind of information an object contains, and thereby indicates the kinds of operations that can be done on the object. In this context, an operation in general is a tool invocation with the APSE object as a parameter. The category attribute therefore is analogous in this respect to types in the Ada language. In the same way that the type of an Ada object determines the meaningful operations upon it, the category of an APSE object determines the tools that can process it meaningfully.

For example, an object with category "Ada source text" can be processed by an Ada compiler, but it is not meaningful for an object of category "project schedule" to be compiled. APSE objects, in this sense, can be considered to be strongly typed.

In general, a tool processes objects of a given category. Some tools, however, can process an object regardless of its category; for example, a tool to rename an

---

[1] The word *object* in this chapter refers to KAPSE database objects unless stated otherwise.

object must be able to process objects of any category within the project. Thus the KAPSE must provide for both strongly typed and weakly typed access.

Access control is another important predefined attribute of APSE objects. The access control *mechanism* determines the kinds of primitive operations (e.g., read, write, execute, and append) available on objects and provides means to permit or deny a given kind of access. The access control *attribute* of an object determines the users (or tools acting on behalf of users) that can access the object using a given primitive operation.

The requirements of large projects dictate that the KAPSE access control mechanism be particularly flexible. In some cases, data and programs may be very sensitive, so that few users are permitted access. On the other hand, sharing and exchange of public or semiprivate objects should be accomplished easily. Regardless of sensitivity, objects should be protected from unauthorized or erroneous access. Many gradations of access control must be provided by the KAPSE, which means that the fundamental KAPSE mechanism must have fine granularity.

If a system is developed by a single programmer, tracking the changes and progress of the system sometimes can be difficult, but often informal conventions regarding source program updates are successful. The programmer simply remembers the state of the system (in this context, "state" refers to degree of completion) and tracks the changes mentally. When a change introduces a new bug, the previous state of the program often can be reconstructed by undoing the most recent changes. If the program is set aside for a while, the detailed evolution is difficult (if not impossible) to reconstruct, making later maintenance and enhancement difficult. The larger the system, the greater is the difficulty.

The problems of tracking system history are far greater if dozens, perhaps hundreds, of programmers are involved in building the system. Coordinating development among many programmers can be exceedingly difficult, and informal conventions rarely, if ever, succeed. Daily editing, compiling, linking, debugging, testing, and tool executions widely alter the state of a project, and the task of reconstructing an earlier state of a project can be impossible.

The KAPSE associates a history attribute with objects to provide the basis for tracking the state of projects. The history attribute records enough information to reconstruct previous states of an object. For a given object, the history attribute records the tools and tool inputs used to create the object. The history attribute is the basis for configuration control tools within the MAPSE.

One of the central requirements of the KAPSE is to promote portability. The Ada language itself has features to support portability, but a language definition cannot cover all the aspects of the programming environment in which the language is implemented. Certain necessary capabilities are simply beyond the scope of a language definition.

An example of such a capability is the ability to invoke a complete Ada program within an executing Ada program. Ada defines subprogram and entry calls within a single program, but it does not define the means to invoke an independent Ada program within a program. Program invocation is an essential capability for certain applications, for example, a command language processor. Without it, it is difficult to compose separately-built tools to perform a combined function. Composition of tools is a very desirable feature in a programming environment.

Moreover, APSE users must be able to suspend or abort executing programs and to resume suspended programs. These facilities, similarly, are beyond the scope of the language definition, yet are very important in an interactive programming environment. To enhance portability of programs that need such capabilities, these facilities are provided by the KAPSE interface.

Another fundamental requirement of the KAPSE is to support *interoperability*. Interoperability is the ability to move database objects between APSEs, maintaining the relationships among the objects, without requiring conversion, manual intervention, or programming new tools. The moved object then can be processed by tools and users on the new host just as it was on its previous host. For example, an Ada program library and its associated objects might be moved between two APSEs that reside on hosts with different architectures and operating systems. The KAPSE database must enable the library to maintain the relationships between the compilation units, documentation, executable code, and other related objects, so that the Ada compiler, documentation tools, configuration tools, and others can use the objects appropriately.

10.7 MAPSE Tools

As stated above, the MAPSE provides a minimal set of tools to support the complete life cycle of Ada programs. MAPSE tools encourage the user to work in Ada language terms, rather than in terms of the host or target machine. These tools, and especially their user interface, should be consistent with Ada and with one another as much as possible, so that the user does not have to learn specialized syntax and conventions for each tool.

The Ada syntax and semantics for declarations, expressions, if statements, loop statements, and other constructs apply to the input languages of MAPSE tools. For example, the command language processor and debugger need similar constructs to control sequencing, declare variables, and so forth. These constructs should be based on the corresponding constructs of Ada.

Interactive languages, of course, should permit compact expression to reduce the typing burden. Because compact expression is not one of Ada's strong points, MAPSE tools generally will relax Ada rules somewhat, such as allowing omission of commas and semicolons in commands. This compromise between the goals of consistency and user-friendliness can cause learning problems for new users, but the productivity advantages make it worthwhile.

10.8 Command Language Processor

One of the main user interfaces to the APSE is the command language processor. It provides the ability to invoke APSE tools and is the user interface to KAPSE services.

Like other MAPSE tools, its user interface adopts Ada constructs where applicable. Many Ada constructs are appropriate to a command language. For example, most command languages allow sequences of commands to be stored in a file to be invoked as a single command. Such a file is often called a "script." In a MAPSE command language, a *command language subprogram* plays the role of scripts. The command language subprogram can be invoked with parameters in a manner similar to Ada subprogram calls.

10.9 Ada Debugger

The MAPSE debugger provides for dynamic analysis and debugging of Ada programs in source language terms. The MAPSE debugger provides the feature typically found in interactive debuggers, such as:

1. tracing

2. breakpoints

3. snapshots

4. single step operation.

Using the MAPSE debugger, the user debugs an Ada program, not a machine language program that has been translated from Ada; that is, the debugger is aware of Ada semantics and mediates between the user view of an Ada program and the executable code generated by the compiler. The user inspects variables by name and sets breakpoints and traces by source statement number.

Given the nature of the Ada application domain, testing and debugging on the final target system are essential. Target debugging varies widely and, in some cases, may be target dependent. Several styles of debugging with regard to the target are possible. If it has sufficient resources available, the target can contain a debugging monitor; a user then debugs on the target, using the APSE debugging interface. In the worst case, the target will have no APSE compatible facilities, and debugging is therefore target and application specific.

10.10 Ada Editor

Although a MAPSE editor may be simply a text editor, a more supportive editor for Ada programming is based upon the syntax and semantics of Ada; that is, the editor is designed to support construction of correct Ada programs. It is specialized for Ada programming rather than being a general-purpose text editor, and is based on Ada constructs rather than upon unstructured text. As an Ada specialist, the editor embodies knowledge of Ada syntax and semantics to help the programmer with clerical details. In addition to (or instead of) commands for manipulating text, it provides commands for constructing and modifying Ada constructs such as loops, blocks, program units, and so forth.

10.11 Configuration Control

The MAPSE provides tools for configuration control. A *configuration* is a collection of objects that comprises a system. A configuration might be a release of a working system or it might be simply a test system for development use. Configurations may differ due to tailoring for a given set of peripheral devices or memory resources.

Configurations may exist as revisions or as versions. A *revision* of a system is a configuration that supersedes previous configurations. Revisions reflect the evolutionary fixes and enhancements of a system. Presumably a new revision includes fixes and improvements to previous revisions and therefore makes them obsolete. A *version* of a system is a configuration that is an alternative to other configurations and does not supersede them. For example, different package bodies for the same package specification could be structured as different versions of the body. These bodies perhaps differ in implementation technique, but they provide the same external behavior and therefore one revision does not supersede another, although one may be the generally preferred version. The preferred version is often the default, so that users who do not explicitly specify a version receive the default version.

The KAPSE provides support for both revisions and versions of objects. Configuration control tools use the history attribute of objects to enable reporting the constituent objects of a configuration and reconstructing previous revisions.

For example, consider the automatic banking application from Section 9.10. To build a configuration for this system, specifications and bodies for each of the library units and subunits (TRANSACTIONS, PROCESS, TELLER, and so forth) must be selected. Each compilation unit may have a history of several revisions. Let us assume, also, that the body of package CUSTOMER_INTERFACE has two alternate versions: one for English-speaking customers and one for French-speaking customers.

Figure 10.2 partially depicts two different configurations referred to as A and B. Configuration A uses the next-to-last revision of procedure PROCESS and the latest revision of CUSTOMER_INTERFACE (version 1). Configuration B uses the latest revision of procedure PROCESS and the latest revision CUSTOMER_INTER-FACE (version 2). It is possible that configuration A is stable and has already been released for commercial use. Configuration B may be undergoing tests for a future release.

A flexible configuration manager allows system builders (the people configuring the system) to select existing configurations and to create new configurations. The builders should be able to dictate easily the versions and revisions to be configured; for example, commands such as "all latest revisions, first versions," or "all latest revisions before October 1," typically are needed.

Conversely, a configuration manager should be able to "unconfigure" a system by recreating the source code of outdated compilation units from which a given configuration was built. For example, after configuration A is released and its revisions are outdated, errors could be discovered. The software supplier then must recreate the source code for configuration A to test and correct it.

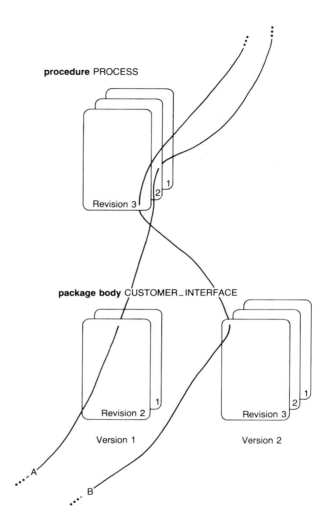

Figure 10.2 Two Configurations for Automatic Banking

10.12 Other APSE tools

An APSE contains tools to support a wide range of methods and projects. It will include support for measurement, verification, documentation, project control, fault reporting, requirements specification, and comprehensive configuration management. The detailed specifications of these tools can be expected to evolve to suit the emerging needs of large Ada projects. An APSE is open-ended, which means that new tools can be added, and these new tools can be used uniformly with existing APSE tools.

10.13 Summary

An Ada programming support environment (APSE) is a layered, integrated, open-ended set of tools to promote Ada programming and life-cycle support. The software life cycle typically is divided into the following phases: requirements analysis, specification, design, implementation, testing, and maintenance and enhancement. The major expense of a large software system often is in the maintenance and enhancement phase. The APSE has built-in support to make all phases of the life cycle more manageable.

An APSE adopts a host/target approach to development. The host system is the computer system upon which the APSE itself executes. The target system is the system for which an application is developed.

An APSE is divided into three layers: KAPSE, MAPSE, and APSE. The lowest layer is the kernel (KAPSE), which provides a database for long-term storage of environment objects and low-level support for executing programs. The KAPSE is built upon either the host operating system or the bare machine.

One of the primary concerns of an APSE is configuration control, which is the tracking of versions and revisions. A version is a software system related to similar versions but suited to slightly different requirements. A revision is a system that includes fixes or enhancements to previous revisions of the same system. To aid configuration control, the KAPSE maintains the history of database objects, so that it is possible to reconstruct previous revisions of objects.

The MAPSE is the minimal APSE which includes the necessary tools for Ada program development: an Ada compiler, a command language processor, an Ada high-level debugger, and an editor. The APSE provides additional tools, such as configuration control and program analysis tools, for more comprehensive support of the entire life cycle.

10.14 Exercises

1. Because Ada is designed for portability, why is it necessary to define the KAPSE to promote Ada tool portability?
2. Describe the difference between revision and version.
3. Should a command language of an APSE be Ada-like? Describe the advantages and disadvantages.

APPENDIX A

Answers to Selected Exercises

Chapter 1

2. With the Ada style, the programmer must write the dashes prior to every comment line. On the other hand, it is impossible for portions of program text to be "omitted" from the program because the programmer inadvertently failed to close a bracketed comment.

5. Because all possible values of AN_INTEGER_EXPRESSION are not covered by the when clauses. The value of AN_INTEGER_EXPRESSION could be other than 1 or 2. A repair:

```
case AN_INTEGER_EXPRESSION is
    when 1        => ITS_ONE;
    when 2        => ITS_TWO;
    when others  => null;
end case;
```

Chapter 2

3. a. 7
   b. 1024
   c. INTEGER'LAST - INTEGER'FIRST + 1

4. Attributes help to make dependencies upon properties explicit. Given the intent of the previous fragment, the following statement is presently equivalent but is more maintainable, especially if additional planets are discovered, or if certain of the larger asteroids (e.g., Ceres) between Mars and Jupiter are redefined to be planets.

    ```
    for WORLD in PLANET'SUCC(MARS) .. PLANET'LAST loop
    ...
    end loop;
    ```

8. Discriminants may also be used to initialize a record component:

    ```
    type BEING(BIRTH_PLACE : PLANET) is record
        AGE  : NATURAL := 0;
        HOME : PLANET  := BIRTH_PLACE;
    end record;

    subtype EARTHLING is BEING(BIRTH_PLACE = ) EARTH);
    subtype MARTIAN   is BEING(BIRTH_PLACE = ) MARS);

    JOHN_Q_PUBLIC : EARTHLING;                       -- HOME
                                                     -- initially EARTH
    CAPTAIN_QUEST : EARTHLING := (EARTH, 45, MARS);  -- HOME
                                                     -- initially MARS
    X2QYZJPX      : MARTIAN;                          -- HOME
                                                     -- initially MARS
    ```

    Discriminants can be used to constrain a component which itself has a discriminant record type:

    ```
    type FAMILY(COMPANION : PET) is record        -- See Section 2.11
        NUMBER_OF_CHILDREN : NATURAL;
        FATHER             : STRING(1..20);
        MOTHER             : STRING(1..20);
        FAMILY_PET         : HOUSE_PET(KIND = ) COMPANION);
    end record;
    ```

9. 1,2

10. The declaration for R is legal. The declaration for A is not because the component subtype of an array must be constrained. It would be legal, however, to write:

```
        subtype R1 is R(J = > 5);
        A : array(1..10) of R1;
```

11. Only the first two assignments are legal. The other two are illegal because A, C, and D all have different types. In particular, the type of A is UA, whereas C and D have different anonymous types.

13. Here is one approach, using variants:

```
        type DOLLAR_LIST is array (INTEGER range <>) of DOLLAR;
        subtype YEAR is POSITIVE range 1984..2000;

        type YEAR_LIST(YR : YEAR) is record
            case YR is
                when 1984 | 1988 | 1992 | 1996 | 2000 = >
                    LEAP_YR_DOLLAR_LIST : DOLLAR_LIST(1..366);
                when others = >
                    NON_LEAP_YR_DOLLAR_LIST : DOLLAR_LIST(1..365);
            end case;
        end record;
```

Chapter 3

2.
```
procedure PAD(N           : in POSITIVE;
              FILL        : in CHARACTER;
              WITHIN      : in out STRING) is
    begin
        if   N <= WITHIN'LENGTH   then
            declare
                K : POSITIVE := WITHIN'LAST - N + 1;
            begin
                WITHIN(K .. WITHIN'LAST) := (1..N = > FILL);
            end;
        end if;
    end PAD;
```

3.
```
type SPACE is array (INTEGER range <>) of TRANSACTION;
type QUEUE_TYPE(SIZE : POSITIVE) is record
    ITEMS : SPACE(1..SIZE);
    HEAD  : POSITIVE := 1;
    TAIL  : POSITIVE := 1;
    COUNT : NATURAL  := 0;
end record;
```

Note that in this definition we are forced to give up the subtype constraints formerly associated with HEAD, TAIL, and COUNT. (Explain.)

8. 1,2

9.
```ada
SIZE : constant := 4;
type SQUARE_MATRIX is array(1..SIZE, 1..SIZE) of FLOAT;
function "*"(A,B : SQUARE_MATRIX) return SQUARE_MATRIX is
    T : SQUARE_MATRIX;
begin
    for A_ROW in 1..SIZE loop
        for B_COL in 1..SIZE loop
            declare
                SUM : FLOAT := 0.0;
            begin
                for J in 1..SIZE loop
                    SUM :=  SUM  +  A(A_ROW,J) * B(J, B_COL);
                end loop;
                T(A_ROW,B_COL) := SUM;
            end;
        end loop;
    end loop;
    return T;
end "*";
```

11.
```ada
function DAY_AFTER(THIS : DAY) return DAY is
begin
    if THIS = DAY'LAST then
        return DAY'FIRST;
    else
        return DAY'SUCC(THIS);
    end if;
end DAY_AFTER;
```

14. The practicality of such a function is questionable but nevertheless illustrative. One definition of "=" would be to say two queues are equal if the queued values are the same and queued in the same order.

```ada
package QUEUE_PACKAGE is
    type QUEUE_TYPE is limited private;
    ...
    function "="(A,B : QUEUE_TYPE) return BOOLEAN;
private
    ...
end QUEUE_PACKAGE;

package body QUEUE_PACKAGE is
    ...
    function "="(A,B : QUEUE_TYPE) return BOOLEAN is
        I       : INDEX := A.HEAD;
        J       : INDEX := B.HEAD;
        A_COUNT : POSITIVE := A.COUNT;
        B_COUNT : POSITIVE := B.COUNT;
```

```
    begin
        while A_COUNT ) 0 and B_COUNT )0 loop
            if A.ITEMS(I) /= B.ITEMS(J) then
                return FALSE;
            end if;
            I := I mod SIZE + 1;
            J := J mod SIZE + 1;
            A_COUNT := A_COUNT - 1;
            B_COUNT := B_COUNT - 1;
        end loop;
        return A_COUNT = B_COUNT;
    end "=";
end QUEUE_PACKAGE;
```

Chapter 4

1. The advantages of exceptions are discussed in several places in the text. There are situations where parameter-passing is more appropriate than exceptions. For example, if the error also has associated information in addition to the nature of the error, which must be returned, a record containing a status flag and the associated information perhaps is more appropriate than exceptions. That is, if the detected error must return more than a status indication, parameter-passing is appropriate. Strictly speaking, the status parameter is more than a status flag, in that it has more structure.

3. The first reraises the same exception that was propagated to this unit. The second converts whatever exception was raised into the exception FATAL_ERROR.

5. The program prints:

   ```
   Exception handled in block.
   Exception handled in P.
   ```

Chapter 5

1. Yes, because a generic formal private type is a formal parameter, not an ordinary private type (which can be declared only in package specifications). A generic formal private type requires no full declaration because it is a generic formal parameter; the actual parameter supplies the full declaration.

3. The first generic specification is more general, because any type that has assignment "=" and "⟨" operations for it can be the actual parameter to ORDER_MAKER. The "⟨" operation must be passed explicitly in the instantiation. The second is less general, because it requires a discrete type as its actual

parameter. Because generic formal discrete types have "⟨" operations defined for them, no "⟨" operation need be included as a generic formal parameter.

5. Add the following declarations:

```
procedure PRINT_YEAR(KEY : NAME_TYPE; INFO : EMPLOYEE_INFO)
is
begin
     PUT_LINE("Employee: " & KEY);
     PUT     ("Year hired: ");
     PUT     (INFO.HIRED);
     NEW_LINE(SPACING = ⟩ 2);
end PRINT_YEAR;

procedure REPORT_YEAR_HIRED is
     new EMPLOYEE.INORDER_TRAVERSE(OPERATION = ⟩
                                      PRINT_YEAR);
```

and the following call in the body of PRINT_REPORTS:

```
PUT_LINE("Year Hired Report");
REPORT_YEAR_HIRED(ROOT_NODE);
```

Chapter 6

3. (a) No, as explained in Section 6.2, subprograms are reentrant.
    (b) One of the calls will occur first and will finish the entry call to QUEUE_TASK.PUT, making the queue full. The second call will get suspended because the selective wait statement in QUEUE_TASK will not accept an entry to PUT until the queue is no longer full.

7. The first part of the exercise is answered. Assume the following two declarations:

```
type INT_ARRAY is array(POSITIVE range ⟨⟩) of INTEGER;
function LARGEST_INT(LIST : INT_ARRAY) return INTEGER;
```

The function LARGEST_INT can be easily written using the same logic as LARGEST_DOLLAR from Section 3.2. Then the following function performs a concurrent array search:

```
function CONCURRENT_LARGEST_INT(LIST : INT_ARRAY)
   return INTEGER is
     LARGEST_ON_LEFT  : INTEGER;
     LARGEST_ON_RIGHT : INTEGER;
     MID_POINT        : INTEGER;

     procedure DO_BOTH_HALVES(LEFT,  RIGHT  : in  INT_ARRAY) is
```

```
        task DO_LEFT;
        task body DO_LEFT is
        begin
            LARGEST_ON_LEFT := LARGEST_INT(LEFT);
        end DO_LEFT;

    begin
            LARGEST_ON_RIGHT := LARGEST_INT(RIGHT);
    end DO_BOTH_HALVES;

begin
    MID_POINT := (LIST'FIRST + LIST'LAST) / 2;
    DO_BOTH_HALVES(LEFT  => LIST(LIST'FIRST .. MID_POINT),
                   RIGHT => LIST(MID_POINT + 1 .. LIST'LAST));
    if LARGEST_ON_LEFT > LARGEST_ON_RIGHT then

        return LARGEST_ON_LEFT;
    else
        return LARGEST_ON_RIGHT;
    end if;
end CONCURRENT_LARGEST_INT;
```

8. A task that calls one of its own entries will deadlock.

9. The accept statement would be abandoned thereby finishing the selective wait statement. The exception would then be raised again after the selective statement and after the entry call in GENERATE_REPORT. Because neither task body has exception handlers, both tasks complete immediately. Assuming neither task created any dependent tasks, they also terminate. The exception does not propagate to REPORT_WRITER. However, this procedure returns as soon as its sequence of statements has been completed.

11. The first two statements are selective waits. In the first case, the task will attempt to rendezvous with a caller, but only if it can do so immediately. If no immediate rendezvous is possible, it will execute the **else** part, which happens to cause a 60 second delay. The second statement is quite different: The task will wait for a caller, but it will wait no longer than 60 seconds. If 60 seconds elapse and rendezvous did not occur, the selective wait is finished.

     The third statement is a timed entry call. Here the task makes a call but withdraws it if rendezvous does not occur within the minute. In the fourth example, a conditional entry call, the task attempts an entry call, but withdraws it if rendezvous is not immediately possible. If no rendezvous can occur, it executes the **else** part of the statement, which happens to delay it for 60 seconds.

13. Yes, for example the text would be legal in the presence of:

```
subtype D is INTEGER range 1..10;
task type TT is
    entry E(D)(N : INTEGER);
end TT;
T : array (D) of TT;
I,J,K : D := 1;
A : array(D) of INTEGER;
```

Chapter 7

1. The following subprogram reads and writes a file of INTEGERs, using TEXT_IO:

```
with TEXT_IO;
procedure COPY_INTEGERS is
    package IO_FOR_INTEGERS is new TEXT_IO.INTEGER_IO(
        NUM => INTEGER);
    AN_INTEGER : INTEGER;
    use IO_FOR_INTEGERS, TEXT_IO;
begin
    while not END_OF_FILE loop
        GET(AN_INTEGER);
        PUT(AN_INTEGER);
        NEW_LINE;
    end loop;
end COPY_INTEGERS;
```

3. The following program unit implements the tree as an anonymous external file which is destroyed after the program completes.

```
with DIRECT_IO;
generic
    type KEY_TYPE      is private;
    type ELEMENT_TYPE is private;
    with function "<"(LEFT, RIGHT : KEY_TYPE) return BOOLEAN is <>;

package BINARY_TREE_MAKER is

    type KIND is private;

    function   MAKE return KIND;
    function   IS_EMPTY(T : KIND) return BOOLEAN;
    procedure INSERT   (T : in out KIND; K : KEY_TYPE;
                        E : ELEMENT_TYPE);
    function   RETRIEVE(T : KIND; K : KEY_TYPE)
                        return ELEMENT_TYPE;
    KEY_NOT_FOUND : exception;
```

```
     generic
         with procedure OPERATION(K : KEY_TYPE;
                                   E : ELEMENT_TYPE);
         procedure INORDER_TRAVERSE(THE_TREE : in KIND);

private
     type KIND is range 0 .. INTEGER'LAST; -- Valid up to
                                           -- TREE_IO.COUNT'LAST.
     type INTERNAL_RECORD is record
         KEY           : KEY_TYPE;
         ELEMENT       : ELEMENT_TYPE;
         LEFT, RIGHT : KIND;
     end record;
     package TREE_IO is new DIRECT_IO(ELEMENT_TYPE =>
                                      INTERNAL_RECORD);

end BINARY_TREE_MAKER;

package body BINARY_TREE_MAKER is

     EMPTY_TREE : constant KIND := KIND'FIRST;
     TREE_FILE   : TREE_IO.FILE_TYPE;              -- the internal file
     CURRENT_RECORD_NUMBER : TREE_IO.COUNT := TREE_
                                   IO.COUNT'FIRST;

     function MAKE return KIND is
     begin
         return EMPTY_TREE;
     end MAKE;

     function IS_EMPTY(T : KIND) return BOOLEAN is
     begin
         return T = EMPTY_TREE;
     end IS_EMPTY;

     procedure INSERT(T : in out KIND; K : KEY_TYPE;
                      E : ELEMENT_TYPE) is
         use TREE_IO; -- For visibility of "+" on TREE_IO.COUNT.
     begin
         if T = EMPTY_TREE then
             CURRENT_RECORD_NUMBER :=
                 CURRENT_RECORD_NUMBER + 1;
             TREE_IO.WRITE(FILE => TREE_FILE,
                     ITEM => (KEY        => K,
                              ELEMENT  => E,
                              LEFT | RIGHT => EMPTY_TREE),
                       TO     => CURRENT_RECORD_NUMBER);
             T := KIND(CURRENT_RECORD_NUMBER);
```

```
        else
            declare
                IS_PARENT : BOOLEAN;      -- Record gets the new child?
                TEMP      : INTERNAL_RECORD;  .
            begin
                READ(FILE  => TREE_FILE,
                     ITEM  => TEMP,
                     FROM  => COUNT(T));

                if K < TEMP.KEY then
                    IS_PARENT := TEMP.LEFT = EMPTY_TREE;
                    INSERT(TEMP.LEFT, K, E);
                else
                    IS_PARENT := TEMP.RIGHT = EMPTY_TREE;
                    INSERT(TEMP.RIGHT, K, E);
                end if;

                if IS_PARENT then   -- Update parent record in file.
                    WRITE(FILE  => TREE_FILE,
                          ITEM  => TEMP,
                          TO    => COUNT(T));
                end if;
            end;
        end if;
end INSERT;




function RETRIEVE(T : KIND; K : KEY_TYPE) return ELEMENT_TYPE is
    FILED_RECORD : INTERNAL_RECORD;
begin
    if T = EMPTY_TREE then
        raise KEY_NOT_FOUND;
    end if;

    READ(FILE  => TREE_FILE,
         ITEM  => FILED_RECORD,
         FROM  => COUNT(T));

    if K = FILED_RECORD.KEY then
        return FILED_RECORD.ELEMENT;
    elsif K < FILED_RECORD.KEY then
        return RETRIEVE(FILED_RECORD.LEFT, K);
    else
        return RETRIEVE(FILED_RECORD.RIGHT, K);
    end if;

end RETRIEVE;
```

```
procedure INORDER_TRAVERSE(THE_TREE : in KIND) is
    FILED_RECORD : INTERNAL_RECORD;
begin
    if THE_TREE /= EMPTY_TREE then

        READ(FILE => TREE_FILE,    -- Read record to operate upon.
             ITEM => FILED_RECORD,
             FROM => COUNT(THE_TREE));

        INORDER_TRAVERSE (FILED_RECORD.LEFT);
        OPERATION(FILED_RECORD.KEY, FILED_RECORD.ELEMENT);
        INORDER_TRAVERSE (FILED_RECORD.RIGHT);

    end if;

end INORDER_TRAVERSE;

begin

    CREATE(TREE_FILE);    -- Create the anonymous internal file.

end BINARY_TREE_MAKER;
```

In many applications, the tree must be preserved after the program completes. To implement this approach, the file name could be "wired in" to the CREATE operation in the package body initialization. Alternatively, it would be useful to add an initialization procedure to the specification, so that calling units could supply a file name. Calling units then would have to add the call to the initialization procedure before using other operations in the package. A finalization procedure also would be needed to ensure that the file was closed before the program completes.

Only the private part of the above specification changed from the version in Section 5.11. Program units that used the earlier specification, however, need not be changed to work with the new implementation, but they must be recompiled, as discussed further in Chapter 9.

Chapter 8

```
1. package body INPUT_DEVICE_HANDLER is
       ...
       task DEVICE_MONITOR;                     -- no entries
       task body DEVICE_MONITOR is
          B : BYTE;
          MASK : constant BYTE :=
              (FALSE, TRUE, TRUE, TRUE, TRUE, TRUE, TRUE, TRUE);
```

```
         begin
           loop
             while not DV.CTRL(FULL) loop
                 delay (0.050);          -- delay 50 milliseconds
             end loop;
             B := DV.DATA and MASK;
             IN_Q.ENTER(TO_CHARACTER(B));
           end loop;
         end DEVICE_MONITOR;
         ...
       begin
           DV.CTRL(INTERRUPTS) := FALSE;
       end INPUT_DEVICE_HANDLER;

  3. package LIST_OPERATIONS is
         -- needed type declarations
         -- other operations
         procedure FREE_LIST(HEAD : in out NODE_POINTER);
       end LIST_OPERATIONS;

       with UNCHECKED_DEALLOCATION;
       package body LIST_OPERATIONS is
         -- other operations

         procedure FREE_NODE is new UNCHECKED_DEALLOCATION(
                               OBJECT => TRANSACTION_NODE,
                               NAME   => NODE_POINTER);

         procedure FREE_LIST(HEAD : in out NODE_POINTER) is
           T : NODE_POINTER;
         begin
           while HEAD /= null loop
             T := HEAD.NEXT_TRANSACTION;
             FREE_NODE(HEAD);
             HEAD := T;
           end loop;
         end FREE_LIST;
       end LIST_OPERATIONS;
```

Chapter 9

1. Yes. Changing the private part changes the package specification, and therefore using units are outdated and must be recompiled.

Chapter 10

1. Ada does not provide all the facilities that are needed in a programming support environment. A major requirement is dynamic binding, which is the ability to call an entire program from within another program. Such a capability is essential to some programs, such as a command language processor. Without a KAPSE, each environment would provide its own program invocation interface, making tools less portable.

3. Opinions vary. The advantages are that many features needed in a command language processor are similar to Ada features; for example, variables, strings, if statements, and loop statements are useful features in a command language. If Ada is used, the command processor is the same as the programming language it supports, which increases uniformity. On the other hand, Ada is a big language and has features that are inappropriate for a command language. The command language inevitably must be a subset of Ada. For increased friendliness of the user interface, the command language also could relax the Ada syntax rules, which decreases uniformity. On the whole, it is probably best to reuse the parts of Ada that are appropriate for a command language, with changes to make the user interface easy to use.

APPENDIX B

Bibliography and Further Reading

Ada. United States Department of Defense. Reference Manual for the Ada Programming Language. ANSI/MIL-STD 1815A. Feb. 1983.

Barnes, J. G. P. Programming in Ada, Reading, MA: Addison-Wesley, 1982. An insightful text by an Ada designer. Examples are well chosen and explanations of Ada rules are clear.

Bohm, C. and Jacopini, G. "Flow Diagrams, Turing Machines and Languages with only Two Formulation Rules," Communications of the ACM 9, 5(May 1966), pp. 366-371. An important paper which proved that structured control statements are sufficient to write any program written with goto statements.

Brender, R. F. and Nassi, I. R. "What Is Ada?," Computer, 14, 6(June 1981), pp. 17-24. Nice presentation of some of key Ada features in a short space.

Brinch Hansen, P. "A Keynote Address on Concurrent Programming," Selected Reprints in Software, IEEE Computer Society, 1980. Makes the point that programming languages should offer features for concurrency and that consistent use of these features should be check automatically by the compiler.

Brooks, F. P. The Mythical Man-Month, Reading, MA: Addison-Wesley, 1979.

Cohen, N. H. "Parallel Quicksort: An Exploration of Concurrent Programming in Ada," Ada Letters, 2, 2(September/October 1982), pp. 61-68. Uses Ada tasks and recursion to implement a concurrent version of the familiar "quicksort" algorithm.

DeRemer, F. and Kron, H. H. "Programming-in-the-Large Versus Programming-in-the-Small," IEEE Transactions on Software Engineering, 2, 2(June,1976), pp. 80-86. Points out the need for a "module interconnection language" to express the relationships among program modules.

Gehani, N. Ada An Advanced Introduction, Englewood Cliffs, NJ: Prentice-Hall, 1983.

Graham, A. K. "Software Design: Breaking the Bottleneck," IEEE Spectrum, (March 1982), pp. 43-50. Argues that the bottlenecks of software productivity will not be eliminated until the development of integrated programming support environments which address all activities involved in software development.

Hibbard, P., Hisgen, A., Rosenberg, A., Shaw, M., and Sherman, M. Studies in Ada Style, New York: Springer-Verlag, 1981. This short book contains an essay on abstraction facilities in modern programming languages, followed by five well-crafted and nontrivial Ada applications.

Hoare, C.A.R. "Communicating Sequential Processes," Communications of the ACM, 21, 8(August 1978), pp. 666-677. Proposes language constructs for communication among concurrent processes which influenced the Ada tasking model.

Hofstadter, D. Gödel, Escher, Bach: An Eternal Golden Braid, Basic Books, New York, 1979. A popular, wide-ranging discourse upon the Godel incompleteness theorem, artificial intelligence, and levels of abstraction.

Ichbiah, J. D., Krieg-Brueckner, B., Wichmann, B. A., Ledgard, H. F., Heliard, J-C., Abrial, J-R., Barnes, J. G. P., and Roubine, O. Preliminary Rationale for the Design of the Ada Programming Language, ACM SIGPLAN Notices (June 1979), Part B. Provides design rationale for many aspects of an early version of Ada. Although Ada changed somewhat since this publication, the changes generally have been consistent with the motivations expressed in the "Rationale".

LeBlanc, R. J. and Goda, J. J. "Ada and Software Development Support: A New Concept in Language Design," Computer, 15, 5(May 1982), pp. 75-82. Some very nice examples of generic program units.

STEELMAN, United States Department of Defense. STEELMAN Requirements for High Order Programming Languages. June 1978.

STONEMAN, United States Department of Defense. "Stoneman": Requirements for the Ada Programming Support Environment. Feb. 1980.

Tanenbaum, A. S. "A Tutorial on Algol 68," Computing Surveys, 8, 2(June 1976), pp. 155-190.

Wirth, N. Algorithms + Data Structures = Programs. Englewood Cliffs NJ: Prentice Hall, 1976.

Wulf, W. A. "Trends in the Design and Implementation of Programming Languages," Selected Reprints in Software, IEEE Computer Society, 1980.

Wulf, W. and Shaw, M. "Global Variable Considered Harmful," SIGPLAN Notices (February 1983), pp. 28-34. Argues that global variables are the goto statements of program data, in their effect on clarity.

APPENDIX C

Predefined Language Attributes

The following appendix is reproduced from the Reference Manual for the Ada Programming Language by permission of the Ada Joint Program Office, OUS-DRE(R&AT). Section numbers in this appendix refer to sections in the reference manual.

P'ADDRESS

For a prefix P that denotes an object, a program unit, a label, or an entry:

Yields the address of the first of the storage units allocated to P. For a subprogram, package, task unit or label, this value refers to the machine code associated with the corresponding body or statement. For an entry for which an address clause has been given, the value refers to the corresponding hardware interrupt. The value of this attribute is of the type ADDRESS defined in the package SYSTEM. (See 13.7.2.)

P'AFT

For a prefix P that denotes a fixed point subtype:

Yields the number of decimal digits needed after the point to accommodate the precision of the subtype P, unless the delta of the subtype P is greater than 0.1, in which case the attribute yields the value one. (P'AFT is the smallest positive integer N for which $(10^{**}N)^*$P'DELTA is greater than or equal to one.) The value of this attribute is of the type *universal_integer*. (See 3.5.10.)

P'BASE

For a prefix P that denotes a type or subtype:

This attribute denotes the base type of P. It is only allowed as the prefix of the name of another attribute: for example, P'BASE'FIRST. (See 3.3.3.)

P'CALLABLE

For a prefix P that is appropriate for a task type:

Yields the value FALSE when the execution of the task P is either completed or terminated, or when the task is abnormal; yields the value TRUE otherwise. The value of this attribute is of the predefined type BOOLEAN. (See 9.9.)

P'CONSTRAINED

For a prefix P that denotes an object of a type with discriminants:

Yields the value TRUE if a discriminant constraint applies to the object P, or if the object is a constant (including a formal parameter or generic formal parameter of mode **in**); yields the value FALSE otherwise. If P is a generic formal parameter of mode **in out**, or if P is a formal parameter of mode **in out** or **out** and the type mark given in the corresponding parameter specification denotes an unconstrained type with discriminants, then the value of this attribute is obtained from that of the corresponding actual parameter. The value of this attribute is of the predefined type BOOLEAN. (See 3.7.4.)

P'CONSTRAINED

For a prefix P that denotes a private type or subtype:

Yields the value FALSE if P denotes an unconstrained nonformal private type with discriminants; also yields the value FALSE if P denotes a generic formal private type and the associated actual subtype is either an unconstrained type with discriminants or an unconstrained array type; yields the value TRUE otherwise. The value of this attribute is of the predefined type BOOLEAN. (See 7.4.2.)

P'COUNT

For a prefix P that denotes an entry of a task unit:

Yields the number of entry calls presently queued on the entry (if the attribute is evaluated within an accept statement for the entry P, the count does not include the calling task). The value of this attribute is of the type *universal_integer*. (See 9.9.)

P'DELTA

For a prefix P that denotes a fixed point subtype:

Yields the value of the delta specified in the fixed accuracy definition for the subtype P. The value of this attribute is of the type *universal_real*. (See 3.5.10.)

P'DIGITS

For a prefix P that denotes a floating point subtype:

Yields the number of decimal digits in the decimal mantissa of model numbers of the subtype P. (This attribute yields the number D of section 3.5.7.) The value of this attribute is of the type *universal_integer*. (See 3.5.8.)

P'EMAX

For a prefix P that denotes a floating point subtype:

Yields the largest exponent value in the binary canonical form of model numbers of the subtype P. (This attribute yields the product 4*B of section 3.5.7.) The value of this attribute is of the type *universal_integer*. (See 3.5.8.)

P'EPSILON

For a prefix P that denotes a floating point subtype:

Yields the absolute value of the difference between the model number 1.0 and the next model number above, for the subtype P. The value of this attribute is of the type *universal_real*. (See 3.5.8.)

P'FIRST

For a prefix P that denotes a scalar type, or a subtype of a scalar type:

Yields the lower bound of P. The value of this attribute has the same type as P. (See 3.5.)

P'FIRST

For a prefix P that is appropriate for an array type, or that denotes a constrained array subtype:

Yields the lower bound of the first index range. The value of this attribute has the same type as this lower bound. (See 3.6.2 and 3.8.2.)

P'FIRST(N)

For a prefix P that is appropriate for an array type, or that denotes a constrained array subtype:

Yields the lower bound of the N-th index range. The value of this attribute has the same type as this lower bound. The argument N must be a static expression of type *universal_integer*. The value of N must be positive (nonzero) and no greater than the dimensionality of the array. (See 3.6.2 and 3.8.2.)

P'FIRST_BIT

For a prefix P that denotes a component of a record object:

Yields the offset, from the start of the first of the storage units occupied by the component, of the first bit occupied by the component. This offset is measured in bits. The value of this attribute is of the type *universal_integer*. (See 13.7.2.)

P'FORE

For a prefix P that denotes a fixed point subtype:

Yields the minimum number of characters needed for the integer part of the decimal representation of any value of the subtype P, assuming that the representation does not include an exponent, but includes a one-character prefix that is either a minus sign or a space. (This minimum number does not include superfluous zeros or underlines, and is at least two.) The value of this attribute is of the type *universal_integer*. (See 3.5.10.)

P'IMAGE

For a prefix P that denotes a discrete subtype:

This attribute is a function with a single parameter. The actual parameter X must be a value of the base type of P. The result type is the predefined type STRING. The result is the image of the value of X, that is, a sequence of characters representing the value in display form. The image of an integer value is the corresponding decimal number; without underlines, leading zeros, exponent, or trailing spaces; but with a one character prefix that is either a minus sign or a space.

The image of an enumeration value is either the corresponding identifier in upper case or the corresponding character literal (including the two apostrophes); neither leading nor trailing spaces are included. The image of a character other than a graphic character is implementation-defined. (See 3.5.5.)

P'LARGE

For a prefix P that denotes a real subtype:

The attribute yields the largest positive model number of the subtype P. The value of this attribute is of the type *universal_real*. (See 3.5.8 and 3.5.10.)

P'LAST

For a prefix P that denotes a scalar type, or a subtype of a scalar type:

Yields the upper bound of P. The value of this attribute has the same type as P. (See 3.5.)

P'LAST

For a prefix P that is appropriate for an array type, or that denotes a constrained array subtype:

Yields the upper bound of the first index range. The value of this attribute has the same type as this upper bound. (See 3.6.2 and 3.8.2.)

P'LAST(N)

For a prefix P that is appropriate for an array type, or that denotes a constrained array subtype:

Yields the upper bound of the N-th index range. The value of this attribute has the same type as this upper bound. The argument N must be a static expression of type *universal_integer*. The value of N must be positive (nonzero) and no greater than the dimensionality of the array. (See 3.6.2 and 3.8.2.)

P'LAST_BIT

For a prefix P that denotes a component of a record object:

Yields the offset, from the start of the first of the storage units occupied by the component, of the last bit occupied by the component. This offset is measured in bits. The value of this attribute is of the type *universal_integer*. (See 13.7.2.)

P'LENGTH

For a prefix P that is appropriate for an array type, or that denotes a constrained array subtype:

Yields the number of values of the first index range (zero for a null range). The value of this attribute is of the type *universal_integer*. (See 3.6.2.)

P'LENGTH(N)

For a prefix P that is appropriate for an array type, or that denotes a constrained array subtype:

Yields the number of values of the N-th index range (zero for a null range). The value of this attribute is of the type *universal_integer*. The argument N must be a static expression of type *universal_integer*. The value of N must be positive (nonzero) and no greater than the dimensionality of the array. (See 3.6.2 and 3.8.2.)

P'MACHINE_EMAX

For a prefix P that denotes a floating point type or subtype:

Yields the largest value of exponent for the machine representation of the base type of P. The value of this attribute is of the type *universal_integer*. (See 13.7.3.)

P'MACHINE_EMIN

For a prefix P that denotes a floating point type or subtype:

Yields the smallest (most negative) value of exponent for the machine representation of the base type of P. The value of this attribute is of the type *universal_integer*. (See 13.7.3.)

P'MACHINE_MANTISSA

For a prefix P that denotes a floating point type or subtype:

Yields the number of digits in the mantissa for the machine representation of the base type of P (the digits are extended digits in the range 0 to P'MACHINE_RADIX - 1). The value of this attribute is of the type *universal_integer*. (See 13.7.3.)

P'MACHINE_OVERFLOWS

For a prefix P that denotes a real type or subtype:

Yields the value TRUE if every predefined operation on values of the base type of P either provides a correct result or raises the exception NUMERIC_ERROR in overflow situations; yields the value FALSE otherwise. The value of this attribute is of the predefined type BOOLEAN. (See 13.7.3.)

P'MACHINE_RADIX

For a prefix P that denotes a floating point type or subtype:

Yields the value of the radix used by the machine representation of the base type of P. The value of this attribute is of the type *universal_integer*. (See 13.7.3.)

P'MACHINE_ROUNDS

For a prefix P that denotes a real type or subtype:

Yields the value TRUE if every predefined arithmetic operation on values of the base type of P either returns an exact result or performs rounding; yields the value FALSE otherwise. The value of this attribute is of the predefined type BOOLEAN. (See 13.7.3.)

P'MANTISSA

For a prefix P that denotes a real subtype:

Yields the number of binary digits in the binary mantissa of model numbers of the subtype P. (This attribute yields the number B of section 3.5.7 for a floating point type, or of section 3.5.9 for a fixed point type.) The value of this attribute is of the type *universal_integer*. (See 3.5.8 and 3.5.10.)

P'POS

For a prefix P that denotes a discrete type or subtype:

This attribute is a function with a single parameter. The actual parameter X must be a value of the base type of P. The result type is the type *universal_integer*. The result is the position number of the value of the actual parameter. (See 3.5.5.)

P'POSITION

For a prefix P that denotes a component of a record object:

Yields the offset, from the start of the first storage unit occupied by the record, of the first of the storage units occupied by the component. This offset is measured in storage units. The value of this attribute is of the type *universal_integer*. (See 13.7.2.)

P'PRED

For a prefix P that denotes a discrete type or subtype:

This attribute is a function with a single parameter. The actual parameter X must be a value of the base type of P. The result type is the base type of P. The result is the value whose position number is one less than that of X. The exception CON-

STRAINT_ERROR is raised if X equals P'BASE'FIRST. (See 3.5.5.)

P'RANGE

For a prefix P that is appropriate for an array type, or that denotes a constrained array subtype:

Yields the first index range of P, that is, the range P'FIRST .. P'LAST. (See 3.6.2.)

P'RANGE(N)

For a prefix P that is appropriate for an array type, or that denotes a constrained array subtype:

Yields the N-th index range of P, that is, the range P'FIRST(N) .. P'LAST(N). (See 3.6.2.)

P'SAFE_EMAX

For a prefix P that denotes a floating point type or subtype:

Yields the largest exponent value in the binary canonical form of safe numbers of the base type of P. (This attribute yields the number E of section 3.5.7.) The value of this attribute is of the type *universal_integer*. (See 3.5.8.)

P'SAFE_LARGE

For a prefix P that denotes a real type or subtype:

Yields the largest positive safe number of the base type of P. The value of this attribute is of the type *universal_real*. (See 3.5.8 and 3.5.10.)

P'SAFE_SMALL

For a prefix P that denotes a real type or subtype:

Yields the smallest positive (nonzero) safe number of the base type of P. The value of this attribute is of the type *universal_real*. (See 3.5.8 and 3.5.10.)

P'SIZE

For a prefix P that denotes an object:

Yields the number of bits allocated to hold the object. The value of this attribute is of the type *universal_integer*. (See 13.7.2.)

P'SIZE

For a prefix P that denotes any type or subtype:

Yields the minimum number of bits that is needed by the implementation to hold any possible object of the type or subtype P. The value of this attribute is of the type *universal_integer*. (See 13.7.2.)

P'SMALL

For a prefix P that denotes a real subtype:

Yields the smallest positive (nonzero) model number of the subtype P. The value of this attribute is of the type *universal_real*. (See 3.5.8 and 3.5.10.)

P'STORAGE_SIZE

For a prefix P that denotes an access type or subtype:

Yields the total number of storage units reserved for the collection associated with the base type of P. The value of this attribute is of the type *universal_integer*. (See 13.7.2.)

P'STORAGE_SIZE

For a prefix P that denotes a task type or a task object:

Yields the number of storage units reserved for each activation of a task of the type P or for the activation of the task object P. The value of this attribute is of the type *universal_integer*. (See 13.7.2.)

P'SUCC

For a prefix P that denotes a discrete type or subtype:

This attribute is a function with a single parameter. The actual parameter X must be a value of the base type of P. The result type is the base type of P. The result is the value whose position number is one greater than that of X. The exception CONSTRAINT_ERROR is raised if X equals P'BASE'LAST. (See 3.5.5.)

P'TERMINATED

For a prefix P that is appropriate for a task type:

Yields the value TRUE if the task P is terminated; yields the value FALSE otherwise. The value of this attribute is of the predefined type BOOLEAN. (See 9.9.)

P'VAL

For a prefix P that denotes a discrete type or subtype:

This attribute is a special function with a single parameter X which can be of any integer type. The result type is the base type of P. The result is the value whose position number is the *universal_integer* value corresponding to X. The exception CONSTRAINT_ERROR is raised if the *universal_integer* value corresponding to X is not in the range P'POS(P'BASE'FIRST) .. P'POS(P'BASE'LAST). (See 3.5.5.)

P'VALUE

For a prefix P that denotes a discrete type or subtype:

This attribute is a function with a single parameter. The actual parameter X must be a value of the predefined type STRING. The result type is the base type of P. Any leading and any trailing spaces of the sequence of characters that corresponds to X are ignored.

For an enumeration type, if the sequence of characters has the syntax of an enumeration literal and if this literal exists for the base type of P, the result is the corresponding enumeration value. For an integer type, if the sequence of characters has the syntax of an integer literal, with an optional single leading character that is a plus or minus sign, and if there is a corresponding value in the base type of P, the result is this value. In any other case, the exception CONSTRAINT_ERROR is raised. (See 3.5.5.)

P'WIDTH

For a prefix P that denotes a discrete subtype:

Yields the maximum image length over all values of the subtype P (the image is the sequence of characters returned by the attribute IMAGE). The value of this attribute is of the type *universal_integer*. (See 3.5.5.)

APPENDIX D

Predefined Language Pragmas

The following appendix is reproduced from the Reference Manual for the Ada Programming Language by permission of the Ada Joint Program Office, OUS-DRE(R&AT). Section numbers in this appendix refer to sections in the reference manual.

Pragma	*Meaning*
CONTROLLED	Takes the simple name of an access type as the single argument. This pragma is only allowed immediately within the declarative part or package specification that contains the declaration of the access type; the declaration must occur before the pragma. This pragma is not allowed for a derived type. This pragma specifies that automatic storage reclamation must not be performed for objects designated by values of the access type, except upon leaving the innermost block statement, subprogram body, or task body that encloses the access type declaration, or after leaving the main program (see 4.8).
ELABORATE	Takes one or more simple names denoting library units as arguments. This pragma is only allowed immediately after the

context clause of a compilation unit (before the subsequent library unit or secondary unit). Each argument must be the simple name of a library unit mentioned by the context clause. This pragma specifies that the corresponding library unit body must be elaborated before the given compilation unit. If the given compilation unit is a subunit, the library unit body must be elaborated before the body of the ancestor library unit of the subunit (see 10.5).

INLINE

Takes one or more names as arguments; each name is either the name of a subprogram or the name of a generic subprogram. This pragma is only allowed at the place of a declarative item in a declarative part or package specification, or after a library unit in a compilation, but before any subsequent compilation unit. This pragma specifies that the subprogram bodies should be expanded inline at each call whenever possible; in the case of a generic subprogram, the pragma applies to calls of its instantiations (see 6.3.2).

INTERFACE

Takes a language name and a subprogram name as arguments. This pragma is allowed at the place of a declarative item, and must apply in this case to a subprogram declared by an earlier declarative item of the same declarative part or package specification. This pragma is also allowed for a library unit; in this case the pragma must appear after the subprogram declaration, and before any subsequent compilation unit. This pragma specifies the other language (and thereby the calling conventions) and informs the compiler that an object module will be supplied for the corresponding subprogram (see 13.9).

LIST

Takes one of the identifiers ON or OFF as the single argument. This pragma is allowed anywhere a pragma is allowed. It specifies that listing of the compilation is to be continued or suspended until a LIST pragma with the opposite argument is given within the same compilation. The pragma itself is always listed if the compiler is producing a listing.

MEMORY_SIZE

Takes a numeric literal as the single argument. This pragma is only allowed at the start of a compilation, before the first compilation unit (if any) of the compilation. The effect of this pragma is to use the value of the specified numeric literal for the definition of the named number MEMORY_SIZE (see 13.7).

OPTIMIZE

Takes one of the identifiers TIME or SPACE as the single argument. This pragma is only allowed within a declarative part and it applies to the block or body enclosing the declarative part. It specifies whether time or space is the primary optimization criterion.

PACK
Takes the simple name of a record or array type as the single argument. The allowed positions for this pragma, and the restrictions on the named type, are governed by the same rules as for a representation clause. The pragma specifies that storage minimization should be the main criterion when selecting the representation of the given type (see 13.1).

PAGE
This pragma has no argument, and is allowed anywhere a pragma is allowed. It specifies that the program text which follows the pragma should start on a new page (if the compiler is currently producing a listing).

PRIORITY
Takes a static expression of the predefined integer subtype PRIORITY as the single argument. This pragma is only allowed within the specification of a task unit or immediately within the outermost declarative part of a main program. It specifies the priority of the task (or tasks of the task type) or the priority of the main program (see 9.8).

SHARED
Takes the simple name of a variable as the single argument. This pragma is allowed only for a variable declared by an object declaration and whose type is a scalar or access type; the variable declaration and the pragma must both occur (in this order) immediately within the same declarative part or package specification. This pragma specifies that every read or update of the variable is a synchronization point for that variable. An implementation must restrict the objects for which this pragma is allowed to objects for which each of direct reading and direct updating is implemented as an indivisible operation (see 9.11).

STORAGE_UNIT
Takes a numeric literal as the single argument. This pragma is only allowed at the start of a compilation, before the first compilation unit (if any) of the compilation. The effect of this pragma is to use the value of the specified numeric literal for the definition of the named number STORAGE_UNIT (see 13.7).

SUPPRESS
Takes as arguments the identifier of a check and optionally also the name of either an object, a type or subtype, a subprogram, a task unit, or a generic unit. This pragma is only allowed either immediately within a declarative part or imme-

diately within a package specification. In the latter case, the only allowed form is with a name that denotes an entity (or several overloaded subprograms) declared immediately within the package specification. The permission to omit the given check extends from the place of the pragma to the end of the declarative region associated with the innermost enclosing block statement or program unit. For a pragma given in a package specification, the permission extends to the end of the scope of the named entity.

If the pragma includes a name, the permission to omit the given check is further restricted: it is given only for operations on the named object or on all objects of the base type of a named type or subtype; for calls of a named subprogram; for activations of tasks of the named task type; or for instantiations of the given generic unit (see 11.7).

SYSTEM_NAME Takes an enumeration literal as the single argument. This pragma is only allowed at the start of a compilation, before the first compilation unit (if any) of the compilation. The effect of this pragma is to use the enumeration literal with the specified identifier for the definition of the constant SYSTEM_NAME. This pragma is only allowed if the specified identifier corresponds to one of the literals of the type NAME declared in the package SYSTEM (see 13.7).

APPENDIX E

Predefined Language Environment

The following appendix is reproduced from the Reference Manual for the Ada Programming Language by permission of the Ada Joint Program Office, OUSDRE(R&AT). Section numbers in this appendix refer to sections in the reference manual.

This annex outlines the specification of the package STANDARD containing all predefined identifiers in the language. The corresponding package body is implementation-defined and is not shown.

The operators that are predefined for the types declared in the package STANDARD are given in comments since they are implicitly declared. Italics are used for pseudo-names of anonymous types (such as *universal_real*) and for undefined information (such as *implementation_defined* and *any_fixed_point_type*).

package STANDARD **is**

type BOOLEAN **is** (FALSE, TRUE);

-- The predefined relational operators for this type are as follows:

-- **function** "="   (LEFT, RIGHT : BOOLEAN) **return** BOOLEAN;
-- **function** "/="   (LEFT, RIGHT : BOOLEAN) **return** BOOLEAN;
-- **function** "⟨"   (LEFT, RIGHT : BOOLEAN) **return** BOOLEAN;
-- **function** "⟨="   (LEFT, RIGHT : BOOLEAN) **return** BOOLEAN;
-- **function** "⟩"   (LEFT, RIGHT : BOOLEAN) **return** BOOLEAN;
-- **function** "⟩="   (LEFT, RIGHT : BOOLEAN) **return** BOOLEAN;

-- The predefined logical operators and the predefined logical negation
-- operator are as follows:

-- **function** "and" (LEFT, RIGHT : BOOLEAN) **return** BOOLEAN;
-- **function** "or"   (LEFT, RIGHT : BOOLEAN) **return** BOOLEAN;
-- **function** "xor" (LEFT, RIGHT : BOOLEAN) **return** BOOLEAN;
-- **function** "not" (RIGHT : BOOLEAN) **return** BOOLEAN;

-- The universal type *universal_integer* is predefined.

type INTEGER **is** *implementation_defined*;

-- The predefined operators for this type are as follows:

-- **function** "="   (LEFT, RIGHT : INTEGER) **return** BOOLEAN;
-- **function** "/="   (LEFT, RIGHT : INTEGER) **return** BOOLEAN;
-- **function** "⟨"   (LEFT, RIGHT : INTEGER) **return** BOOLEAN;
-- **function** "⟨="   (LEFT, RIGHT : INTEGER) **return** BOOLEAN;
-- **function** "⟩"   (LEFT, RIGHT : INTEGER) **return** BOOLEAN;
-- **function** "⟩="   (LEFT, RIGHT : INTEGER) **return** BOOLEAN;

-- **function** "+"   (RIGHT : INTEGER) **return** INTEGER;
-- **function** "-"   (RIGHT : INTEGER) **return** INTEGER;
-- **function** "abs" (RIGHT : INTEGER) **return** INTEGER;

-- **function** "+"   (LEFT, RIGHT : INTEGER) **return** INTEGER;
-- **function** "-"   (LEFT, RIGHT : INTEGER) **return** INTEGER;
-- **function** "*"   (LEFT, RIGHT : INTEGER) **return** INTEGER;
-- **function** "/"   (LEFT, RIGHT : INTEGER) **return** INTEGER;
-- **function** "rem" (LEFT, RIGHT : INTEGER) **return** INTEGER;
-- **function** "mod" (LEFT, RIGHT : INTEGER) **return** INTEGER;

-- **function** "**"   (LEFT : INTEGER; RIGHT : INTEGER)
--   **return** INTEGER;

-- An implementation may provide additional predefined integer types. It
-- is recommended that the names of such additional types end with
-- INTEGER as in SHORT_INTEGER or LONG_INTEGER. The
-- specification of each operator for the type *universal_integer*, or for any
-- additional predefined integer type, is obtained by replacing INTEGER
-- by the name of the type in the specification of the corresponding
-- operator of the type INTEGER, except for the right operand of the
-- exponentiating operator.

-- The universal type *universal_real* is predefined.

type FLOAT **is** *implementation_defined*;

-- The predefined operators for this type are as follows:

-- **function** "=" (LEFT, RIGHT : FLOAT) **return** BOOLEAN;
-- **function** "/=" (LEFT, RIGHT : FLOAT) **return** BOOLEAN;
-- **function** "⟨" (LEFT, RIGHT : FLOAT) **return** BOOLEAN;
-- **function** "⟨=" (LEFT, RIGHT : FLOAT) **return** BOOLEAN;
-- **function** "⟩" (LEFT, RIGHT : FLOAT) **return** BOOLEAN;
-- **function** "⟩=" (LEFT, RIGHT : FLOAT) **return** BOOLEAN;

-- **function** "+" (RIGHT : FLOAT) **return** FLOAT;
-- **function** "-" (RIGHT : FLOAT) **return** FLOAT;
-- **function** "abs" (RIGHT : FLOAT) **return** FLOAT;

-- **function** "+" (LEFT, RIGHT : FLOAT) **return** FLOAT;
-- **function** "-" (LEFT, RIGHT : FLOAT) **return** FLOAT;
-- **function** "*" (LEFT, RIGHT : FLOAT) **return** FLOAT;
-- **function** "/" (LEFT, RIGHT : FLOAT) **return** FLOAT;

-- **function** "**" (LEFT : FLOAT; RIGHT : INTEGER) **return** FLOAT;

-- An implementation may provide additional predefined floating point
-- types. It is recommended that the names of such additional types end
-- with FLOAT as in SHORT_FLOAT or LONG_FLOAT. The
-- specification of each operator for the type *universal_real*, or for any
-- additional predefined floating point type, is obtained by replacing
-- FLOAT by the name of the type in the specification of the
-- corresponding operator of the type FLOAT.

```
-- In addition, the following operators are predefined for universal
-- types:

-- function "*" (LEFT : universal_integer; RIGHT : universal_real)
--   return universal_real;
-- function "*" (LEFT : universal_real;    RIGHT : universal_integer)
--   return universal_real;
-- function "/" (LEFT : universal_real;    RIGHT : universal_integer)
--   return universal_real;


-- The type universal_fixed is predefined. The only operators declared for
-- this type are

-- function "*" (LEFT : any_fixed_point_type;
--               RIGHT : any_fixed_point_type) return universal_fixed;
-- function "/" (LEFT : any_fixed_point_type;
--               RIGHT : any_fixed_point_type) return universal_fixed;


-- The following characters form the standard ASCII character set.
-- Character literals corresponding to control characters are not identifiers;
-- they are indicated in italics in this definition.

type CHARACTER is

    (nul,  soh,  stx,  etx,     eot,  enq,  ack,  bel,
     bs,   ht,   lf,   vt,      ff,   cr,   so,   si,
     dle,  dc1,  dc2,  dc3,     dc4,  nak,  syn,  etb,
     can,  em,   sub,  esc,     fs,   gs,   rs,   us,

     ' ',  '!',  '"',  '#',     '$',  '%',  '&',  ''',
     '(',  ')',  '*',  '+',     ',',  '-',  '.',  '/',
     '0',  '1',  '2',  '3',     '4',  '5',  '6',  '7',
     '8',  '9',  ':',  ';',     '<',  '=',  '>',  '?',

     '@',  'A',  'B',  'C',     'D',  'E',  'F',  'G',
     'H',  'I',  'J',  'K',     'L',  'M',  'N',  'O',
     'P',  'Q',  'R',  'S',     'T',  'U',  'V',  'W',
     'X',  'Y',  'Z',  '[',     '\',  ']',  '^',  '_',

     '`',  'a',  'b',  'c',     'd',  'e',  'f',  'g',
     'h',  'i',  'j',  'k',     'l',  'm',  'n',  'o',
     'p',  'q',  'r',  's',     't',  'u',  'v',  'w',
     'x',  'y',  'z',  '{',     '|',  '}',  '~',  del );
```

for CHARACTER **use** --   128 ASCII character set without holes
(0, 1, 2, 3, 4, 5, ..., 125, 126, 127);

-- The predefined operators for the type CHARACTER are the same
-- as for any enumeration type.

package ASCII **is**

-- Control characters:

NUL	: **constant** CHARACTER := *nul*;	SOH	: **constant** CHARACTER := *soh*;
STX	: **constant** CHARACTER := *stx*;	ETX	: **constant** CHARACTER := *etx*;
EOT	: **constant** CHARACTER := *eot*;	ENQ	: **constant** CHARACTER := *enq*;
ACK	: **constant** CHARACTER := *ack*;	BEL	: **constant** CHARACTER := *bel*;
BS	: **constant** CHARACTER := *bs*;	HT	: **constant** CHARACTER := *ht*;
LF	: **constant** CHARACTER := *lf*;	VT	: **constant** CHARACTER := *vt*;
FF	: **constant** CHARACTER := *ff*;	CR	: **constant** CHARACTER := *cr*;
SO	: **constant** CHARACTER := *so*;	SI	: **constant** CHARACTER := *si*;
DLE	: **constant** CHARACTER := *dle*;	DC1	: **constant** CHARACTER := *dc1*;
DC2	: **constant** CHARACTER := *dc2*;	DC3	: **constant** CHARACTER := *dc3*;
DC4	: **constant** CHARACTER := *dc4*;	NAK	: **constant** CHARACTER := *nak*;
SYN	: **constant** CHARACTER := *syn*;	ETB	: **constant** CHARACTER := *etb*;
CAN	: **constant** CHARACTER := *can*;	EM	: **constant** CHARACTER := *em*;
SUB	: **constant** CHARACTER := *sub*;	ESC	: **constant** CHARACTER := *esc*;
FS	: **constant** CHARACTER := *fs*;	GS	: **constant** CHARACTER := *gs*;
RS	: **constant** CHARACTER := *rs*;	US	: **constant** CHARACTER := *us*;
DEL	: **constant** CHARACTER := *del*;		

-- Other characters:

EXCLAM	: **constant** CHARACTER := '!';	QUOTATION	: **constant** CHARACTER := '"';
SHARP	: **constant** CHARACTER := '#';	DOLLAR	: **constant** CHARACTER := '$';
PERCENT	: **constant** CHARACTER := '%';	AMPERSAND	: **constant** CHARACTER := '&';
COLON	: **constant** CHARACTER := ':';	SEMICOLON	: **constant** CHARACTER := ';';
QUERY	: **constant** CHARACTER := '?';	AT_SIGN	: **constant** CHARACTER := '@';
L_BRACKET	: **constant** CHARACTER := '[';	BACK_SLASH	: **constant** CHARACTER := '\';
R_BRACKET	: **constant** CHARACTER := ']';	CIRCUMFLEX	: **constant** CHARACTER := '^';
UNDERLINE	: **constant** CHARACTER := '_';	GRAVE	: **constant** CHARACTER := '`';
L_BRACE	: **constant** CHARACTER := '{';	BAR	: **constant** CHARACTER := '	';
R_BRACE	: **constant** CHARACTER := '}';	TILDE	: **constant** CHARACTER := '_';

-- Lower case letters:

LC_a : **constant** CHARACTER := 'A';

...

LC_z : **constant** CHARACTER := 'Z';

end ASCII;

-- Predefined subtypes:

subtype NATURAL **is** INTEGER **range** 0 .. INTEGER'LAST;
subtype POSITIVE **is** INTEGER **range** 1 .. INTEGER'LAST;

-- Predefined string type:

type STRING **is array**(POSITIVE **range** ⟨⟩) **of** CHARACTER;

pragma PACK(STRING);

-- The predefined operators for this type are as follows:
-- **function** " = "   (LEFT, RIGHT : STRING) **return** BOOLEAN;
-- **function** "/ = "   (LEFT, RIGHT : STRING) **return** BOOLEAN;
-- **function** "⟨"   (LEFT, RIGHT : STRING) **return** BOOLEAN;
-- **function** "⟨ = "   (LEFT, RIGHT : STRING) **return** BOOLEAN;
-- **function** "⟩"   (LEFT, RIGHT : STRING) **return** BOOLEAN;
-- **function** "⟩ = "   (LEFT, RIGHT : STRING) **return** BOOLEAN;

-- **function** "&" (LEFT : STRING;   RIGHT : STRING)
--   **return** STRING;
-- **function** "&" (LEFT : CHARACTER; RIGHT : STRING)
--   **return** STRING;
-- **function** "&" (LEFT : STRING;   RIGHT : CHARACTER)
--   **return** STRING;
-- **function** "&" (LEFT : CHARACTER; RIGHT : CHARACTER)
--   **return** STRING;

       type DURATION **is delta** *implementation_defined*
                range *implementation_defined*;

-- The predefined operators for the type DURATION are the same
-- as for any fixed point type.

-- The predefined exceptions:

CONSTRAINT_ERROR   : **exception**;
NUMERIC_ERROR   : **exception**;
PROGRAM_ERROR   : **exception**;
STORAGE_ERROR   : **exception**;
TASKING_ERROR   : **exception**;

end STANDARD;

Certain aspects of the predefined entities cannot be completely described in the language itself. For example, although the enumeration type BOOLEAN can be written showing the two enumeration literals FALSE and TRUE, the short-circuit control forms cannot be expressed in the language.

Note:

The language definition predefines the following library units:

- The package CALENDAR   (see 9.6)

- The package SYSTEM   (see 13.7)
- The package MACHINE_CODE (if provided)   (see 13.8)
- The generic procedure UNCHECKED_DEALLOCATION   (see 13.10.1)
- The generic function UNCHECKED_CONVERSION   (see 13.10.2)

- The generic package SEQUENTIAL_IO   (see 14.2.3)
- The generic package DIRECT_IO   (see 14.2.5)
- The package TEXT_IO   (see 14.3.10)
- The package IO_EXCEPTIONS   (see 14.5)
- The package LOW_LEVEL_IO   (see 14.6)

Glossary

The following appendix is reproduced from the Reference Manual for the Ada Programming Language by permission of the Ada Joint Program Office, OUS-DRE(R&AT). Section numbers in this appendix refer to sections in the reference manual.

This appendix is informative and is not part of the standard definition of the Ada programming language. Italicized terms in the abbreviated descriptions below either have glossary entries themselves or are described in entries for related terms.

Accept statement. See *entry*.

Access type. A value of an access type (an *access value*) is either a null value, or a value that *designates* an *object* created by an allocator. The designated object can be read and updated via the access value. The definition of an access type specifies the type of the objects designated by values of the access type. See also *collection*.

Actual parameter. See *parameter*.

Aggregate. The evaluation of an aggregate yields a value of a *composite type*. The value is specified by giving the value of each of the *components*. Either *positional association* or *named association* may be used to indicate which value is associated with which component.

Allocator. The evaluation of an allocator creates an *object* and returns a new *access value* which designates the object.

Array type. A value of an array type consists of *components* which are all of the same *subtype* (and hence, of the same type). Each component is uniquely distinguished by an index (for a one-dimensional array) or by a sequence of indices (for a multidimensional array). Each index must be a value of a *discrete type* and must lie in the correct index *range*.

Assignment. Assignment is the *operation* that replaces the current value of a *variable* by a new value. An *assignment statement* specifies a variable on the left, and on the right, an *expression* whose value is to be the new value of the variable.

Attribute. The evaluation of an attribute yields a predefined characteristic of a named entity; some attributes are *functions*.

Block statement. A block statement is a single statement that may contain a sequence of statements. It may also include a *declarative part*, and *exception handlers*; their effects are local to the block statement.

Body. A body defines the execution of a *subprogram, package, or task*. A *body stub* is a form of body that indicates that this execution is defined in a separately compiled *subunit*.

Collection. A collection is the entire set of *objects* created by evaluation of *allocators* for an *access* type.

Compilation unit. A compilation unit is the *declaration* or the *body* of a *program unit*, presented for compilation as an independent text. It is optionally preceded by a *context clause*, naming other compilation units upon which it depends by means of one more *with clauses*.

Component. A component is a value that is a part of a larger value, or an *object* that is part of a larger object.

Composite type. A composite type is one whose values have *components*. There are two kinds of composite type: *array types* and *record types*.

Constant. See *object*.

Constraint. A constraint determines a subset of the values of a *type*. A value in that subset *satisfies* the constraint.

Context clause. See *compilation unit*.

Declaration. A declaration associates an identifier (or some other notation) with an entity. This association is in effect within a region of text called the *scope* of the declaration. Within the scope of a declaration, there are places where it is possible to use the identifier to refer to the associated declared entity. At such places the identifier is said to be a *simple name* of the entity; the *name* is said to *denote* the associated entity.

Declarative Part. A declarative part is a sequence of *declarations*. It may also contain related information such as *subprogram bodies* and representation clauses.

Denote. See *declaration*.

Derived Type. A derived type is a *type* whose operations and values are replicas of those of an existing type. The existing type is called the *parent type* of the derived type.

Designate. See *access type, task*.

Direct visibility. See *visibility*.

Discrete Type. A discrete type is a *type* which has an ordered set of distinct values. The discrete types are the *enumeration* and *integer types*. Discrete types are used for indexing and iteration, and for choices in case statements and record *variants*.

Discriminant. A discriminant is a distinguished *component* of an *object* or value of a *record type*. The subtypes of other components, or even their presence or absence, may depend on the value of the discriminant.

Discriminant constraint. A discriminant constraint on a *record type* or *private type* specifies a value for each *discriminant* of the *type*.

Elaboration. The elaboration of a *declaration* is the process by which the declaration achieves its effect (such as creating an *object*); this process occurs during program execution.

Entry. An entry is used for communication between *tasks*. Externally, an entry is called just as a *subprogram* is called; its internal behavior is specified by one or more *accept statements* specifying the actions to be performed when the entry is called.

Enumeration type. An enumeration type is a *discrete type* whose values are represented by enumeration literals which are given explicitly in the *type declaration*. These enumeration literals are either *identifiers* or *character literals*.

Evaluation. The evaluation of an *expression* is the process by which the value of the expression is computed. This process occurs during program execution.

Exception. An exception is an error situation which may arise during program execution. To *raise* an exception is to abandon normal program execution so as to signal that the error has taken place. An *exception handler* is a portion of program text specifying a response to the exception. Execution of such a program text is called *handling* the exception.

Expanded name. An expanded name *denotes* an entity which is *declared* immediately within some construct. An expanded name has the form of a *selected component*: the *prefix* denotes the construct (a *program unit*; or a *block*, loop, or *accept statement*); the *selector* is the *simple name* of the entity.

Expression. An expression defines the computation of a value.

Fixed point type. See *real type*.

Floating point type. See *real type*.

Formal parameter. See *parameter*.

Function. See *subprogram*.

Generic unit. A generic unit is a template either for a set of *subprograms* or for a set of *packages*. A subprogram or package created using the template is called an *instance* of the generic unit. A *generic instantiation* is the kind of *declaration* that creates an instance. A generic unit is written as a subprogram or package but with the specification prefixed by a *generic formal part* which may declare *generic formal parameters.* A generic formal parameter is either a *type*, a *subprogram*, or an *object*. A generic unit is one of the kinds of *program unit*.

Handler. See *exception*.

Index. See *array type*.

Index constraint. An index constraint for an *array type* specifies the lower and upper bounds for each index *range* of the array type.

Indexed component. An indexed component *denotes* a *component* in an *array*. It is a form of *name* containing *expressions* which specify the values of the *indices* of the array component. An indexed component may also denote an *entry* in a family of entries.

Instance. See *generic unit*.

Integer type. An integer type is a *discrete type* whose values represent all integer numbers within a specific *range*.

Lexical element. A lexical element is an identifier, a *literal*, a delimiter, or a comment.

Limited type. A limited type is a *type* for which neither assignment nor the predefined comparison for equality is implicitly declared. All *task* types are limited. A *private type* can be defined to be limited. An equality operator can be explicitly declared for a limited type.

Literal. A literal represents a value literally, that is, by means of letters and other characters. A literal is either a numeric literal, an enumeration literal, a character literal, or a string literal.

Mode. See *parameter*.

Model number. A model number is an exactly representable value of a *real type*. *Operations* of a real type are defined in terms of operations on the model numbers of the type. The properties of the model numbers and of their operations are the minimal properties preserved by all implementations of the real type.

Name. A name is a construct that stands for an entity: it is said that the name *denotes* the entity, and that the entity is the meaning of the name. See also *declaration, prefix*.

Named association. A named association specifies the association of an item with one or more positions in a list, by naming the positions.

Object. An object contains a value. A program creates an object either by *elaborating* an *object declaration* or by *evaluating* an *allocator*. The declaration or allocator specifies a *type* for the object: the object can only contain values of that type.

Operation. An operation is an elementary action associated with one or more *types*. It is either implicitly declared by the *declaration* of the type, or it is a *subprogram* that has a *parameter* or *result* of the type.

Operator. An operator is an operation which has one or two operands. A unary operator is written before an operand; a binary operator is written between two operands. This notation is a special kind of *function call*. An operator can be declared as a function. Many operators are implicitly declared by the *declaration* of a *type* (for example, most type declarations imply the declaration of the equality operator for values of the type).

Overloading. An identifier can have several alternative meanings at a given point in the program text: this property is called *overloading*. For example, an overloaded enumeration literal can be an identifier that appears in the definitions of two or more *enumeration types*. The effective meaning of an overloaded identifier is determined by the context. *Subprograms, aggregates, allocators,* and string *literals* can also be overloaded.

Package. A package specifies a group of logically related entities, such as *types, objects* of those types, and *subprograms* with *parameters* of those types. It is written as a *package declaration* and a *package body*. The package declaration has a *visible part,* containing the *declarations* of all entities that can be explicitly used outside the package. It may also have a *private part* containing structural details that complete the specification of the visible entities, but which are irrelevant to the user of the package. The *package body* contains implementations of *subprograms* (and possibly *tasks* as other *packages*) that have been specified in the package declaration. A package is one of the kinds of *program unit*.

Parameter. A parameter is one of the named entities associated with a *subprogram, entry,* or *generic unit,* and used to communicate with the corresponding subprogram body, *accept statement* or generic body. A *formal parameter* is an identifier used to denote the named entity within the body. An *actual parameter* is the particular entity associated with the corresponding formal parameter by a *subprogram call, entry call,* or *generic instantiation.* The *mode* of a formal parameter specifies whether the associated actual parameter supplies a value for the formal parameter, or the formal supplies a value for the actual parameter, or both. The association of actual parameters with formal parameters can be specified by *named associations,* by *positional associations,* or by a combination of these.

Parent type. See *derived type*.

Positional association. A positional association specifies the association of an item with a position in a list, by using the same position in the text to specify the item.

Pragma. A pragma conveys information to the compiler.

Prefix. A prefix is used as the first part of certain kinds of name. A prefix is either a *function call* or a *name*.

Private part. See *package*.

Private type. A private type is a *type* whose structure and set of values are clearly defined, but not directly available to the user of the type. A private type is known only by its *discriminants* (if any) and by the set of *operations* defined for it. A private type and its applicable operations are defined in the *visible part* of a *package*, or in a *generic formal part*. *Assignment*, equality, and inequality are also defined for private types, unless the private type is *limited*.

Procedure. See *subprogram*.

Program. A program is composed of a number of *compilation units*, one of which is a *subprogram* called the *main program*. Execution of the program consists of execution of the main program, which may invoke subprograms declared in the other compilation units of the program.

Program unit. A program unit is any one of a *generic unit, package, subprogram,* or *task unit*.

Qualified expression. A qualified expression is an *expression* preceded by an indication of its *type* or *subtype*. Such qualification is used when, in its absence, the expression might be ambiguous (for example as a consequence of *overloading*).

Raising an exception. See *exception*.

Range. A range is a contiguous set of values of a *scalar type*. A range is specified by giving the lower and upper bounds for the values. A value in the range is said to *belong* to the range.

Range constraint. A range constraint of a *type* specifies a *range*, and thereby determines the subset of the values of the type that *belong* to the range.

Real type. A real type is a *type* whose values represent approximations to the real numbers. There are two kinds of real type: *fixed_point_types* are specified by absolute error bound; *floating point_types* are specified by a relative error bound expressed as a number of significant decimal digits.

Record type. A value of a record type consists of *components* which are usually of different *types* or *subtypes*. For each component of a record value or record *object*, the definition of the record type specifies an identifier that uniquely determines the component within the record.

Renaming declaration. A renaming declaration declares another *name* for an entity.

Rendezvous. A rendezvous is the interaction that occurs between two *parallel* tasks when one task has called an *entry* of the other task, and a corresponding *accept statement* is being executed by the other task on behalf of the calling task.

Representation clause. A representation clause directs the compiler in the selection of the mapping of a *type*, an *object*, or a *task* onto features of the underlying machine that executes a program. In some cases, representation clauses completely specify the mapping; in other cases, they provide criteria for choosing a mapping.

Satisfy. See *constraint, subtype.*

Scalar type. An *object* or value of a scalar *type* does not have *components.* A scalar type is either a *discrete type* or a *real type.* The values of a scalar type are ordered.

Scope. See *declaration.*

Selected component. A selected component is a *name* consisting of a *prefix* and of an identifier called the *selector.* Selected components are used to denote record components, *entities,* and *objects* designated by access values; they are also used as *expanded names.*

Selector. See *selected component.*

Simple name. See *declaration, name.*

Statement. A statement specifies one or more actions to be performed during the execution of a *program.*

Subcomponent. A subcomponent is either a *component,* or a component of another subcomponent.

Subprogram. A subprogram is either a *procedure* or a *function.* A procedure specifies a sequence of actions and is invoked by a *procedure call* statement. A function specifies a sequence of actions and also returns a value called the *result,* and so a *function call* is an *expression.* A subprogram is written as a *subprogram declaration,* which specifies its *name, formal parameters,* and (for a function) its result; and a *subprogram body* which specifies the sequence of actions. The subprogram call specifies the *actual parameters* that are to be associated with the formal parameters. A subprogram is one of the kinds of *program unit.*

Subtype. A subtype of a *type* characterizes a subset of the values of the type. The subset is determined by a *constraint* on the type. Each value in the set of values of a subtype *belongs* to the subtype and satisfies the constraint determining the subtype.

Subunit. See *body.*

Task. A task operates in parallel with other parts of the program. It is written as a *task specification* (which specifies the *name* of the task and the names and *formal parameters* of its entries), and a *task body* which defines its execution. A *task unit* is one of the kinds of *program unit.* A *task type* is a *type* that permits the subsequent *declaration* of any number of similar tasks of the type. A value of a task type is said to *designate* a task.

Type. A type characterizes both a set of values, and a set of *operations* applicable to those values. A *type definition* is a language construct that defines a type. A particular type is either an *access type,* an *array type,* a *private type,* a *record type,* a *scalar type,* or a *task type.*

Use clause. A use clause achieves *direct visibility* of *declarations* that appear in the *visible parts* of named *packages.*

Variable. See *object.*

Variant part. A variant part of a *record* specifies alternative record *components,* depending on a *discriminant* of the record. Each value of the discriminant establishes a particular alternative of the variant part.

Visibility. At a given point in a program text, the *declaration* of an entity with a certain identifier is said to be visible if the entity is an acceptable meaning for an occurrence at that point of the identifier. The declaration is *visible* by *selection* at the place of the selector in a *selected component* or at the place of the name in a *named association.* Otherwise, the declaration is *directly visible,* that is, if the identifier alone has that meaning.

Visible part. See *package.*

With clause. See *compilation unit.*

APPENDIX G

Syntax Summary

The following appendix is reproduced from the Reference Manual for the Ada Programming Language by permission of the Ada Joint Program Office, OUSDRE (R&AT). Section numbers in this appendix refer to sections in the reference manual.

2.1

```
graphic_character ::= basic_graphic_character
    | lower_case_letter | other_special_character

basic_graphic_character ::=
        upper_case_letter | digit
    | special_character | space_character

basic_character ::=
        basic_graphic_character | format_effector
```


2.3

```
identifier ::=
    letter {[underline] letter_or_digit}

letter_or_digit ::= letter | digit

letter ::= upper_case_letter | lower_case_letter
```

2.4

numeric_literal ::= decimal_literal I based_literal

2.4.1

decimal_literal ::= integer [.integer] [exponent]

integer ::= digit {[underline] digit}

exponent ::= E [+] integer I E - integer

2.4.2

based_literal ::=
    base # based_integer [.based_integer] # [exponent]

base ::= integer

based_integer ::=
    extended_digit {[underline] extended_digit}

extended_digit ::= digit I letter

2.5

character_literal ::= 'graphic_character'

2.6

string_literal ::= "{graphic_character}"

2.8

pragma ::=
    pragma identifier [(argument_association {, argument_association})];

argument_association ::=
    [*argument*_identifier =⟩] name
    I [*argument*_identifier =⟩] expression

3.1

basic_declaration ::=
           object_declaration   I number_declaration
      I type_declaration   I subtype_declaration
      I subprogram_declaration I package_declaration
      I task_declaration   I generic_declaration
      I exception_declaration   I generic_instantiation
      I renaming_declaration   I deferred_constant_declaration

3.2

object_declaration ::=
      identifier_list : [**constant**] subtype_indication [:= expression];
    I identifier_list : [**constant**] constrained_array_definition [:= expression];

number_declaration ::=
      identifier_list : **constant** := *universal_static*_expression;

identifier_list ::= identifier {, identifier}

3.3.1

type_declaration ::= full_type_declaration
    I incomplete_type_declaration I private_type_declaration

full_type_declaration ::=
  type identifier [discriminant_part] **is** type_definition;

type_definition ::=
      enumeration_type_definition I integer_type_definition
    I real_type_definition   I array_type_definition
    I record_type_definition   I access_type_definition
    I derived_type_definition

3.3.2

subtype_declaration ::=
  subtype identifier **is** subtype_indication;

subtype_indication ::= type_mark [constraint]

type_mark ::= *type*_name I *subtype*_name

constraint ::=
    range_constraint | floating_point_constraint | fixed_point_constraint
    | index_constraint | discriminant_constraint

3.4

derived_type_definition ::= **new** subtype_indication

3.5

range_constraint ::= **range** range

range ::= *range*_attribute
    | simple_expression .. simple_expression

3.5.1

enumeration_type_definition ::=
    (enumeration_literal_specification {, enumeration_literal_specification})

enumeration_literal_specification ::= enumeration_literal

enumeration_literal ::= identifier | character_literal

3.5.4

integer_type_definition ::= range_constraint

3.5.6

real_type_definition ::=
    floating_point_constraint | fixed_point_constraint

3.5.7

floating_point_constraint ::=
    floating_accuracy_definition [range_constraint]

floating_accuracy_definition ::= **digits** *static*_simple_expression

3.5.9

fixed_point_constraint ::=
    fixed_accuracy_definition [range_constraint]

fixed_accuracy_definition ::= **delta** *static*_simple_expression

3.6

array_type_definition ::=
    unconstrained_array_definition | constrained_array_definition

unconstrained_array_definition ::=
    array(index_subtype_definition {, index_subtype_definition}) **of**
                *component*_subtype_indication

constrained_array_definition ::=
    array index_constraint **of** *component*_subtype_indication

index_subtype_definition ::= type_mark **range** ⟨⟩

index_constraint ::= (discrete_range {, discrete_range})

discrete_range ::= *discrete*_subtype_indication | range

3.7

record_type_definition ::=
    record
        component_list
    end record

component_list ::=
        component_declaration {component_declaration}
    | {component_declaration} variant_part
    | **null**;

component_declaration ::=
    identifier_list : component_subtype_definition [:= expression];

component_subtype_definition ::= subtype_indication

3.7.1

discriminant_part ::=
    (discriminant_specification {; discriminant_specification})

```
discriminant_specification ::=
    identifier_list : type_mark [:= expression]
```

3.7.2

```
discriminant_constraint ::=
    (discriminant_association {, discriminant_association})
```

```
discriminant_association ::=
    [discriminant_simple_name {| discriminant_simple_name} =>] expression
```

3.7.3

```
variant_part ::=
    case discriminant_simple_name is
        variant
        {variant}
    end case;
```

```
variant ::=
    when choice {| choice} =>
        component_list
```

```
choice ::= simple_expression
    | discrete_range | others | component_simple_name
```

3.8

```
access_type_definition ::= access subtype_indication
```

3.8.1

```
incomplete_type_declaration ::= type identifier [discriminant_part];
```

3.9

```
declarative_part ::=
    {basic_declarative_item} {later_declarative_item}
```

```
basic_declarative_item ::= basic_declaration
    | representation_clause | use_clause
```

```
later_declarative_item  ::=  body
    | subprogram_declaration | package_declaration
    | task_declaration       | generic_declaration
    | use_clause             | generic_instantiation
```

```
body  ::=  proper_body | body_stub
```

```
proper_body  ::=  subprogram_body | package_body | task_body
```

4.1

```
name  ::=  simple_name
    | character_literal  | operator_symbol
    | indexed_component  | slice
    | selected_component | attribute
```

```
simple_name  ::=  identifier
```

```
prefix  ::=  name | function_call
```

4.1.1

```
indexed_component  ::=  prefix(expression {, expression})
```

4.1.2

```
slice  ::=  prefix(discrete_range)
```

4.1.3

```
selected_component  ::=  prefix.selector
```

```
selector  ::=  simple_name
    | character_literal | operator_symbol | all
```

4.1.4

```
attribute  ::=  prefix'attribute_designator
```

```
attribute_designator  ::=  simple_name [(universal_static_expression)]
```

4.3

```
aggregate ::=
    (component_association {, component_association})

component_association ::=
    [choice {| choice}  =〉 ] expression
```

4.4

```
expression ::=
        relation {and relation} | relation {and then relation}
    | relation {or relation}  | relation {or else relation}
    | relation {xor relation}

relation ::=
        simple_expression [relational_operator simple_expression]
    | simple_expression [not] in range
    | simple_expression [not] in type_mark

simple_expression ::= [unary_adding_operator] term {binary_adding_operator
    term}

term ::= factor {multiplying_operator factor}

factor ::= primary [** primary] | abs primary | not primary

primary ::=
        numeric_literal | null | aggregate | string_literal | name | allocator
    | function_call | type_conversion | qualified_expression | (expression)
```

4.5

```
logical_operator   ::=  and | or | xor

relational_operator   ::=  = | /= | 〈 | 〈= | 〉 | 〉=

binary_adding_operator   ::=  + | - | &

unary_adding_operator   ::=  + | -

multiplying_operator   ::=  * | / | mod | rem

highest_precedence_operator   ::=  ** | abs | not
```

4.6

type_conversion ::= type_mark(expression)

4.7

qualified_expression ::=
    type_mark'(expression) **|** type_mark'aggregate

4.8

allocator ::=
    new subtype_indication **|** **new** qualified_expression

5.1

sequence_of_statements ::= statement {statement}

statement ::=
    {label} simple_statement **|** {label} compound_statement

simple_statement ::= null_statement
    | assignment_statement **|** procedure_call_statement
    | exit_statement   **|** return_statement
    | goto_statement   **|** entry_call_statement
    | delay_statement   **|** abort_statement
    | raise_statement   **|** code_statement

compound_statement ::=
      if_statement   **|** case_statement
    | loop_statement   **|** block_statement
    | accept_statement **|** select_statement

label ::= ⟨⟨*label*_simple_name⟩⟩

null_statement ::= **null**;

5.2

assignment_statement ::=
    *variable*_name := expression;

5.3

```
if_statement ::=
    if condition then
        sequence_of_statements
    {elsif condition then
        sequence_of_statements}
    [else
        sequence_of_statements]
    end if;

condition ::= boolean_expression
```

5.4

```
case_statement ::=
    case expression is
        case_statement_alternative
        {case_statement_alternative}
    end case;

case_statement_alternative ::=
    when choice {| choice } =>
        sequence_of_statements
```

5.5

```
loop_statement ::=
    [loop_simple_name:]
        [iteration_scheme] loop
            sequence_of_statements
        end loop [loop_simple_name];

iteration_scheme ::= while condition
    | for loop_parameter_specification

loop_parameter_specification ::=
    identifier in [reverse] discrete_range
```

5.6

```
block_statement ::=
    [block_simple_name:]
        [declare
                declarative_part]
```

begin
        sequence_of_statements
[**exception**
        exception_handler
        {exception_handler}]
    end [*block*_simple_name];

5.7

exit_statement ::=
    exit [*loop*_name] [**when** condition];

5.8

return_statement ::=   **return** [expression];

5.9

goto_statement ::=   **goto** *label*_name;

6.1

subprogram_declaration ::= subprogram_specification;

subprogram_specification ::=
        procedure identifier [formal_part]
    | **function** designator   [formal_part] **return** type_mark

designator ::= identifier | operator_symbol

operator_symbol ::= string_literal

formal_part ::=
    (parameter_specification {; parameter_specification})

parameter_specification ::=
    identifier_list : mode type_mark [:= expression]

mode ::= [**in**] | **in out** | **out**

6.3

```
subprogram_body ::=
      subprogram_specification is
            [declarative_part]
      begin
            sequence_of_statements
      [exception
            exception_handler
            {exception_handler}]
      end [designator];
```

6.4

```
procedure_call_statement ::=
      procedure_name [actual_parameter_part];

function_call ::=
      function_name [actual_parameter_part]

actual_parameter_part ::=
      (parameter_association {, parameter_association})

parameter_association ::=
      [formal_parameter =>] actual_parameter

formal_parameter ::= parameter_simple_name

actual_parameter ::=
      expression | variable_name | type_mark(variable_name)
```

7.1

```
package_declaration ::= package_specification;

package_specification ::=
      package identifier is
            {basic_declarative_item}
      [private
            {basic_declarative_item}]
      end [package_simple_name]

package_body ::=
      package body package_simple_name is
            [declarative_part]
```

```
    [begin
            sequence_of_statements
    [exception
            exception_handler
            {exception_handler}]]
      end  [package_simple_name];
```

7.4

```
private_type_declaration  ::=
      type identifier [discriminant_part] is [limited] private;
```

```
deferred_constant_declaration  ::=
      identifier_list  :  constant  type_mark;
```

8.4

```
use_clause  ::=  use package_name {, package_name};
```

8.5

```
renaming_declaration  ::=
            identifier  :  type_mark    renames object_name;
      |  identifier  :  exception      renames exception_name;
      |  package identifier            renames package_name;
      |  subprogram_specification  renames subprogram_or_entry_name;
```

9.1

```
task_declaration  ::=  task_specification;
```

```
task_specification  ::=
      task [type] identifier [is
          {entry_declaration}
          {representation_clause}
      end [task_simple_name]]
```

```
task_body  ::=
      task body task_simple_name is
          [declarative_part]
      begin
            sequence_of_statements
```

[**exception**
exception_handler
{exception_handler}]
end [*task*_simple_name];

9.5

entry_declaration ::=
entry identifier [(discrete_range)] [formal_part];

entry_call_statement ::= *entry*_name [actual_parameter_part];

accept_statement ::=
accept *entry*_simple_name [(entry_index)] [formal_part] [**do**
sequence_of_statements
end [*entry*_simple_name]];

entry_index ::= expression

9.6

delay_statement ::= **delay** simple_expression;

9.7

select_statement ::= selective_wait
| conditional_entry_call | timed_entry_call

9.7.1

selective_wait ::=
select
select_alternative
{**or**
select_alternative}
[**else**
sequence_of_statements]
end select;

select_alternative ::=
[**when** condition =⟩]
selective_wait_alternative

selective_wait_alternative ::= accept_alternative
  | delay_alternative | terminate_alternative

accept_alternative ::= accept_statement [sequence_of_statements]

delay_alternative ::= delay_statement [sequence_of_statements]

terminate_alternative ::= **terminate**;

9.7.2

conditional_entry_call ::=
    select
        entry_call_statement
        [sequence_of_statements]
    else
        sequence_of_statements
    end select;

9.7.3

timed_entry_call ::=
    select
        entry_call_statement
        [sequence_of_statements]
    or
        delay_alternative
    end select;

9.10

abort_statement ::= **abort** *task*_name {, *task*_name};

10.1

compilation ::= {compilation_unit}

compilation_unit ::=
    context_clause library_unit | context_clause secondary_unit

library_unit ::=
    subprogram_declaration | package_declaration
    | generic_declaration | generic_instantiation
    | subprogram_body

secondary_unit ::= library_unit_body | subunit

library_unit_body ::= subprogram_body | package_body

10.1.1

context_clause ::= {with_clause {use_clause}}

with_clause ::= **with** *unit*_simple_name {, *unit*_simple_name};

10.2

body_stub ::=
    subprogram_specification **is separate**;
    | **package body** *package*_simple_name **is separate**;
    | **task body** *task*_simple_name **is separate**;

subunit ::= **separate** (*parent_unit*_name) proper_body

11.1

exception_declaration ::= identifier_list : **exception**;

11.2

exception_handler ::=
    when exception_choice {| exception_choice} =⟩
        sequence_of_statements

exception_choice ::= *exception*_name | **others**

11.3

raise_statement ::= **raise** [*exception*_name];

12.1

generic_declaration ::= generic_specification;

generic_specification ::=
     generic_formal_part subprogram_specification
  | generic_formal_part package_specification

generic_formal_part ::= **generic** {generic_parameter_declaration}

generic_parameter_declaration ::=
     identifier_list : [**in** [**out**]] type_mark [:= expression];
  | **type** identifier **is** generic_type_definition;
  | private_type_declaration
  | **with** subprogram_specification [**is** name];
  | **with** subprogram_specification [**is** ⟨⟩];

generic_type_definition ::=
     (⟨⟩) | **range** ⟨⟩ | **digits** ⟨⟩ | **delta** ⟨⟩
  | array_type_definition | access_type_definition

12.3

generic_instantiation ::=
     package identifier **is**
          new *generic_package*_name [generic_actual_part];
  | **procedure** identifier **is**
          new *generic_procedure*_name [generic_actual_part];
  | **function** designator **is**
          new *generic_function*_name [generic_actual_part];

generic_actual_part ::=
     (generic_association {, generic_association})

generic_association ::=
     [generic_formal_parameter =⟩] generic_actual_parameter

generic_formal_parameter ::= *parameter*_simple_name | operator_symbol

generic_actual_parameter ::= expression | *variable*_name
  | *subprogram*_name | *entry*_name | type_mark

13.1

representation_clause ::=
     type_representation_clause | address_clause

type_representation_clause :: = length_clause
    | enumeration_representation_clause | record_representation_clause

13.2

length_clause :: = **for** attribute **use** simple_expression;

13.3

enumeration_representation_clause :: = **for** *type*_simple_name **use** aggregate;

13.4

record_representation_clause :: =
    for *type*_simple_name **use**
      record [alignment_clause]
        {component_clause}
      end record;

alignment_clause :: = **at mod** *static*_simple_expression;

component_clause :: =
    *component*_name **at** *static*_simple_expression **range** *static*_range;

13.5

address_clause :: = **for** simple_name **use at** simple_expression;

13.8

code_statement :: = type_mark'*record*_aggregate;

INDEX